D0829764

INSIDERS' GUIDE® TO
ORANGE COUNTY

HELP US KEEP THIS GUIDE UP-TO-DATE

We would love to hear from you concerning your experiences with this guide and how you feel it could be improved and kept up-to-date. Please send your comments and suggestions to:

editorial@GlobePequot.com

Thanks for your input, and happy travels!

INSIDERS' GUIDE® SERIES

INSIDERS' GUIDE® TO

ORANGE COUNTY

ELIZABETH BORSTING

INSIDERS' GUIDE

GUILFORD, CONNECTICUT
AN IMPRINT OF GLOBE PEQUOT PRESS

All the information in this guidebook is subject to change. We recommend that you call ahead to obtain current information before traveling.

To buy books in quantity for corporate use or incentives, call **(800) 962–0973** or e-mail **premiums@GlobePequot.com**.

INSIDERS' GUIDE ®

Copyright © 2010 Morris Book Publishing, LLC

ALL RIGHTS RESERVED. No part of this book may be reproduced or transmitted in any form by any means, electronic or mechanical, including photocopying and recording, or by any information storage and retrieval system, except as may be expressly permitted in writing from the publisher. Requests for permission should be addressed to Globe Pequot Press, Attn: Rights and Permissions Department, P.O. Box 480, Guilford, CT 06437.

Insiders' Guide is a registered trademark of Morris Book Publishing, LLC.

Editorial Director, Travel: Amy Lyons
Project Editor: Ellen Urban
Layout Artist: Kevin Mak
Text Designer: Sheryl Kober
Maps by Design Maps Inc. © Morris Book Publishing, LLC

ISBN: 978-0-7627-5961-3

Printed in the United States of America
10 9 8 7 6 5 4 3 2 1

CONTENTS

CONTENTS

Directory of Maps

ACKNOWLEDGMENTS

Though I now live just across the county line in Long Beach, California's fifth largest city and part of Los Angeles County, I am still an Orange County girl at heart. I spent my formative years in Orange County, where I attended elementary school, junior high, and high school. Looking back now, growing up in Orange County during the early 1980s was as wonderful as I remember. Summers were reserved for the beach, nighttime bonfires, and hanging out at the mall with friends. When winter came we still hung out at the beach because, let's face it, Southern California is rarely without sunshine. We might also head to the local mountains to ski, spend a school holiday roaming about Disneyland, or graze on popcorn and Junior Mints while watching a double feature at the local movie theater. Life was simple back then, and Orange County, as many discovered, was an ideal location to raise a family.

It was only once I moved away from Orange County that I learned of other people's perceptions about the place I called home. Angelenos referred to those who lived in Orange County as "living behind the Orange Curtain," a reference to the region's political leanings. Valley Girls, a pseudo teen subculture that briefly emerged during the 1980s, thought their Orange County counterparts lived "way out there." Orange County had a reputation, unbeknownst to me, of being a boring bedroom community that counted Disneyland as its only claim to fame. Really? That's why I find it so ironic that Orange County, now referred to as The OC, is suddenly haute and hip thanks to the imaginations of Hollywood heavyweights. It's been amazing for me to watch the region evolve and blossom into one of Southern California's most desirable destinations. Its reputation went from drab, according to outsiders, to absolutely fab, with *USA Today* touting it as the "capital of cool." Imagine that! But, of course, those of us raised in The OC always knew it was something special.

Writing a guidebook of this magnitude takes a lot of time and effort, and there can be some casualties along the way as you scurry to meet deadlines. While I might be credited as the author, I certainly had a lot of help. First and foremost, I'd like to thank my husband Kurt and our children, Jake and Katie, for being understanding when I had to lug the laptop on vacations or needed to sequester myself behind my office door in order to frantically write, rewrite, and edit during this process. I'd also like to thank my mom and dad for simply being wonderful and nurturing parents. Had they not purchased our OC house on Hacienda Street in 1975, I wouldn't be writing this book. I would also like to thank my brother Steven for babysitting our 16-year-old dog Ruby Jean while I visited countless hotels and restaurants. And, finally, I'd like to say thank you to Amy Lyons, my editor at Globe Pequot, for giving me the green light and go ahead to write the first edition of this book.

ABOUT THE AUTHOR

Elizabeth Arrighi Borsting is a freelance writer and public relations consultant for the hospitality industry. Her writing credits include *Celebrity Weddings & Honeymoon Getaways*, *Open Road's Southern California Guide*, *Open Road's Northern California Guide*, *California's Best B&Bs*, and *LA With Kids*, plus Peter Pauper Press's *Top 101 Honeymoon Destinations*. She has served as a contributing editor for both *Honeymoon Magazine* and *Preferred Destinations*, and her work has also appeared in the *Los Angeles Times* and *National Geographic Traveler*. She resides with her husband Kurt and their two children, Jake and Katie, plus pup Ruby Jean along the coast in Long Beach, California, just south of Los Angeles and adjacent to Orange County.

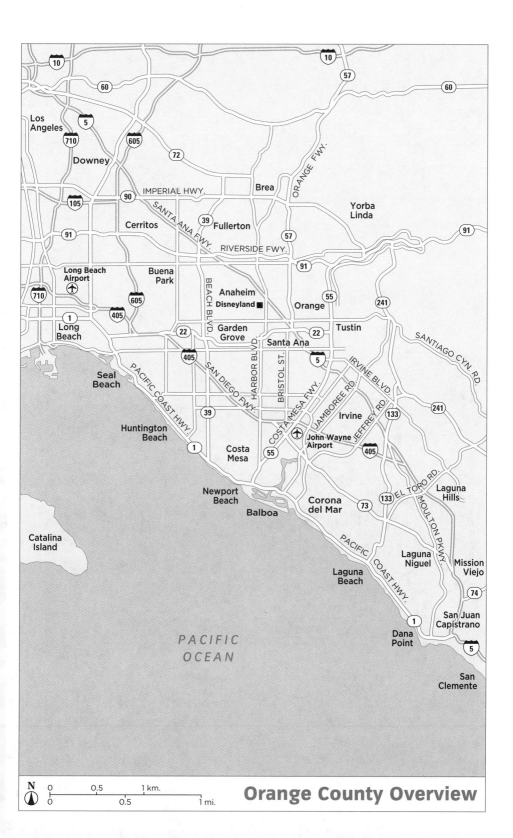

Orange County Overview

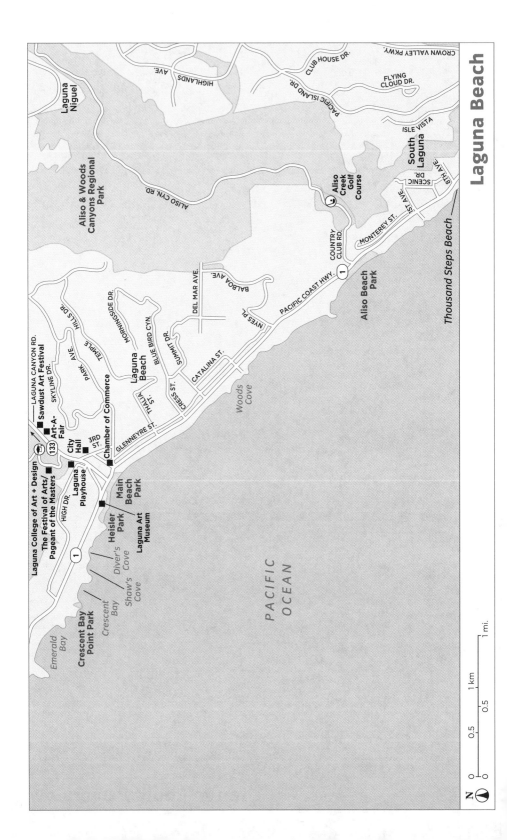

Laguna Beach

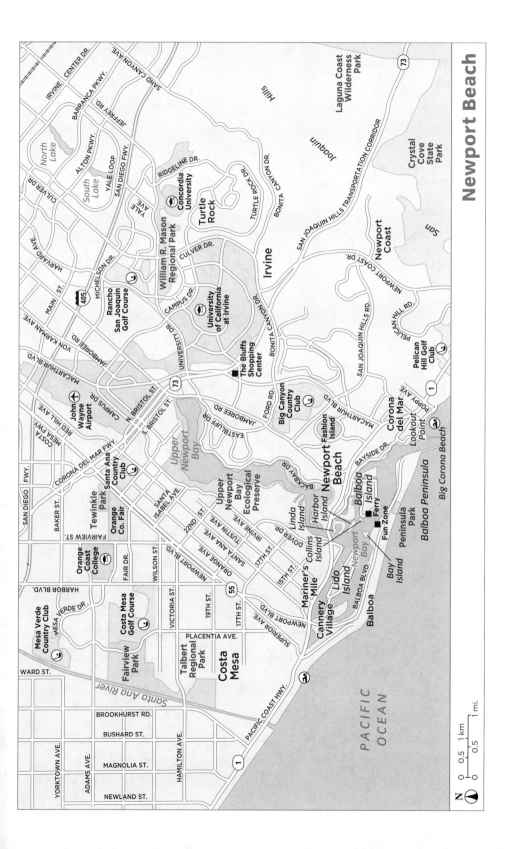

Newport Beach

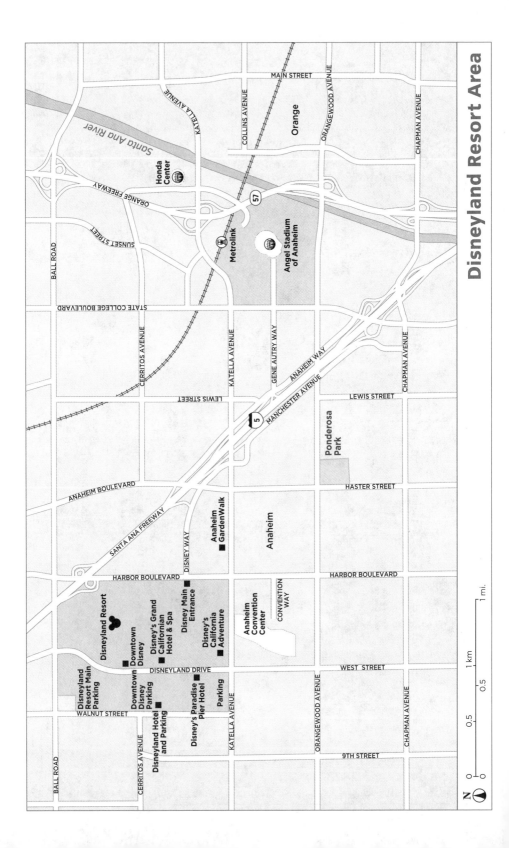

Disneyland Resort Area

PREFACE

Congratulations! You've arrived at one of the most desirable places in Southern California and, perhaps, the entire United States—Orange County. Whether you are here for a much-needed getaway, are a longtime resident, or have decided to relocate to the land of palm trees and sunshine, you will undoubtedly fall in love with all that Orange County has to offer. The *Insiders' Guide to Orange County* was conceived to help with the transition by arming you with all the necessary information without burdening you with frivolous details that will be no use to you whatsoever.

Orange County is no longer hiding in the shadows of its much larger neighbor, Los Angeles, as it has finally come into its own. Once lampooned as the place "behind the Orange Curtain," a reference that speaks to the county's more conservative political stance, Orange County has slowly evolved into a more progressive and upscale community. These days it's referred to as The OC, a hipper moniker that came into fashion during the run of a TV show by the same name. Reality shows such as *The Real Housewives of Orange County* and *Laguna Beach* also put the spotlight on Orange County, though it's hard to say whether the participants of these so-called reality shows did more harm than good. Gwen Stefani, lead singer of No Doubt, has also helped to catapult the county's image by touting her Anaheim roots and often referring to Orange County in her lyrics.

It's likely that you purchased this book prior to your departure, or maybe you've just arrived and are thumbing through the possibilities while lounging poolside. But, make no mistake, there is a lot more to Orange County than swimming pools and television dramas. Let's start with the incredible climate and topography. Orange County enjoys more than 300 days of sunshine a year, with an average temperature of 70 degrees and very little precipitation—just enough to keep things lush and green. If you cast your eyes in one direction you're likely to see snow-covered mountains during the winter, where in less than 90 minutes you can be traversing the slopes on a pair of skis. In the opposite direction are 42 miles of pristine coastline with pounding surf, silvery sands, and idyllic weather conditions that make it possible to sunbathe in the dead of winter. To the east is the Coachella Valley where the desert resort communities, such as Palm Springs, are located. They make for a great weekend getaway and take only 90 minutes to reach as well. Just 26 miles across the sea is Catalina Island, an enchanting isle with roaming bison, a single seaside hamlet, a handful of inns, and lots of recreational opportunities.

Orange County seems caught somewhere between urban and suburbia. The region is made up of bedroom communities where tidy streets are lined with one- and two-story homes, conveniences that are strategically placed nearby, and a Starbucks found on just about every corner. But there is also a sophisticated side to The OC, and a dominant resort influence lies along the magnificent coastline. Here you'll find a collection of four- and five-star waterfront resorts, fabulous seaside restaurants, tony day spas, and parking lots filled with luxury vehicles. Orange County also has some great shopping destinations, such as Fashion Island and South Coast Plaza, as well as unique cultural and historic stops, such as the 18th-century Mission San Juan Capistrano. Of course, you may have plans to spend a day at Disneyland Resort, home to the original Disneyland theme park and the decade-old Disney's California Adventure, which is in the midst of a major multimillion-dollar makeover. Not far from this theme park mecca is Knott's Berry Farm in Buena Park, which features a seasonal water park and a collection of stomach-churning thrill rides. Southern California is fortunate to have not one, but two presidential libraries. History buffs and politico types will enjoy sleuthing around the Richard Nixon Library and

Birthplace in Yorba Linda. But a daytrip to Simi Valley, about 90 minutes north of Orange County, will put you behind the gates of the Ronald Reagan Presidential Library, too.

While there is no "downtown" Orange County to speak of, there are charming downtown areas and villages in some of the individual cities. Along Harbor Boulevard in Fullerton you'll find a fleet of shops, restaurants, and club venues tucked behind the doors of historic buildings. The same can be said of Old Towne Orange, where an historic circular plaza, as well as the streets that jut from the loop, are lined with antique shops, restaurants, and nightclubs. Balboa Island, part of Newport Beach, has a charming two-lane road lined with shops and restaurants, and Laguna Beach, an artists' village, is brimming with individual businesses, galleries, restaurants, and lounges.

So what if Orange County doesn't have a professional football team? Neither does the much larger Los Angeles. The county's major league baseball team, the Los Angeles Angels of Anaheim, are World Series champs. The OC also has a professional hockey team, the Ducks, and a quarter horse racetrack. Huntington Beach, the original Surf City USA, is home to a number of surfing competitions including the US Open of Surfing, which draws thousands of spectators every summer. Volleyball competitions are played on the sand as well. And with great surf, an abundance of golf courses, public tennis courts, and organized sports leagues, athletic types aren't relegated to just the sidelines. It's easy to be active in The OC, and many people can be found riding their bikes along the beach path or bodysurfing in the blue Pacific.

When it comes to education, you won't find a more well-rounded or diverse place to study. There are some 80 post-secondary institutions in Orange County including close to a dozen public colleges and universities, plus 15 private schools and more than 50 professional schools. The region is one of the nation's most educated as well, with more than 60 percent of high school graduates pursuing post-secondary educations.

Linking all these destinations and elements together is a labyrinth of freeways and surface streets. But for a truly mesmerizing experience that requires some patience due to vehicle congestion and continuous stoplights, motor down Pacific Coast Highway from Seal Beach to Dana Point. This original long and winding road meanders through Orange County's coastal communities with long stretches resulting in breathtaking ocean views, glimpses of million-dollar mansions, small seaside communities that beckon to be explored on foot, and roadside eateries worthy of a stop.

Orange County is a work in progress that continues to evolve through development and commerce. Dirt lots are transitioning into new residential communities offering hip, loft-style living and single family homes as people continue to arrive in pursuit of the California dream. The Orange County Great Park in Irvine is being developed in phases. Once complete, it will be nearly twice the size of New York City's Central Park, replete with extensive open areas coupled with an abundance of recreational and cultural uses. Communities such as the area surrounding Disneyland and the city of Brea, which once seemed trapped in a long-forgotten era, have undergone gentrification and are attracting a new breed of dwellers by offering mixed-use retail and residential space.

Bottom line—whatever the reason for your pilgrimage to Orange County, this book's goal is to provide you with the necessary information to make the most of your time. Whether you're visiting for a short spell and need hotel and restaurant recommendations or are here for the long haul, you are now armed with a format intended to guide you to the best Orange County has to offer. No book can ever capture the essence of a great destination like Orange County, but we've done our best to present a concise and informative overview, leaving out any useless information or half-hearted suggestions. The places we've profiled are places we frequent and would recommend to friends and family ourselves. So get to know Orange County if you're a first time visitor, whether that means locating the best hospital facility or discovering who makes the meanest martini—once you've had a chance to unload the moving van, of course. And, if you're a longtime resident, why not reacquaint yourself with the place you call home? All you need is a little sunscreen, a pair of cool shades, and some attitude to give you that edge.

HOW TO USE THIS BOOK

Unlike other regions of the United States, Southern California is often the backdrop for Hollywood drama. Usually it's Los Angeles enjoying the limelight. Remember *Beverly Hills 90210*, *LA Law*, and *Melrose Place*? Then came the new millennium, and suddenly Orange County was thrust into the spotlight. Once known as the home of Mickey Mouse, this suburban region was quickly transformed from Orange County into *The OC,* thanks to the now defunct television show of the same name. Yes, in true Hollywood fashion Orange County got a bona fide makeover while the cameras were rolling and America was watching. Reality shows, such as *Laguna Beach*, have managed to paint an unrealistic, but entertaining, depiction of life in The OC. And, while *The Real Housewives of Orange County* makes for mindless entertainment, the line between fact and fiction is clearly drawn.

Orange County for the most part is a tapestry of towns and cities. Sandwiched between Los Angeles and San Diego, it's a hybrid of sorts with both suburban sensibilities and urban nuances. Named for the abundant orange groves that once thrived in these parts, the county is now a collection of residential and commercial developments with little trace of its agricultural origins; although, if you look hard enough, there are still some wide open spaces and patches of farmland. The prevailing philosophy is the *bigger the better, the newer the nicer.* Brand spanking new homes reek of square footage; theme parks, such as Disneyland and Knott's Berry Farm, continue to expand and reinvent themselves; and modest beach hotels have given way to new, plush coastal resorts sporting five-star status, celebrity chefs, and sprawling spa sanctuaries.

This book highlights the usual suspects—the high-profile attractions, the unbelievable stretches of coastline, the sandy beaches and pounding surf, and the incredible places to shop—but it also gives you some insight from a local's perspective. Put this book to work by discovering some of The OC's better kept and most closely guarded secrets: Parks frequented by locals, hiking trails that traverse the county's outback and wetlands, hands-on cooking classes for adults and children, spectacular events, and must-see venues. Feast on fabulous Mexican fare, nosh on succulent sushi, and graze on fresh seafood within a sandal-toss of the beach. We feel confident that you'll be able to find the big chain restaurants on your own, so we've chosen to feature mostly individual eateries run by dedicated restaurateurs.

Orange County is also an idyllic home base for exploring some of Southern California's other destinations. Weekend getaways to enchanting islands, bucolic mountains, historic mining towns, palm-laden deserts, and vine-covered hills ripe with plump grapes are all within reach. Daytrips to Los Angeles, from its gentrified downtown to the tinsel-laden streets of Hollywood, are just a short car ride away. While Orange County might be considered the quintessential California getaway existing beneath a veil of sunshine and surf, less than two hours away are snow-covered mountains where you can ski and snowboard with the best of 'em.

But none of these enticing offerings—the theme parks, the hidden treasures, the day trippin' treks—are of any use unless you know how to get from Point A to Point B. Ah, that's where this book comes in handy to first-time visitors and recent transplants. It will help guide you onto freeways and along surface streets to get you where you need to go, while occasionally pointing out places of interest as you motor along. The first several chapters comprise a crash course in Orange County 101, covering the necessary and vital information for visitors, such as accommodations and restaurants—which, for some, is a matter of basic survival. Between these pages is also a brief history on Orange County, as well as demographics and basic need-to-know information, such as standard business hours and average gratuity for restaurant servers and hotel housekeeping staff. You'll also learn about the rules of the road, including child-safety laws, what law enforcement considers "under the influence," and whether or not you can chat on your cell phone while the wheels are in motion.

This *Insiders' Guide* aims not only to acquaint you with Orange County, but to empower you by directing you to the most interesting, innovative, and significant destinations within the county lines and beyond. At the same time, this book paints an accurate picture—warts and all—of The OC, whether it's touting the virtues of its higher education opportunities or wrestling with the fallout of the housing market due to the economic downturn. It also arms you with knowledge of important laws, how to navigate the web of freeways, and how best to use public transportation. As for areas of interest, for the most part this book tends to stick close to the two main areas that visitors find most alluring: the Disneyland Resort Area in Anaheim and the coastal communities that truly define the meaning of California dreamin'. The book is divided into areas of interest—accommodations, restaurants, attractions, and so on—and then broken out either by region (inland vs. coastal) or by city in alphabetical order. And while the most significant attractions, landmarks, and points of interest take center stage, make no mistake that those with supporting roles—the lesser known, off-the-beaten-path wonders—are included as well.

Moving to Orange County or already live here? Be sure to check out the blue-tabbed pages at the back of the book, where you will find the **Living Here** appendix that offers sections on relocation, real estate, education, and health care.

Yes, Orange County certainly has plenty of drama, as well as a comedic side that makes it a favorite destination for visitors. And, while it certainly has exceeded its 15 minutes of fame, visitors, transplants, and even longtime residents continue to crave more of what The OC has to offer. Mr. DeMille, The OC is ready for its close-up.

AREA OVERVIEW

Even if you've never visited Orange County, it still probably has an air of familiarity—perhaps even a sense of déjà vu. For more than half a century it has enjoyed plenty of attention as the home of Disneyland. In more recent years, it has invaded American living rooms with such television shows as *The OC, Laguna Beach,* and *The Real Housewives of Orange County*. None of these dramas or reality shows were able to truly capture the real Orange County.

Sandwiched between Los Angeles and San Diego Counties and abutting Riverside County to the north, there is no urban center in this suburban county. But whatever cosmopolitan vibe it lacks, Orange County more than makes up for it with its traditional downtown areas and villages, including those belonging to Laguna Beach, Corona del Mar, Orange, Huntington Beach, San Clemente, Seal Beach, and Fullerton, as well as its more than 40 miles of sandy beaches. In recent years, some cities have managed to fabricate their own town centers, including Brea, which completely bulldozed its original downtown and rebuilt it from the ground up, as well as Anaheim, which reinvented itself by creating residential lofts and adding restaurants and shops. South Coast Metro in Costa Mesa and Newport Center, home to Fashion Island, in Newport Beach are city-style developments that cater more to the business community with high-rise office space and weekday conveniences. Santa Ana serves as the county's governmental seat, while Irvine gets kudos for being its business and financial hub.

Orange County's population has climbed steadily in the last few decades with residents now exceeding three million spread across 34 incorporated cities, up from 2.85 million in 2000—a 5.8 percent increase. It is the second most densely inhabited county in California, trailing behind Los Angeles but surpassing San Diego. Orange County is also home to two major theme parks, Disneyland and Knott's Berry Farm. It also has two of Southern California's best shopping destinations, Fashion Island and South Coast Plaza, and is well known for its houses of worship, including the monumental Crystal Cathedral and *Purpose Drive Life* author Rick Warren's Saddleback Church.

The county is divided into three regions: North, central, and south. North is home to the Richard M. Nixon Presidential Library and Birthplace as well as the Happiest Place on Earth, Disneyland. Knott's Berry Farm, the Crystal Cathedral, and South Coast Plaza all call the central portion of the county home. And Laguna Beach, Dana Point, and San Clemente, all beach communities, are found in the south close to the San Diego County line. On the other end of the spectrum, the coastal communities of Huntington Beach and Sunset Beach are near the Los Angeles County line; in fact, Seal Beach abuts the LA County line.

The county is known for its affluence. The county-wide median home price is $429,000, but in communities such as Laguna Beach and Newport Beach the median home prices are $1.3 million and $2.7 million respectively. The median household income exceeds $73,000, with 8.9 percent of the population living below poverty level. And nearly one-third of Orange County residents 25 and older have earned a bachelor's degree or higher, according to the 2000 census.

Orange County has several interesting neighborhoods, as well as many bedroom communities where there is not much more than strip malls and grocery stores. Visitors tend to gravitate towards two regions—the Anaheim resort area and the coastal enclaves with their glistening beaches and million-dollar homes.

GENERAL ORANGE COUNTY INFO

If you're visiting the area from another state or country, or if you've just relocated to Orange County, it's wise to arm yourself with some practical information. Having basic knowledge, such as the various area codes within the county (they continue to split, which confuses even lifelong residents) or standard tipping practices for restaurants and cabs, can help to eliminate the guesswork.

Business hours can vary depending on how *business* is defined. Service-oriented businesses, such as dry cleaners and automotive repair shops, typically operate from 9 a.m. to 5 p.m. weekdays and Saturdays. National retailers and shopping malls seem to be expanding their hours and are open seven days a week from 10 a.m. to 9 p.m. (some remain open until 10 p.m. or later), until 7 p.m. on Saturday, and usually from 11 a.m. to 6 p.m. on Sunday. Then there are those open 24 hours—the grocery and pharmacy chains, such as CVS, Walgreens, and Rite-Aid. Banks still have bankers' hours for the most part, while museums close their doors Monday and Tuesday, but it's always wise to call ahead.

There's not much to say about the climate and weather in Orange County other than it's absolutely wonderful. Rarely does it get much above 75 degrees at the beach, but inland temperatures can exceed double digits during the peak of summer. It's also a dry climate, although in recent summers the region has experienced waves of humidity—but nothing severe like you find in Florida. Rain usually presents itself in the winter and early spring.

The standard electrical current for Orange County, as well as the entire U.S., is 110 volts.

For emergencies—life-threatening conditions, crime, fire, medical—call 9-1-1. This call is always toll-free from any private or public phone. From a hotel room you may need to dial a "9" first to get an outside line or simply press "0" to connect to the hotel operator.

As a traveler, or resident for that matter, take precautions like you would anywhere else. Lock your car once you're behind the wheel and be sure to keep it locked when it's parked and unoccupied. It's also wise not to leave expensive or personal items out in the open. Hotel guests should hang the "privacy please" sign on the outside of the door once it's been serviced by housekeeping—this gives the appearance that someone is inside the room. Also, never open your hotel room door without first looking through the peephole, and if someone knocks on the door saying they've come to make a repair, first call the front desk to make sure it's legitimate. Usually the hotel clears these types of inconveniences with the guest first.

There used to be a time when smoking was acceptable, but that's no longer the case. In fact, smoking is prohibited on all public transportation vehicles and in public buildings, as well as inside restaurants and bars. Smoking is also banned in public outdoor places, including some public beaches. Definitely ask before you light up. Tobacco buyers must be at least 18 years old and may be asked to provide proof of age.

For decades Orange County had just one area code—714. But with advancements in technology came fax machines, cell phones, Blackberries, and a lack of new number combinations. So a new area code was created for south Orange County—949—while north Orange County retained 714. Eventually, cities to the west, such as Sunset Beach and Seal Beach, were given the 562 area code, which is shared with southeast Los Angeles County. Just recently another split took place, adding 657 as a fourth area code. Consumers who already have a 714 area code will keep the status quo, but consumers needing a new or additional telephone number may be given the new 657 area code. The entire campus of Cal State Fullerton has voluntarily transitioned to the 657 area code. What this means is that if you have a 657 area code and your next door neighbor has a 714 number, you will be required to dial the area code plus the number.

Orange County, like the rest of the state, operates on Pacific Standard Time (Greenwich Mean Time minus eight hours) trailing three hours behind the East Coast. Daylight Savings Time is also observed.

It's customary to leave a gratuity of 15 to 20 percent at restaurants on the total, pre-tax bill for meals and just 10 percent at counter service-only or buffet dining. If you doubled the sales tax, which is 8.75 percent in Orange County, you would be leaving a 17.5 percent tip. In most of Los Angeles County, tax is 9.75 percent, which is nearly a 20 percent tip if you double it. The typical tip for cab drivers is 10 percent, valet $2 to $3, bellhops 50 cents to $1 per bag, and hotel housekeepers $1 to $2 per day.

Travelers can contact the California Department of Tourism (www.visitcalifornia.com) to request travel guides for the entire state or a designated region. The Web site also has a plethora of information you can download and print out instantly. If you prefer to talk directly to a representative at the bureau, call 877-CALIFORNIA. Local convention and visitors bureaus are also great sources for getting information on hotels, restaurants, attractions, and more. For Orange County, the Anaheim/Orange County Visitor & Convention Bureau (714-765-8888, www.anaheimoc.org) can provide you with maps, guides, information on hotel specials, and more.

ANAHEIM/NORTH ORANGE COUNTY

During the past few years Anaheim has undergone a major transformation. Yes, it's still widely known for being home to Disneyland, as well as California Adventure, which is getting a $1.1 billion facelift after being open just a decade, and Downtown Disney, which links the two parks. But Anaheim now has much more to offer visitors. Kitschy motels that once surrounded the theme park creating a jumbled landscape with their hodgepodge signs now adhere to a new signage plan that gives Harbor Boulevard and the surrounding avenues a more unified and finished look. The city also gets credit for having two successful sports franchises—the Los Angeles Angels of Anaheim, which plays baseball at Angel Stadium, and the Anaheim Ducks, which offers NHL puck-to-puck action at the Honda Center. During the Ducks hiatus, the Honda Center is a popular stop for pop artists promoting their latest CDs. Recent acts have included Miley Cyrus and Gwen Stefani. Disney on Ice and the Ringling Bros. Circus also use the Honda Center to entertain the masses. Anaheim has also added stylish residential lofts along State College Boulevard and surrounding streets, which gives these once drab avenues a bit of urban panache. Another enhancement, especially for conventioneers attending events at the Anaheim Convention Center, is the new Shops at Anaheim GardenWalk. This two-story, outdoor lifestyle center features recognizable restaurants, such as PF Chang's, as well as retail, an upscale bowling alley, and state-of-the-art movie theaters.

NORTH AND CENTRAL ORANGE COUNTY

While Anaheim, which is 28 miles south of Los Angeles, remains the main thrust for tourism in the inland region, north and central Orange County also have their share of attractions. West of Anaheim is Buena Park where Knott's Berry Farm and Soak City can be found, as well as themed restaurants, including Medieval Times and Pirate's Dinner Adventure. North of Anaheim is Yorba Linda, which until the early 1990s was nothing more than tract homes and horse trails. It now features the Richard Nixon Library and Birthplace on the site of the president's childhood home, built by his father, where he was born on January 9, 1913. Nearby is Brea, which includes a newly built downtown area (the old one was bulldozed) as well as the Brea Mall. The town has also upgraded its main thoroughfare, Brea Boulevard, to include new residential lofts and commerce. Downtown Fullerton, south of Brea, has a charming downtown area. Founded in 1887, downtown still retains many of its original structures or, at minimum, the edifices. Lining Harbor Boulevard, Downtown Fullerton's main street, as well as many of its crossroads, are hip restaurants, bars, coffeehouses, and shops. The town's focal point, the Fox Fullerton Theatre, was built during Hollywood's Golden era and was on the demolition hit list until citizens rallied to save the theater. It will soon reopen as a center for independent and art films. The Santa Fe Depot, a charming Spanish Colonial building, is where AMTRAK and Metrolink, which quickly transports commuters to and from Los Angeles, make frequent daily stops. The Old Spaghetti Factory is also located adjacent to the depot and was once a depot itself for the Union Pacific Railroad. And a few miles away is California State University, Fullerton (CSUF).

If you want to do some real time travel, the historic Orange Circle in Old Towne Orange, east of Anaheim, looks much the way it did at the turn of the 20th century. This historic district has National Register of Historic Places status and includes more than 1,300 vintage homes and buildings sporting more than 50 different architectural styles, from Victorian to Craftsman. Packed within its 1 square mile is the Orange Circle, which is flanked with awning-covered shops, restaurants, sidewalk cafes, residential flats, and a center fountain. There are four spokes that branch off from the circle and run north to south, east to west. These streets, Chapman and Glassell, along with smaller avenues, hold steepled churches, schools, the old Santa Fe Depot, packing houses, and parks. There are also a few bars and lounges, which cater to the students attending Chapman University a few blocks away. Every Labor Day weekend the Orange Circle hosts the three-day International Street Fair, featuring cuisines from around the world, live entertainment, and arts and crafts.

COASTAL ORANGE COUNTY

Pacific Coast Highway, the original long and winding road, is the common thread linking Orange County's beach communities together. It begins at the Los Angeles County line in the southwestern region of the county in Seal Beach and continues for some 40 miles to Dana Point, where it ends at I-5. Sandwiched in between are glistening beaches, quaint seaside towns and hamlets, jutting piers, and multimillion-dollar resorts as well as vintage inns, art galleries, harbors and marinas filled with bobbing yachts, sidewalk cafes, and fine dining restaurants.

Seal Beach and Old Town

Starting at the most western point is Seal Beach, named for the many seals that once policed the waters. The town has retained much of its seaside charm. There is a real sense of community in Old Town, which lies on the south side of Pacific Coast Highway. Main Street, which ends at Ocean Avenue at the foot of the pier, offers lots of shops and restaurants as well as pubs, wine bars, services, and an historic single-screen movie theater. Except for a Coffee Bean and Tea Leaf and a Subway sandwich shop, both of which flank the start of Main Street, as well as businesses along Pacific Coast Highway, Old Town doesn't really have any national retailers or restaurants to speak of. It is also the only Orange County beach community (probably the only beach community in all of Southern California) that hasn't installed parking meters on its Main Street, although meters do line Ocean Avenue, which fronts the beach. However, the issue of whether to install parking meters or not remains a hot topic for city officials, residents, and business owners, and it probably is just a matter of time before the city goes ahead and installs meters to create additional revenue. Surrounding Old Town are many vintage seaside cottages that fan out in both directions. In recent years many of these structures have been torn down, including an enchanting 1920s-era bed and breakfast, to make way for new McMansions. The beach itself is a great place to spend the day, and there is an enclosed playground right on the sand. At the end of the pier is a Ruby's Diner, too. The only other attraction is the Red Car Museum, where car #1734 sits on the old Pacific Electric Right of Way. The museum is small, as big as the red car itself, but offers an interesting peek into pre-freeway travel. Often called the "Mayberry by the Sea," Seal Beach hosts an annual Christmas Parade the first Friday night in December, summer concerts, a spring fish fry, and Fourth of July celebrations.

Sunset Beach

Several years ago there was a soap opera called *Sunset Beach*, which supposedly took place in this small town. Much of it was actually filmed in neighboring Seal Beach. The real Sunset Beach is a folksy, unincorporated community with a mix of huge oceanfront homes and eclectic dwellings positioned on a small inlet on the opposite side of Pacific Coast Highway. This century-old community has its share of annual events as well as several bars and restaurants. The beach doesn't have crowds like Newport and Huntington beaches, which is a plus. But there are no beach concessions either, so be sure to bring some beverages and snacks if you plan on making a day of it. The tiny bay is ideal for launching kayaks or small row boats. Sunset Beach's only real landmark is a huge shingled water tower, which has been transformed into a vacation rental home.

Huntington Beach

Once you cross Warner Avenue, you have entered Huntington Beach, a town that embraces an "endless summer" attitude. Established in the late 1880s, eventually christened Pacific City, and finally incorporated in 1909, Huntington Beach was renamed for railroad magnate Henry Huntington, who orchestrated the city's development. Ocean swells, endless sunshine, and a fleet of bobbing longboards have played an instrumental role in earning Huntington Beach its well-deserved—and official—"Surf City" moniker, not to mention attracting some 11 million visitors annually. At the corner of Warner and Pacific Coast Highway begins the Bolsa Chica Ecological Reserve, where nearly 200 species of birds nest on an abundance of unspoiled acreage on the east side of the highway. To the west, which will be rather obvious, is Bolsa Chica Beach. Further south at the intersection of Main Street and Pacific Coast Highway is the start of downtown Huntington Beach and its many boutiques, surf shops, restaurants, and bars. The International Surf Museum, Surfing Walk of Fame, and Surfers'

Hall of Fame are all found here as well. The strand, which runs along the beach, is 8.5 miles long and nearly as crowded as the city streets with inline skaters, skateboarders, bicyclers, joggers, and walkers.

Skirting the eastern perimeter of downtown is a neighborhood full of vintage homes, but more modern, linear homes are found along Pacific Coast Highway. A new retail center, the Strand, has opened in downtown and offers a more sophisticated surf vibe with a smattering of shops, a pedestrian breezeway, a boutique hotel, and collection of restaurants. In addition, two ocean view properties, the Waterfront Hilton and the Huntington Hyatt Regency Resort and Spa, will soon be joined by a W Hotel, further transitioning Huntington Beach from a surf ghetto into a bona fide resort town. The pier, which is a major landmark, juts out into the ocean and houses a Ruby's Diner at the very end. Several annual events take place near the pier including national surfing competitions, afternoon concerts, a weekly farmers' market, and much more.

Further inland are several residential tracts built mostly during the 1960s, '70s, and '80s that are tucked behind such major streets as Beach Boulevard, Golden West Avenue, Edinger Avenue, and Warner Avenue. Golden West Community College is located in Huntington Beach, and neighboring the college is Bella Terra, an open-air center located off the 405 at Beach Boulevard featuring shops, restaurants such as Cheesecake Factory, department stores, and Barnes & Noble, just to name a few. Old World, a German marketplace known for its annual Oktoberfest, is located behind Bella Terra.

Newport Beach

From Huntington Beach it's on to the more tony and moneyed Newport Beach. And, even though Newport Beach exudes wealth, there are some charming enclaves that seem to harken back to a simpler era. Nothing illustrates this better than Balboa Peninsula and Balboa Island, separated by Newport Bay. Overlooking the bay on the peninsula side is the Balboa Fun Zone, which has shrunk to only two rides, a Ferris wheel and a merry-go-round, and vintage arcades that house a mix of old amusements and state-of-the-art video games. You can also take a peek inside the historic Balboa Pavilion or rent an electric Duffy boat and cruise the waters. There are several rental stores along the side streets where you can rent inline skates, tandem bikes, beach cruisers, and surfboards. On the beach side is the pier where the original Ruby's Diner is located, and small swells of waves that don't attract surfers, but families seem to feel right at home.

From the peninsula you can take the Balboa Ferry across to Balboa Island. The ferry holds three cars per crossing, but also transports bicyclists, walkers, and skaters across the bay. Once you reach the island, it's just a short walk along the waterfront, where you'll pass charming beach cottages, until you reach the small downtown area along Marine Avenue. There aren't any national retailers, except a single Starbucks, but there are plenty of original shops and restaurants. Dad's, with its tiny walk-up window, serves classic Balboa bars, vanilla ice-cream bars dipped in a vat of chocolate and rolled in sprinkles or nuts. If you're looking to purchase island property, there is no shortage of realtors.

If you cross the small bridge leading away from the island's hamlet and head up the hill, you've reached Pacific Coast Highway. Turn right, and you're heading towards Fashion Island, which is on the immediate left. Less than a mile later is Corona del Mar, which is still part of Newport Beach proper. Both sides of Pacific Coast Highway are lined with more shops, restaurants, pubs, and galleries. Continuing south on Pacific Coast Highway, Newport Coast, a planned multimillion-dollar community and home to the Crystal Cove Promenade and its handful of upscale shops, is located on the left-hand side of the road with Crystal Cove State Park positioned beachside. Here you can camp or stay in one of the vintage clapboard cottages and enjoy all the beach has to offer. There are 18 miles of hiking and equestrian trails, too.

Laguna Beach

Just over the hill from Crystal Cove is the artists' colony of Laguna Beach. Set along the Pacific Ocean with seven stunning miles of coastline, Laguna Beach is just 9.1 square miles with less than 25,000 full-time residents. Laguna Beach's reputation as an artists' colony began during the early part of the 20th century with the arrival of plein-air artist Norman St. Claire. Today there are nearly 100 galleries showcasing an array of art forms from local, national, and international artists. Galleries are concentrated in three primary areas: Gallery Row, located along the 300 and 400 blocks of Coast Highway; the Downtown Village area; and the South Village area, which covers the 1100 to 1600 block of Coast Highway.

In addition, Laguna Beach is home to several summer art festivals, including the renowned Festival of Arts and Pageant of the Masters presented in July and August. The festival is a juried exhibit of fine, strictly original works by more than 140 gifted artists, while the pageant presents a mesmerizing stage production of living art recreations. The Sawdust Festival is an outdoor festival with nearly 200 local artists displaying their works in a village of booths connected by paths of sawdust. The Art-A-Fair Festival is another summer gathering showcasing several artists from around the world. The Laguna Art Museum is another artistic attraction. Performing arts also play a major role at the award-winning Laguna Playhouse, the West Coast's oldest continuously operating professional theater company, and Laguna Beach Live!, designed to nurture young talents. In addition, visitors can enjoy First Thursdays Art Walk, a festive cultural evening hosted the first Thursday of each month from 6 to 9 p.m. with free shuttle service to more than 40 galleries. Coast Highway and the Downtown Village area are home to a number of unique and unusual shops. Among the treasures likely to be found are vintage and contemporary hand-crafted jewelry, ceramics and pottery, gourmet foods and wines, antiques, home furnishings, surf gear, collectibles, designer fashions, and much more. Two of Orange County's top resorts—the Montage and Surf and Sand—are

Best of Orange County

Finding out the best places to go doesn't happen overnight. We've sped up the process by recommending these local favorites:

Nicest Place to Exchange Nuptials: Overlooking the Beach at the Surf and Sand Resort & Spa in Laguna Beach

Most Likely Place to Spot a Former NBA Star: Josh Slocum's in Newport Beach, whose owner is none other than Dennis Rodman

Best Classroom Atmosphere: Corky Carroll's Surf School, Huntington Beach

Best Celebrity-Style Crib to Rent: Sunset Cove Villas, Laguna Beach

Best Place to Sip a Salty Margarita: Las Brisas in Laguna Beach

Best Place to People Watch: Along Main Street, Downtown Huntington Beach

Tastiest Annual Event: A Taste of Newport at Fashion Island in September

Best Place for Original and Affordable Art: The Annual Sawdust Festival held every summer in Laguna Beach

Perfect Place to Be Pampered: Pacific Waters Spa at the Hyatt Resort, Huntington Beach

Best Place for Rare Books: Barnaby Rudge Booksellers, Laguna Beach

Premium Place to Putt: Pelican Hill Golf Club, Newport Beach

Best Beer Joint: Yard House at Fashion Island

Hautest Horticulture Retreat: Sherman Library and Gardens, Corona del Mar

Best Place to Get Cookin': Laguna Culinary Arts, Laguna Beach

Best Place for a Sopranos-Style Dinner: Spaghettini in Seal Beach

Best Place for a Beach Bonfire: Bolsa Chica State Beach, Huntington Beach

Place with the Best Stage Presence: The Laguna Playhouse, Laguna Beach

Cheapest Waterfront Meal: Ruby's Diner at the end of the Huntington Beach Pier

Best Oceanfront Dining: The Beach House, Laguna Beach

found in Laguna Beach. Celebrities such as Bette Midler and Heather Locklear have homes here as well. Strewn across the Laguna coastline is an impressive collection of beaches and coves—30 in all. Visitors can choose their location based on their interests; whether it's a desire to explore tide pools or participate in an impromptu game of beach volleyball, each seaside nook offers its own brand of recreation. Some favorite pastimes include sunbathing, whale watching, bird watch-ing, beachfront basketball, swimming, surfing, boogie and body boarding, scuba diving, and kayaking, just to name a few.

Dana Point

Dana Point—home to the oceanfront Ritz-Carlton, St. Regis Resort & Spa, the charming New England-style Blue Lantern Inn, and the contemporary Laguna Cliffs Marriott—was named for Richard Henry Dana, the 19th-century seafaring

Vital Statistics

Founding: The name Orange County was more common than you might think back in 1880. Six other states had counties by the same name as well as many towns dubbed Orange. For Orange County, California, the name seemed apropos considering its thriving citrus industry; however, these days only a few lingering orange groves remain. Prior to separating from Los Angeles County in 1889, several attempts were made on the part of citizens and leaders to become independent from Los Angeles. The first attempt took place in 1870 and it passed the State Assembly, but died with the committee in the State Senate. It took nearly 20 years, five more attempts, several name suggestions including the County of Anaheim and Santa Ana County, and perseverance on the part of residents.

Population: As of July 2007, the U.S. Census Bureau estimated that Orange County had nearly three million residents—2,997,033 to be exact—with 574,193 owner-occupied houses and condominiums.

Location: Orange County is sandwiched between Los Angeles and San Diego Counties and rests between the San Gabriel foothills and the Pacific Ocean. The county spans nearly 800 square miles and is blessed with 42 miles of coastline. Although independent, it is considered part of the Los Angeles–Long Beach–Santa Ana metro area.

Altitude: Orange County's highest point, Santiago Peak, which rises 5,687 feet above sea level, exceeds that of Denver, which is dubbed the Mile High City. The county's lowest point is, of course, sea level.

Climate: In a word, Orange County's climate is idyllic. New Year's Day, while most of America is shivering from the cold, Southern California is sitting beneath sun-kissed skies watching the annual Tournament of Roses Parade in jeans, T-shirts, and lightweight jackets. The region's climate is not unlike the Mediterranean, especially along the coast. Temperatures rarely drop below 40 degrees in the winter and seldom climb much above the 80-degree mark in the summer. It's not uncommon to awaken to a thick marine fog layer hanging like Spanish moss over the beach cities, but this fog typically burns off by the late morning or early afternoon. The hottest months in Orange County tend to be August and September with average temperatures ranging from the mid-70s to low 80s. Move a bit inland, and the temperatures begin to rise slightly and can be 10 degrees warmer once you move away from the

writer who penned *Two Years before the Mast*, in which he describes the headlands. In the 1920s, oil tycoon Edward Doheny helped to pioneer the development of Capistrano Beach, which failed less than a decade later. Doheny ended up donating 40 acres of prime oceanfront property to the state of California, which became the first state beach and is known as Doheny State Beach Park or, less formally, Doheny Beach. Surfers discovered this southern outpost in the 1950s when Hobie Alter, of Hobie Surfboards and Hobie Cat sailboat fame, opened the first retail surf shop on the mainland in Dana Point. Construction of the harbor followed in the late 1960s with the installation of breakwater jetties constructed from stone. Dedicated in 1971, the harbor contains a pair of yacht-bobbing marinas with slips and mooring for some 2,500 boats. There are also shops and restaurants, and many of the town's special events are staged at the harbor and marina as well. The 1970s also saw the beginning of residential development, but the town is still a sleepy region. That could very well change, as city officials are pushing for a revitalization of the town center, making the stretch along Coast Highway more inviting to pedestrians by courting shop owners, gallery curators, and restaurateurs to open businesses along this route. The Ocean Institute, where marine-education and related events are held, includes a replica of the tall ship *Pilgrim*—Richard Henry Dana sailed on the original vessel.

coast. December and January are the chilliest months when temperatures tend to fluctuate in the 50s. For the most part, Orange County has a dry climate with an occasional swell of humidity during some summer months. As for rain, drizzles and downpours usually take place during the winter months.

Government: Orange County is a chartered county governed by a five-member Board of Supervisors, each of whom is elected from a specific geographic district. The board as a whole determines policy, authorizes expenditures, and oversees the various county departments and agencies. A chairman and vice chairman are annually selected from among the elected supervisors, and the county executive, who is a municipal manager, is a non-elected position. This post is hired by the Board of Supervisors. Each city has its own mayor and council representatives.

Politics: Orange County has always been a conservative region, which is a contrast to its neighbor, the much more liberal Los Angeles. During the 1970s and '80s the county was one of the state's leading Republican voting blocks. It still has a strong Republican core and helped to elect George W. Bush to office in both 2000 and 2004. The 2008 election was an almost evenly matched race in this conservative block, with Barack Obama taking 48 percent of the vote and John McCain taking 50 percent.

Famous Orange County residents: Comedian and *Saturday Night Live* alum Will Ferrell was raised in Irvine and graduated from University High; actor Patrick Warburton, best known for his role as Elaine's boyfriend, David Puddy, on *Seinfeld* as well as his voiceover work, was raised in Huntington Beach, graduated from the all-boys Catholic High School Servite in Anaheim, and briefly attended Orange Coast College in Costa Mesa; actor Kevin Costner graduated from Villa Park High School before attending Cal State Fullerton, where he was a member of the Delta Chi fraternity; actress Michelle Pfeiffer was born and raised in Orange County, where she attended Fountain Valley High and Golden West Community College and was a checker at a local Vons grocery store; President Richard Nixon was born and raised in Yorba Linda, where his childhood home still stands and is now part of the Richard Nixon Library compound; actress, director, and preservationist Diane Keaton is a graduate of Santa Ana High; comedian Steve Martin was raised in Garden Grove and worked at Disneyland's Magic Shop on Main Street; golfer Tiger Woods was born in Cypress and is a graduate of Western High School; singer and designer Gwen Stefani of No Doubt fame and the creator of the L.A.M.B. label was raised in Anaheim near Disneyland, was a member of the swim team at Loara High School, and attended Cal State Fullerton.

San Clemente

San Clemente, which spans just 15 square miles of coastline and scenic foothills, was founded by former Seattle mayor Ole Hanson, who purchased and designed a 2,000-acre community in 1925. Buildings were erected in the classic Spanish style with alabaster exteriors, crowning red tile roofs, and black iron accents. San Clemente arrived on the national stage when President Richard Nixon, who had grown up in the northern Orange County town of Yorba Linda, purchased a 1927 Spanish estate in 1969 that was quickly dubbed the Western White House by the media. It became the backdrop for many historic meetings and, after Mr. and Mrs. Nixon left the White House, the couple retired to La Casa Pacifica, where Nixon penned his memoirs. The infamous Frost/Nixon interviews were originally to take place here, but the neighboring Coast Guard's transmitters interfered with the signal and the interview was moved to a home nearby belonging to a Nixon supporter. The Nixons eventually sold their waterfront home in the late 1980s and moved east to a New York City suburb. Today, La Casa Pacifica is a private residence and concealed from public view.

San Clemente, which borders San Diego County, is still a quaint discovery with a downtown area, sandy beaches where the train runs right along the sand, and well-preserved architecture. Forecasts predict that the city's population and service area will double over the next two decades as new residential developments and retail centers come on the scene. Talega, located on the north side of I-5 in the "backwoods" of town, is one such planned community flanked with many spacious homes. Such additions have drawn criticism by some who believe the developments will erode San Clemente's charm. Only time will tell.

OTHER NOTEWORTHY COMMUNITIES

Irvine

Orange County has many other towns and neighborhoods that add to its diverse tapestry. Irvine—whose neighborhoods adhere to strict rules that dictate what color homeowners are allowed to paint their houses and forbid leaving garbage cans in plain sight—is a major retail and financial force. Touted as one of the nation's largest planned communities, Irvine is home to the University of California, Irvine, the largest of the UC campuses, as well as the Irvine Spectrum, a mélange of Moorish architecture with endless dining options, shops, and entertainment venues including a massive Ferris wheel. By 2011 Irvine will be also known as the home of the nearly 1,400-acre Orange County Great Park, which will consist of a sports park, exhibition space, orchard and farm, community gardens and food labs, picnic meadow, and much more. A hot air balloon, tethered and fashioned after an orange, can be seen from the freeway and marks the spot where all of this will occur.

Santa Ana

The county seat, Santa Ana, remains a large settlement for Mexican immigrants. All along 4th Street are Mexican shops, markets, and services advertising "*Habla Español*," and street vendors roam the avenues selling fruit bars and other wares. But there is another side to Santa Ana—one that has slowly transitioned its downtown into an artists' village with stylish lofts, galleries, and studios. Santa Ana is also home to the renowned Bower's Museum, the county's only zoo, and the Old County Courthouse, which has been cast in several movie and television productions but is now an historical museum. The county's only major daily newspaper, *The Orange County Register*, is also located in Santa Ana on Grand Avenue.

San Juan Capistrano

And, finally, the mission bells still resonate on the streets of San Juan Capistrano, the birthplace of Orange County. Home to the historic Mission San Juan Capistrano, founded by Father Junípero Serra in 1776 and built by the natives that once roamed this land, the town still oozes with Spanish charm. March marks the Return of the Swallows, when the feathered fowl return to San Juan Capistrano to nest in the mission's eaves and are heralded by locals and visitors alike. Downtown, where the mission is located, retains much of its early California charm with roofs cloaked in red tiles and structures supported by wood beam accents. The Los Rios Historic District, with its nearly three dozen significant structures lining both sides of Los Rios Street between Del Obispo and Mission Streets, is one of Orange County's oldest continuing neighborhoods. There is a trio of adobe homes built for the mission families in 1794, as well as the O'Neill Museum, another historic dwelling filled with history and artifacts. The district also contains a collection of single-wall board and batten homes built between 1887 and 1910 that shelter retail shops and restaurants. Some are even occupied by residents.

The outlying areas of downtown conceal horse ranches and stately homes that easily pass the $10 million mark. The region is a highly regarded equestrian destination filled with stables and boarding facilities. Trails traverse the landscape and the sound of horses' hoofs is as common in these parts as the hum of automobiles is in other, more urban areas.

No matter what city or region you happen upon in Orange County, you won't be disappointed. It has something to offer most everyone, from pounding waves and velvety sands to luxurious resorts and some of the best shopping destinations. Orange County is California dreamin' at its best.

GETTING HERE, GETTING AROUND

Orange County is a suburban sanctuary made up of 34 independent municipalities, each one blending in with the next. Getting from Point A to Point B can be simple if you familiarize yourself with major roadways, the freeway system, and Orange County's public transportation system. The major roads and freeways typically run east to west or north to south. To help give you a better sense of direction, the San Gabriel Mountains, visible on clear days, are to the north and the Pacific Ocean is to the south.

Unlike other regions, whose streets may run in chronological or alphabetical order, there really is no rhyme or reason to the naming of Orange County's streets, with the exception of those named for the region's early settlers. There are more than 35,000 streets of varying sizes in Orange County, including some 14 Main Streets and a handful of Oak Streets. Many of the major streets are named for significant people, such as Warner, Glassell, Chapman, and Yorba Linda. Other monikers are a bit more obvious, such as State College Boulevard, which runs alongside the campus of Cal State Fullerton, or Beach Boulevard, which cuts a path through the inland cities before ending at Pacific Coast Highway in Huntington Beach with the ocean straight ahead.

When traveling along the freeway, you may encounter delays, especially during rush hour. But if there is a major event taking place, such as a concert at the Honda Center or a baseball game at Angel Stadium, you may find yourself coming to a sudden halt and will continue moving at a snail's pace the closer you get to the venue. Surface streets can be equally slow with their fleet of traffic signals, unexpected roadwork, or when three lanes suddenly transition into two. For the latest freeway traffic conditions and major road blocks, tune in to KNX 1070 AM for frequent traffic reports and updates.

DRIVING

Navigating the Freeway System

Orange County residents, like those in the rest of Southern California, spend most of their time in their cars. It's not that public transportation isn't readily available or that people are in any way opposed to using the system; it's just not part of the everyday culture. So, they sit behind their wheels inching along in rush-hour traffic trying to reach their destinations in a reasonable amount of time and, more importantly, with their sanity intact.

There are two interstate freeways that make their way through Orange County—the 405/San Diego Freeway and the I-5/Santa Ana Freeway. The former gained a bit of notoriety, if that's possible for a patch of pavement, when a white Ford Bronco concealing O.J. Simpson (Al Cowlings was actually driving) became involved in a slow-speed, nationally televised police pursuit that ended with the former football star's arrest for the murder of his ex-wife Nicole Simpson and her friend Ronald Goldman at his Los Angeles estate. The 405 freeway originates in Orange County at the El Toro Y, where the 405 merges with I-5. It then continues through Orange County, heading north through west Los Angeles before terminating in the San Fernando Valley. I-5, on the other hand, is the West Coast's major interstate, beginning in San Diego and traveling north through Orange County, past Disneyland and onward through Los Angeles before continuing to Oregon and Washington states.

Orange County Freeways

Chances are your travels will take you beyond Orange County, thrusting you onto some of Southern California's other freeways. And just when you think you've mastered the region's roadway system, a confusing web of merging lanes and fast-moving vehicles, you find yourself shaking your head in frustration. Just remember, most freeways have both a number and a name, which indicates the road's final destination. But this isn't always the case. Consider the San Diego Freeway, which runs through Orange County and is also known as the 405. Not only does it not end in San Diego, it never even makes it into the county; instead, the roadway merges in Orange County with I-5, the Santa Ana Freeway, which actually trails down through San Diego to the Mexican border. There are other freeway names that break the rule as well. Below is a cheat sheet to help get you acclimated. An asterisk (*) indicates that the freeway also runs through Orange County.

2	Glendale	10	Santa Monica/San Bernardino
22	Garden Grove*	57	Orange*
71	Chino Valley Freeway	91	Riverside/Artesia*
105	Glen Anderson	118	Simi Valley/San Fernando Valley
101	Hollywood		
710	Long Beach	405	San Diego*
14	Antelope Valley	5	Golden State/Santa Ana*
60	Pomona	90	Marina
101	Ventura/Hollywood	110	Pasadena/Harbor
134	Ventura	210	Foothill
605	San Gabriel	55	Newport*

A handful of state routes also weave their way through the county, including the 22/Garden Grove Freeway, a 12-mile multi-lane roadway intersecting with most of the county's major north and south corridors. The 55/Newport Freeway begins in the south at Costa Mesa and continues north to Anaheim Hills. The 57/Orange Freeway will take you from Brea to the city of Orange where you can then transition either onto the 22/Garden Grove Freeway or I-5. The 91/Riverside Freeway, which also crosses with the 57/Orange Freeway, travels between Orange County and Riverside County, slicing its way through the northern part of the county from Yorba Linda and Anaheim Hills, and continuing past Knott's Berry Farm in Buena Park before crossing into Los Angeles County in the city of Cerritos.

Perhaps the county's most scenic and interesting byway is Pacific Coast Highway, simply known by its initials of PCH. The four-lane road is the common thread that links the beach communities together beginning in Dana Point and continuing north through Laguna Beach, Newport Beach, Huntington Beach, Sunset Beach, and, finally, Seal Beach near the Los Angeles County Line.

Rules of the Road

The Carpool Lane

While driving in Orange County, or the entire state of California for that matter, it's wise to learn the rules of the road. High Occupancy Vehicles (HOVs), cars that carry two or more persons with some HOV lanes requiring a three-person minimum, can travel in the HOV (carpool) lane. Each child counts as an occupant, but don't try passing off a pet, baby in the belly, or inflatable doll as a passenger. If you do and get caught by the California Highway Patrol (CHP), the fine is a minimum of $381. Motorcycles are the exception and can use the lane even if it's just the driver riding solo. Be sure to check the signage of the HOV lane on the freeway on which you are traveling because some lanes only require the multi-person minimum during certain hours, which means in the "off" hours they are open to all vehicles.

Cell Phones

Hands-free wireless telephones may be used while driving, but drivers 18 and under are prohibited from using such devices while operating a vehicle. If you are caught using a handheld cell phone, whether you are a resident of California or simply visiting from another state, the base fine of $20 is for the first offense only and $50 for subsequent convictions. While this may sound inexpensive as far as penalties go, additional assessments can be added and the total amount may more than triple the base fine fee. Texting while driving, including reading text messages, is also illegal and carries basically the same penalties.

Child Safety Seats

For legal purposes, there's no need to worry about safety or booster seats for your children as long as they are at least six years old or weigh a minimum of 60 pounds. The California Highway Patrol (CHP) recommends that children should continue using a booster seat until they reach 80 pounds; however, at press time this remains optional. Babies must ride rear-facing up to a year old and less than 20 pounds. Children over 12 months of age and weighing at least 20 pounds are required to ride face forward. Once the child reaches 40 pounds he or she can transition to a belt-positioning booster seat.

Driving Under the Influence (DUI)

California's drunk-driving laws are some of the nation's strictest. You are considered under the influence if your blood alcohol level is 0.08 or higher and, should the attending officer determine that your blood alcohol exceeds the legal limit, you will be arrested on the spot and taken into custody. For drivers 21 and under, there is a zero-tolerance limit. The CHP often conducts sobriety checkpoints, which are well publicized in the newspaper and considered to be a deterrent in preventing unnecessary accidents and deaths. If you are going to drink, be sure to designate a non-drinking driver. Many bars and lounges are more than willing to call a cab for you and some even have courtesy phones that connect you directly to a taxi company.

Move Over Law

Drivers are required to slow down and vacate the lane by moving to the shoulder of the road to allow emergency vehicles, such as police, fire, or paramedics with flashing and audible sirens, the ability to quickly pass.

Red Light-Right Turn

In most instances, you can turn right at a red light after coming to a complete stop as long as there is no oncoming traffic. But be sure there are no signs posted prohibiting this maneuver to avoid getting a traffic ticket.

Road Conditions

Earthquakes are not the only unpredictable occurrences in Southern California. Traffic can be extremely erratic with clear road conditions one minute and a multi-car pile-up the next minute. If you are concerned about road conditions, road closures, or reduced lanes you can contact Caltrans at (800) 427-7623 to be updated on the latest conditions.

Seatbelts and Helmets

All drivers and passengers are required to wear seatbelts when the car is in motion, and motorcyclists, along with their passengers, are required to wear helmets.

Teen Driving Laws

It may be the same roads, but it's not the same rules for teen drivers. Teenagers who have had a license for less than 12 full months are not allowed to drive non-family members under the age of 20 unless a passenger 25 years or older is riding in the front seat. Teens that have had their license less than a year are also prohibited from driving between the hours of 11 p.m. and 5 a.m. except under certain circumstances. Seventeen is the minimum age for an unrestricted license.

i Nothing is more frustrating than having your car break down, especially on the freeway. Thankfully, California freeways have call boxes located every quarter mile and operators will connect you either to your auto club, family members, or your insurance company.

Familiarizing Yourself with Major Roads

Orange County has several main arteries to get you where you need to go. Keep in mind, these major roads will intersect with other major roads resulting in several traffic light stops, which could cause delays depending on your timing, or the timing of the light. AAA and car rental agencies offer free maps of the region to members and customers.

Imperial Highway

This major east to west highway works its way through Los Angeles County and the northern part of Orange County beginning in Anaheim Hills and traveling through Yorba Linda and Brea before crossing over the county line.

Yorba Linda Boulevard

Yorba Linda Boulevard is another north county thoroughfare that runs parallel to Imperial Highway and begins at the 91 Freeway in Yorba Linda traveling through Placentia into Fullerton and terminating at State College Boulevard near the campus of Cal State Fullerton.

State College Boulevard

State College Boulevard begins at Brea Boulevard in northern Orange County before becoming the City Drive at the 5 Freeway and terminating shortly after that. This north to south roadway travels past Cal State Fullerton, Angel Stadium, and the Block of Orange.

Harbor Boulevard

Traveling from Costa Mesa to La Habra, where it becomes Fullerton Road once it reaches Los Angeles County, Harbor Boulevard is a major street running north to south through the county's mid cities. Probably the most notable point of interest on this route, which will take you through Santa Ana, Garden Grove, and Anaheim, is Disneyland Resort. The road is also riddled with several hotels and motels in and around the Disneyland area. Anaheim native Gwen Stefani, lead singer of No Doubt, references Harbor Boulevard in her song "Cool."

Katella Boulevard

Running east to west, Katella Boulevard begins near the 55 Freeway and continues to the 605 Freeway. East of the 55 Freeway the road becomes Villa Park and, eventually, Santiago Canyon, while west of the 605 Freeway at the Los Angeles County line it becomes Willow in the city of Long Beach and, eventually, Sepulveda Boulevard. Major points of interest, all within Anaheim city limits, are Angel Stadium, the Anaheim Convention Center, and Disneyland Resort.

Beach Boulevard

With a name like Beach Boulevard, you might expect this busy road to cross section all of Orange County's seaside cities. But its name indicates its point of termination, which basically dead ends near the sand at Huntington Beach (at Pacific Coast Highway). Beach Boulevard, also known as Highway 39, runs north to south for several miles through Los Angeles and Orange Counties. It enters The OC in La Habra and travels past Knott's Berry Farm in Buena Park and Bella Terra shopping center in the northern section of

Huntington Beach before reaching Pacific Coast Highway in the coastal area of Huntington Beach.

Pacific Coast Highway

Pacific Coast Highway, or PCH, which runs east to west along the Pacific Ocean, is the road linking all the beach communities together. It begins in the south at Dana Point at the 5 Freeway and travels through Laguna Beach, Newport Beach, Huntington Beach, Sunset Beach, and Seal Beach before crossing into Los Angeles County in Long Beach. For the most part, it's a scenic drive with million-dollar views of the glistening ocean, but some stretches are lined with entrances to gated communities, shopping districts, and rows of restaurants. You will find many major resorts along PCH, including the Ritz-Carlton, Montage, Surf and Sand Resort and Spa, and the St. Regis in south Orange County, as well as the Hyatt Regency Resort and Spa and the Waterfront Hilton, both located in Huntington Beach. PCH also skirts Fashion Island, Balboa Island, and the Bolsa Chica Wetlands.

Rental Cars

Most major hotels and resorts have at least one on-site car rental agency to assist you. If you are staying at a hotel that doesn't offer this service, enlist the help of the concierge. Of course, the airport has several companies to choose from, but there are also car rental companies, such as Hertz and Enterprise, located in freestanding buildings within neighborhoods and major resort areas.

Limousines

There is an abundance of limousine and town car service in Orange County. These private companies typically require an advance reservation and, especially for limousines, a minimum time limit. You will also find party buses, stretch Hummers, and other unusual modes of transportation available. Classique Limousines, (714) 288-8853, and Orange County Limousine, (888) 856-1938, are just two such companies that can carry a carload and then some in style.

Taxis

Taxi service in Orange County is rather limited, but readily available at the airport, most major hotels and resorts, and major attractions such as Disneyland. However, unlike major urban centers, you can't just step off the curb and hail a cab. When you need a taxi, have your hotel concierge or restaurant host call ahead for you.

Public Transportation

The Orange County Transportation Authority (OCTA) offers county-wide service with 80 bus routes and 6,500 bus stops. It also operates Metrolink, a rail service with three lines and 11 stations in Orange County with connections to Metrolink lines in Los Angeles, Ventura, San Bernardino, and Riverside counties. The OCTA's online trip planner, www.octa.net, can help you plot your trek, calculate fares, determine the length of your trip, and provide you with walking directions.

Bikeways

Because Orange County is such a sprawling region, most people are prone to riding bikes for pleasure rather than necessity. The favorable climate and some 1,000 miles of bike paths and lanes make it a perfect environment for two-wheeling. Bicyclists share equal rights and responsibilities with their four-wheeled counterparts, but many areas provide bicycle-specific lanes to further promote safety.

AIRPORTS

JOHN WAYNE AIRPORT
18601 Airport Way, Santa Ana
(949) 252-5200
www.ocair.com

Thankfully, you can bypass LAX in most instances and fly directly into John Wayne Airport (SNA), Orange County's only commercial airport and the world's 15th busiest for takeoffs and landings. Centrally located just off the 405 Freeway in Santa Ana, abutting Newport Beach, John Wayne Airport was founded in the 1920s as a private landing

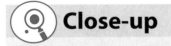

Close-up

California Car Rentals

Renting a car should be easy, and it usually is. But, as a smart consumer, you should always take the "buyer beware" approach. Be sure you read and understand the fine print on the contract.

RENTAL CAR TAXES

In addition to the flat daily or weekly rate paid for a rental car, you will also incur taxes and airport fees, which quickly increase the overall tab. These taxes don't benefit the rental car companies, but rather the ever depleting pockets of city and state government.

GPS SYSTEMS

Many car rental companies have also begun installing global positioning systems (GPS) in their fleets not only to track vehicles if lost or stolen, but to monitor clients as well. Some rental agencies do not allow their vehicles to be driven over state lines, so if you plan on taking a quick trip to Las Vegas be sure you won't accrue any additional charges as a result. Also, keep in mind that rates are constantly changing in both directions.

RATES

Fares are likely to increase during busy holiday weekends, but if cars aren't moving off the lot the agency has more flexibility with their rates. Shop around by calling the agencies directly, visit their Web sites for any unpublished specials, and use travel Web sites, such as Priceline or

---

strip by aviation pioneer Eddie Martin and served as a military base during World War II. In 1967, the first terminal was erected, a 22,000-square-foot facility named for Mr. Martin. The airport's growth was slow going for the next couple of decades with not much happening other than a name change from Orange County Airport to John Wayne Airport, in honor of the late actor who resided in neighboring Newport Beach. It wasn't until 1990 that the airport really took on a life of its own with the opening of a new 337,900-square-foot terminal replete with 14 loading bridges, four carousels, a pair of club lounges, and an array of food and gift concessions. Eventually, the original terminal was demolished.

Perhaps the airport's best asset is its location, a mere 11 miles from the Anaheim/Disneyland district and even closer to the coastal communities. With its close proximity to Laguna Beach, a community with a thriving artists' colony, John Wayne Airport has an impressive arts program that presents museum-quality exhibitions throughout its terminal and sponsors an annual county-wide

Student Art Contest and Exhibition. Among the airport's permanent collection is *The John Wayne Statue,* a bronze sculpture of the Duke designed by sculptor Robert Summers, which stands 9 feet tall and is centered inside the terminal on the arrival level resting atop a two-tiered marble pedestal.

Ground Transportation from the Airport

Airport Shuttles

The Ground Transportation Center (GTC) is the clearinghouse for shuttle service and other transportation and is located a short walk from the Baggage Claim Area on the Arrival/Lower Level in the center of the East Parking Structure. There are several shuttle companies operating within the county with Super Shuttle, (800) 258-3826, and Primetime, (800) 733-8267, among the more well known. Rates will vary depending on your final destination, and it's wise to call ahead to make advance arrangements. You can also visit the airport Web site, www.ocair.com, for more options.

Travelocity, to see if you can get an even better rate. With Priceline's "Name Your Own Price," you can often rent a car at well below the asking price.

MINIMUM AGE

Most rental agencies require that the driver be at least 25 years or older. In most instances, married couples can both get behind the wheel even if only one partner signed the rental agreement. You will also be asked to provide a valid driver's license from your home state or country as well as a major credit card for incidentals, such as returning the vehicle later than the agreement states or bringing the car back with less fuel than when you left. Fuel charges at the rental agency can be nearly twice as much than they are at the pump.

INSURANCE

One way a car rental agency makes money is by selling its own insurance, but it's likely you don't need this supplemental coverage. Chances are you may already be covered through your own insurance policy and many major credit card companies automatically insure their card holders as well when the rental expense is charged on that particular credit card. Check to see if your policy covers collision and damage as well as liability. The former repairs and replaces any physical damage done to the vehicle, while the latter shields you from lawsuits in the event you have a collision and injure someone or damage their property. If you do decide to accept additional insurance from the rental agency, expect to pay an additional $10 to $25 per day for the privilege.

Hotel Shuttles

Several Orange County hotels provide complimentary shuttle service to and from the airport as well. Be sure to ask at the time of reservation if your hotel offers this service or visit the airport Web site, www.ocair.com, for a complete listing of participating hotels.

Taxis

Hailing a taxi in The OC doesn't have quite the cachet it does in larger cities. For one thing, there aren't a lot of taxi drivers aimlessly driving around in search of their next fare. But you will find a queue of taxis in the GTC most any time of day or night. Cabs can ferry up to five passengers, and rates are $2.95 for the first quarter mile, plus 65 cents for each additional quarter mile with a $30 wait fee per hour prorated at 50 cents per minute. You can also possibly negotiate a flat rate with the driver, but do so before entering the cab. Fares are subject to change. You can also call ahead to Yellow Cab (800-535-2211 or 714-535-0156) for the most current rates.

Rental Cars

The major rental car companies are all on site on the Arrival Level (Lower Level) between terminals A and B, across from the iconic John Wayne statue. The rental car return is on the lower level of parking structures A2 and B2, which can be accessed from the GTC.

ON-SITE RENTAL CAR COMPANIES

Alamo Rent-A-Car: (800) 327-9633
Avis Rent-A-Car: (800) 230-4898
Budget Rent-A-Car: (800) 527-0700
Enterprise Rent-A-Car: (800) 736-8222
Hertz Corporation: (800) 654-3131
National Car Rental: (800) 227-7368
Thrifty Car Rental: (800) 847-4389

OFF-SITE RENTAL CAR COMPANIES

These off-site rental car companies are licensed to pick up passengers from the terminal and shuttle them to their pick-up locations off-site.

Alternative Airports

In addition to John Wayne Airport, there is Los Angeles International Airport (LAX), the world's fifth busiest passenger airport with more than 90 national and international airline carriers; and Long Beach Airport (LGB), a regional airport located a few miles west of the Los Angeles/ Orange County line, with easy in, easy out convenience. Currently LGB is serviced by Alaska Airlines, Delta, JetBlue Airways, and US Airways.

Bottom line: If your final destination is Orange County, then John Wayne Airport is the obvious and most convenient choice with Long Beach Airport running a close second. LAX, because of its sheer size and the amount of airport traffic, is the airport to avoid if at all possible.

American Eagle Car Rental: (877) 323-9595 or (714) 432-1313

AM-PM Rent-A-Car: (800) 220-4310

Fox/Payless Rent-A-Car: (800) 220-4310

Go Rent-A-Van: (800) 464-8267

United Auto Rental: (888) 660-0101

U-Save Car & Truck Rental/Newport Beach Rent A Car: (888) 755-6664 or (949) 752-6664

ARRIVING BY TRAIN OR BUS

AMTRAK
(800) 872-7245
www.amtrak.com

Reaching Orange County via Amtrak can also be a very fulfilling travel experience. There are seven train depots within the county, including Irvine, Santa Ana, Orange, Anaheim, Laguna Niguel, Fullerton, and San Juan Capistrano. Depending on where your train originates, it could very well travel directly into Orange County. The Pacific Surfliner, which travels from Seattle to downtown San Diego, makes four stops in Orange County. If there is not direct rail service to Orange County from where your trip originates, chances are you will have to transfer in downtown Los Angeles at Union Station, then board a southbound train headed to Orange County.

GREYHOUND
(800) 231-2222
www.greyhound.com

With a promise to "get you where you're going," Greyhound is an alternative to air or train travel. Often motoring along the back roads of America, stopping in smaller communities and hamlets while en route to big city destinations, those arriving in Orange County will do so at one of two bus terminals. The Anaheim Greyhound Station at 100 West Winston Rd. is extremely close to Disneyland Resort, while the Santa Ana Greyhound Station at 1000 East Santa Ana Blvd. is located close to the 5 Freeway.

i "Know before you go" is a motto that serves travelers well. The California Department of Tourism (www.visitcali fornia.com) can supply you with information on the entire state as well as select regions. The Anaheim/Orange County Visitors & Convention Bureau (714-765-8888 or www.anaheimoc.org), will send you visitors' guides, brochures, maps, and special publications to help you better plan your trip to Orange County.

HISTORY

Orange County may be Southern California's hip and well-heeled corner, but turn the clock back a century or two and life in The OC was one of perseverance and determination coupled with a pioneering spirit from the men and women who helped to settle the land.

Native American tribes, such as the Tongva, Gabrielinos, Juaneño, Shoshones, Ute-Aztecas, and Luiseño, roamed the land long before the arrival of the Spanish. But once explorer Gaspar de Portola discovered the region, life for the natives, unbeknown to them, would change drastically. They were recruited to help the Spanish develop the area during a time when colonial America was struggling for independence some 3,000 miles away on the opposite side of the New World. Orange County's evolution began with the construction of Mission San Juan Capistrano, the seventh mission to be built in the 21-mission chain, and eventually segued to the region's rancho period when adobes and vast farmland were dominant. Land grants, given by both the Spanish and Mexican governments during their reigns, were eventually divided and sold with a group of German settlers reaping the benefits by purchasing several acres at $2 a plot. Their land, christened Anaheim, became a successful wine-producing region during he mid to late 1800s before blight completely destroyed thousands of grapevines. While the region was no longer conducive to grape growing, its rich soil launched another agricultural renaissance, and soon the smell of orange blossoms permeated the air as hundreds of groves produced plump and succulent fruit. Orange County remained a sleepy farming community for much of the nineteenth as well as the first half of the twentieth centuries. Following World War II, a rash of housing developments were built as GIs returned from their tours of duty to settle down and raise families. As the latter part of the twentieth century got underway, Orange County began to evolve as a major tourist destination with the opening of Disneyland. Its metamorphosis as a vacation hotspot continued with the expansion of John Wayne Airport and the addition of plush, coastal resorts. From its humble beginnings to its present-day panache, The OC continues to evolve with each passing year.

THE NATIVE AMERICANS

The first true inhabitants of Orange County were the Native Americans, which consisted of two tribes—the Gabrielinos and the Juaneños. These dwellers were known to roam as they hunted and gathered food. Leadership was handed down from generation to generation creating a monarchy of sorts with one ruling family. For the natives, this was life as they knew it.

THE ARRIVAL OF THE SPANISH

That all changed in the late 1700s when the Spaniards landed along the West Coast of the New World in hopes of colonizing the land, thus forming a tighter bond with Spain. Their goal was to make Spanish citizens of the natives. While England was engaged in the Revolutionary War on the other side of the New World, the Spanish were busy plotting and strategizing how to colonize the west coast, which included what is now Orange County, as well as much of Southern California, and explains the region's heavy Spanish influence. Native Americans were promised land grants, and interracial marriages were very much encouraged as young and old Spanish men took Native American women as wives.

Bet You Didn't Know

According to the travel Web site Legends of America, Orange County has some little known quirky facts. Did you know . . .

- Orange County was once home to a buffalo ranch in Newport Beach and an alligator farm in Buena Park.

- Legend has it that in 1922 a gigantic sea creature was spotted at Three Arch Bay in Laguna Beach.

- Walt Disney, the creator of Mickey Mouse, was afraid of mice.

- In Dana Point, using your own restroom while the window is open is prohibited.

- California is the birthplace of the Internet, the Mazda Miata, Barbie, Frisbees, and skateboards.

- In Tomorrowland inside the original Disneyland, all plants are edible, including bananas, strawberries, tomatoes, and more.

THE MISSIONARY ERA

In the meantime, Spanish missionaries had very different motives and intentions for the natives. Under the guidance of Father Junípero Serra and funded by the Spanish Empire, Christian missionaries, along with Jesuits from Baja California, recruited the Indians to build their missions while educating them on Christian values. Conversion took place up and down the California coast. On November 1, 1776, the seventh of the 21 California missions, but the first and only mission to be erected in what would become Orange County, was built by the natives who were soon taught skills, such as wine making and blacksmithing, as they continued their Christian education. While many assume violence contributed to the decline of the American Indian in California, it was actually a duo of major epidemics that were brought to the region by the Spaniards. These diseases—smallpox and measles—were incurable at the time and fueled doubt among the natives in regards to the Christian faith.

MEXICO DEFEATS SPAIN AND GAINS CONTROL OF CALIFORNIA

Spain was still in control of California's land, including Orange County, with very few land concessions held by individual families. In 1810 things began to shift as the Mexican and Spanish governments began fighting for the rights to the land in a period known as the Mexican War of Independence. Mexico was able to unclench the grip Spain had on the country by winning the war in 1821 and declaring themselves an independent nation. The Spanish flag, which had flown for several years on Orange County soil, was quickly retired and replaced with the Mexican flag. Mexico's victory proved to be a defeat for the Native Americans as well. The land they were promised under Spanish rule was denied under the new government. Land rights were given to individuals who could prove they had the resources to build on the soil in a year or less and who were further willing to cultivate the land for the Mexican government. Deeply upset over this ruling, the American Indians began abandoning the missions as the resources and supplies provided by the Spanish dried up. The Mexican government seized all the missions from the church in 1833 as part of a secularization movement, thus ending the era of the mission system. Following the period of secularization in the 1800s, many missions were rebuilt or restored with all 21 missions enticing visitors with their ruins, museums, artifacts, and interesting stories. Restoration of the missions is an ongoing task.

Many of the missions were rebuilt and restored following the period of secularization. Most are simply reconstructed replicas of the

🔍 Close-up

The Mission System

Just like any other landmark, the missions are a part of California's rich history and tell a story from within their walls. Not only are these stone and adobe structures historically significant, they have also been instrumental in defining California architecture with a heavy Spanish influence that includes crisp white exteriors, wrought-iron accents, red tile roofs, and picturesque courtyards. The Spanish government implemented the mission system in order to secure its claims to the New World. Under the tutelage of Father Junípero Serra, the 21-mission system began when the first mission was established in 1769 in San Diego and concluded when the final stone was laid at the 21st mission in Sonoma in 1823. The missions are found along the historic Mission Trail, which roughly traces El Camino Real—the Royal Road—along I-5 from San Diego to Orange County, Highway 101 from Los Angeles to the San Francisco, Highway 82 from San Francisco to Santa Clara, and Highway 37, which leads to the last mission built in Sonoma. Bronze mission bells, installed during the 1920s, were placed along El Camino Real to alert motorists that they were traveling on the historic highway. The missions were cleverly positioned about 30 miles apart to ensure that each could be reached in a day, from sunrise to sunset, and built near the coast so the Spanish could establish towns and trade with ships. Ironically, they were not built in geographic order. The first mission was established in San Diego and the second mission was built in Carmel along the Central Coast, creating more than a 400-mile gap between the two. But the convenience of spacing them 30 miles apart and establishing coastal trading towns tells only part of the story; the main reason for the mission system was to convert the natives to Christianity.

Each mission shared a common architectural design, which continues to be an influential force today in the design of homes and buildings throughout California. The stone and adobe structures were crowned with hewn timber cloaked in red clay tiles with the interiors coated in whitewashed mud plaster. Each mission has a quadrangle where the shops and rooms were kept and the church, along with additional buildings, helped to enclose the cloistered courtyard. Minor structures were used to house friars, native workers, servants, and soldiers,. A single bell tower was also an integral part of the mission design with Santa Barbara being the only mission to display two bell towers. The church also needed to be built at the same height as the highest tree so that it could easily be spotted from a distance. Today many of the missions have active parishes where people go to worship weekly.

original churches. And many of the missions have a representation of the quadrangle, which was an important design element. All of the missions have ruins to see, museums to visit, and unique stories to tell. Nearly all of the missions are used as parish churches serving a local community. The restoration continues to this day and will always be an important part of California's Spanish history. These historic compounds are open to visitors, and fourth grade students attending California public schools learn of missions and their histories as part of their curriculum.

THE MEXICAN-AMERICAN WAR

The Mexican-American war of 1846 to 1848 ended with the Treaty of Guadalupe Hidalgo and a loss of land control for Mexico. The Gold Rush of 1849 had people flocking to California, which became a state in 1850, but statehood posed an entirely new set of problems for land owners. Many lost what they had acquired due to the liberal distribution under the Spanish and Mexican governments. Citizens were now required to show documentation of ownership in order to retain their holdings and many simply lost their land as a result. Entrepreneurs, such as

James Irvine, seized this opportunity by purchasing large amounts of land and planted more drought-resistant crops that could thrive in California's dry climate, such as walnuts, avocados, and oranges—hence the name Orange County. The expansion of the railroad spawned several additional settlements, and with the invention of the electric trolley system, which ferried passengers to and from Los Angeles, residents became more mobile and regions more accessible. As a result, people from Los Angeles and other areas began flocking to the new resort communities of Huntington Beach and neighboring Seal Beach.

LAND GRANTS, GRAPES, AND ORANGE GROVES

During the 1870s, as the land grants were challenged and the ranchos divided and sold, another phenomenon was taking place. A group of German settlers had purchased one of the land grants for $2 an acre and named it Anaheim, or "home by the river." Long before Napa Valley was growing grapes to make grappa, Anaheim was the state's chief wine producing region. It was a thriving industry that abruptly ended during the 1880s as disease completely destroyed thousands of grapevines, leaving vintners to ponder what to do next. The area's rich soil spawned another agricultural renaissance for the region and soon orange blossoms permeated the air with groves blanketing fields where grapevines once stood.

A SECTION OF LA SECEDES AND BECOMES ORANGE COUNTY

While gold may have been lacking in the hills of Orange County, there was no shortage of silver. In 1887 prospectors began flocking to the Santa Ana Mountains in hopes of striking it rich and, as a result, the population swelled. Residents and officials, unsatisfied with how Los Angeles was governing the region and tired of the long commute to the city, began a campaign to annex themselves from LA. To use a more modern term, the region was geographically undesirable due to the distance between it and LA proper. Many

felt their needs were not being addressed. In 1889 it became official: Orange County was its own, self-governing region.

TOURISM AND TRACT HOMES

The trolley lines helped to promote tourism and growth at the start of the 20th century, and soon piers and picturesque harbors were established. But Orange County still remained a sleepy farming community until the invention of the automobile and the implementation of a freeway system made it even more accessible. Hollywood moguls and movie stars often fled to Orange

OC, Inc.

The development of any county or region is never an overnight proposition. It's a slow process of growth that takes years, even decades, and Orange County is no different. Anaheim, Santa Ana, and Orange were the first cities in the county to incorporate and did so between 1876 and 1888, before the region separated from Los Angeles. W. H. Spurgeon bought 74 acres, laid out a town center he called Santa Ana, and sold downtown lots to investors for $15 a plot. Alfred Beck Chapman and Andrew Glassell, two enterprising lawyers, acquired nearly 1,400 acres of land as barter in return for legal counsel and turned it into a fruit packing and shipping center known as Orange. Cypress and La Palma were prosperous dairy farms, while northern and central Orange County harvested barley, wheat, grapes, citrus, and walnuts. Today, several Fortune 500 and Fortune 1000 companies have their headquarters in Orange County.

County for a quick or extended getaway in what was still considered a semi-rural region. But it was the outbreak of World War II that jolted Orange County out of its daze as thousands of troops trained at military bases throughout the area. As the war came to an end, many servicemen and women decided to stay put. After all, the weather was idyllic and the lifestyle laid back—it was the perfect place to raise a family and live out the American dream in a brand spanking new tract home. Agriculture quickly gave way to commerce and slowly the blossoming orange groves, which once covered this bucolic region, were replaced by planned communities and business parks.

THE ARRIVAL OF MICKEY MOUSE

During the latter part of the 20th century, Orange County attracted national attention when Walt Disney, at the suggestion of the Stanford Research Company, opened his first theme park in Ana-heim on a hot day in July of 1955. Many thought the park would fail because of its rural location, but on opening day thousands of visitors flocked to the new theme park and, even though not everything went as smoothly as anticipated, it became an instant success. Disneyland, along with Knott's Berry Farm, helped Orange County to become a major tourist destination.

PRESENT DAY: THE OC

Orange County is no longer hiding in the shadows of Los Angeles. Even though many still consider Orange County a suburb of Los Angeles (it is part of the Greater Los Angeles–Long Beach–Santa Ana metro area) county officials are quick to point out that Orange County separated from the County of Los Angeles more than a century ago and is its own entity. The land that once harvested grapes and oranges now thrives with an entirely new crop that appeals to the masses—jousting knights, stagecoach rides, magic castles, and buccaneer adventures.

ACCOMMODATIONS

When it comes to hunkering down in The OC, visitors usually gravitate towards hotel properties near Disneyland, or they have a strong desire to go coastal and do a little California dreamin' at a seaside resort. And, with 500 hotel properties and nearly 55,000 guest rooms, chances are you will find a hotel, motel, boutique inn, or private cottage to fit both your needs and budget.

In the last decade Orange County has given birth to a wave of plush, coastal properties. Four- and five-star resorts with their ocean views, out-of-this-world amenities, fine dining, and spa sanctuaries, aside from the Ritz-Carlton Laguna Niguel and Surf and Sand Resort, simply didn't exist before 2000. The same can be said about the Disneyland Resort area in Anaheim, which for many years consisted of the Disneyland Hotel and countless kitschy motels with faux snow-covered roofs and candy-cane icons surrounding the theme park. But, in the last decade, Disney has also freshened up its look with a head-to-toe makeover of its original hotel and the addition of the Grand Californian, an upscale lodge-like property and the centerpiece of Downtown Disney. The hotels surrounding the theme park have also been given a facelift, and a new signage program implemented by the city of Anaheim has given what was once a hodgepodge of motels and tired buildings a crisp, uniform look.

But if you're willing to stay a few miles inland, rather than right on the coast, or can be content with a non-Disney hotel or one that's not within walking distance of the park, you're more likely to find a better rate. It's like the old saying among realtors: "location, location, location." But, don't forget, location usually comes with a price. In this chapter, hotels and resorts are listed in alphabetical order by region or city.

RESERVING YOUR ROOM

With the recent recession and dip in tourism, Orange County has certainly felt the effects of the economy. Sure, people are still arriving in droves, but hotel properties have gotten creative when it comes to packages, rates, and amenities. Central reservation line operators, usually at toll-free numbers, do not have the same flexibility or permission to offer a better rate, but if you call the hotel directly you may be able to get a lower rate or upgrade because hotel-based reservationists have access to occupancy rates, last-minute cancellations, and other pertinent information that may not be readily available to an outside or central reservationist. You may also want to check the hotel Web site for special rates. Travel Web sites, such as Priceline.com and Hotels.com, are other good sources of information. The Anaheim Convention and Visitors Bureau can also assist with online reservations at (800) 901-9655.

RATE INFORMATION

Orange County's high season is typically from Memorial Day through Labor Day with a spike in tourism between Christmas and the New Year, as well as during spring break. Some hotels may hike their rates during the peak season as well as on weekends or require a minimum stay on weekends and holidays. You may also want to inquire about extended stay discounts, AAA rates, and discounted rates if you are a senior citizen. And, finally, don't forget that in addition to the room rate, you will also have to pay a 10 to 15 percent bed tax, depending on the city, plus a resort tax, up to $2, for the state of California. Many properties also charge a daily parking fee and may also tack on a resort fee, so be sure to ask about any additional charges above and beyond room and tax.

PET-FRIENDLY HOTELS

Pet owners are a special breed that consider their four-legged companions as much a part of the family as their offspring. In recent years the lodging industry has begun catering to travelers and their pets by providing designated hotel rooms especially for pet owners. Typically a non-refundable and/or daily cleaning fee is associated, so it's wise to inquire what additional costs may be added to the nightly rate. Also, some may add restrictions, such as a maximum weight limit. Hotel chains that now welcome pets include Motel 6, La Quinta Inn & Suites, Red Roof Inns, Travelodge, Days Inn, Loews, and Four Season Hotels. Additional hotel groups go above and beyond by rolling out the welcome mat, such as Westin, where dogs receive a Heavenly Dog Bed to sleep on, plus their own robes. W Hotels offer tail waggers nightly turndown service, in-room massage, and nighttime treats, while Starwood Hotels and Resorts offer a variety of pet perks with their Starwood LTD (Love that Dog) program. Specific Orange County pet-friendly properties include the Waterfront Hilton in Huntington Beach, many Residence Inn properties, Vacation Village, and Casa Laguna Inn—both in Laguna Beach and at Embassy Suites in Irvine.

GAY-FRIENDLY HOTELS

California, especially the Greater Los Angeles area including Orange County, has a large gay population that is very much out of the closet and welcomed by the community. Same-sex couples check in and check out of hotels just like everyone else. But some hotels, which must meet a certain list of criteria, have been TAG (Travel Alternative Groups) Approved and identified as being gay-welcoming hotels, resorts, and bed and breakfast inns. Orange County has several TAG hotels that can be specifically searched and targeted on Travelocity.com, which has formed an alliance with TAG. Included are Casa Laguna Inn and Spa (Laguna Beach), Shorebreak Hotel and the Hilton Waterfront (Huntington Beach), Sheraton Anaheim Hotel (Disneyland Resort area), Hyatt Regency Newport Beach, Hyatt Regency Orange County (Garden Grove/Disneyland Resort area), Hyatt Regency Huntington Beach Resort and Spa, Wyndham Orange County Hotel (Costa Mesa), the hotels at Disneyland Resort, and many others. There are also many, many Orange County hotels, motels, resorts, and inns that may not be TAG approved, but are welcoming and gay-friendly nonetheless.

PER NIGHT
$.................. Under $150
$$ $150–300
$$$ $301–500
$$$$ .... $501 and above

INLAND ORANGE COUNTY

Anaheim/Disney

ANAHEIM HARBOR RV PARK $
1009 South Harbor Blvd.
(714) 535-6495
www.anaheimharborrvpark.com
Anaheim Harbor RV Park is the closest RV park to Disneyland and is a clean enclave with accommodations for 40-foot RVs plus tip-outs, full hookups, 30 and 50 AMP service, a heated swimming pool, laundry room, new bathrooms, free wireless Internet access and cable TV hook-ups, a five-hole putting green, and video arcade. There is also shuttle service to Disneyland and several restaurants within walking distance.

ANAHEIM RV VILLAGE $
333 West Ball Rd.
(888) 318-5520
www.anaheimvillage.reachlocal.com
This may not be the closest RV park to Disneyland (it's a mere 4 miles away) but it's the newest and the largest with 293 sites including 23 premium

sites for 64- to 70-foot vehicles, free Wi-Fi, playground, swimming pool, arcade center, laundry facilities, and convenience store, plus it's pet-friendly, too.

CANDY CANE INN $
1747 South Harbor Blvd.
(714) 774-5284 or (800) 345-7057
www.candycaneinn.net

Gone are the kitschy red and white ornaments that once gave credence to this former motel's name. While the name is here to stay, most of the candy cane embellishments are gone or at least discreetly displayed. The inn has transitioned nicely from a roadside motel into a value-oriented inn just 250 yards from Disneyland's main gate and is a Disney Good Neighbor property. There are 171 rooms including a collection of new premium rooms, which are a bit more spacious with newer appointments. Each stay includes a complimentary breakfast buffet, free shuttle to Disneyland, parking, and a fitness room. There are also a heated swimming pool and children's wading pool.

DISNEYLAND HOTEL $$
1150 Magic Way
(714) 778-6600
www.disneyland.disney.go.com

The original Disneyland Hotel features nearly 1,000 rooms and suites housed in a trio of towers. It, too, is conveniently located to Downtown Disney with magical touches, such as an oversized Sorcerer's Hat and the Never Land themed pool. The hotel also offers 19 "Character Quarters" with either a Mickey Mouse or Disney Princess motif and ample space for families of five or more. Despite its age (the hotel opened in 1955) it has undergone several renovations over the years and offers contemporary and comfortable surroundings. There are also several casual, themed, and upscale restaurants within the hotel and poolside, with more dining options at neighboring Downtown Disney.

DISNEY'S GRAND CALIFORNIAN HOTEL & SPA $$$
1600 South Disney Dr.
(714) 635-2300
www.disneyland.disney.go.com

Putting you at the center of Disney's magic is this vintage-style resort adjacent to Downtown Disney. With 745 rooms and suites, plus a collection of newly opened residence-style guestrooms complete with kitchens and living areas, this is the newest and most elegant of the Disney properties. Reminiscent of a grand wilderness lodge and fashioned after the Craftsman era of architecture, the public rooms are nicely appointed with rich woods and conversational areas. Guestrooms are equally cozy and offer one or two beds, ample-size bathrooms, and balconies. With an entrance just off Downtown Disney's main pathway, where there are plenty of dining options, the resort is also just a short jaunt from the main entrances of Disneyland and California Adventure. There are also three restaurants located within the hotel, including Napa Rose, a fine dining establishment.

i If your travel plans call for a chunk of time to be spent at Disneyland Resort, then you'll find it convenient to stay within the Magic Kingdom or a neighboring hotel. Be sure to inquire about special travel packages, which bundle together your hotel, theme park tickets, and dining. All three Disney properties have dining options, swimming pools, and concierge levels, and are within walking distance to the main admission gate.

DISNEY'S PARADISE PIER $$
1717 South Disney Dr.
(714) 999-0990
www.disneyland.disney.go.com

This hotel, the furthest from the entrance gate, was once the Pan Pacific Hotel before Disney acquired it several years ago. Disney's Paradise Pier is a three-diamond property offering standard rooms or suites with a single king or two queen-size beds. The concierge level features priority check-in, cabana or poolside rooms, assistance with vacation planning, complimentary continental breakfast and evening wine and cheese reception, nightly turndown service, DVD players, and complimentary movies. While it's not as close to Downtown Disney or the theme park's main entrance, it is still within an easy walking distance.

HOTEL MENAGE $
1221 South Harbor Blvd.
(888) 462-7275
www.hotelmenage.com

A tired Holiday Inn gets a hip transformation and is reborn as Hotel Menage. Touted as Anaheim's first boutique property, the hotel is a nice departure from the big box hotels and no-name motels that populate the area surrounding Disneyland. While the architecture is still reminiscent of its former self, with rooms opening up onto exterior corridors, the rooms are a departure from the old guard with exposed concrete floors, loft-like ceilings, work stations or coloring tables depending on who is occupying the room, and free wireless Internet. The hotel's lobby is lounge-like and the bar is abuzz too. The pool area has a leafy appeal with an outdoor bar, teak loungers, and private cabanas that can be rented for the day. There is also a restaurant on the premises serving Pacific Rim fare, and the hotel is a mouse-toss from Disneyland, which adds an element of convenience for the theme-park bound.

Buena Park

KNOTT'S BERRY FARM RESORT HOTEL $
7675 Crescent Ave.
(866) 752-2444
www.knottshotel.com

Located along the fringes of this popular Orange County theme park, Knott's Berry Farm Resort Hotel is convenient for those visiting Knott's Berry Farm, Soak City, and even Disneyland. The hotel rises nine stories and houses a collection of nice rooms including Snoopy theme rooms where Snoopy himself pays a visit and provides tuck-in service. Telephone bedtime stories are another feature of these novelty rooms. The hotel features a decent size pool plus an all-day dining restaurant. Nearby are additional themed eateries including Medieval Times and Pirates Dinner Adventure. Disneyland is just 6 miles away and can be reached via car or by public bus.

RADISSON SUITES HOTEL $
7762 Beach Blvd.
(714) 739-5600 or (800) 395-7046
www.radisson.com

With 200 rooms offering 500 square feet of living space plus separate bedroom, living area, and bath, the Spanish-style Radisson Suites Hotel enjoys a central location just blocks from Knott's Berry Farm, Soak City, and Beach Boulevard's themed restaurants. The hotel has an atrium lobby and a swimming pool, plus a complimentary breakfast buffet is served each morning and there is a restaurant on the premises, too. There are also coin laundry facilities on the property. Free shuttle service ferries guests to Disneyland or Knott's Berry Farm, eliminating the need to pay for parking at either place. You can also purchase tickets to Disneyland at the front desk, saving you further time at the park's front gate.

Costa Mesa/South Coast Plaza

MARRIOTT SUITES COSTA MESA $
500 Anton Blvd.
(714) 957-1100
www.marriotthotels.com

Located in the heart of South Coast Metro just minutes from Irvine and John Wayne Airport, this all-suite hotel is best suited for business but has all the accoutrements for a leisurely stay, including a swimming pool; decent location near South Coast Plaza; mere minutes from Newport Beach; and rooms designated just for families. The Marriott, which recently underwent a cosmetic upgrade, also has a fitness center. Located inside the hotel is Hemingway's, an upscale bistro with rich woods, marble accents, and imposing columns that is open for breakfast and dinner with poolside dining available when weather permits. There are also several restaurants within walking distance including TGI Friday's, Mastro's Steakhouse, and Scott's Seafood Grill and Bar. South Coast Plaza is also within easy reach.

THE WESTIN SOUTH COAST PLAZA $$
686 Anton Blvd.
(714) 540-2500
www.westinsouthcoastplaza.com

On a recent tour to promote their book *Read all About It*, former First Lady Laura Bush and daughter Jenna stayed at this upscale hotel within charging distance to South Coast Plaza. Newly redesigned with the expected Westin touch, guests are unaware of the sensory experiences taking place around them—the soft lighting, aromatherapy, fresh botanicals and background music—all part of the Westin repositioning intended to soothe and stimulate. Rooms are equipped with the signature Westin Heavenly Bed, flat screen televisions, and soothing color schemes. Pinot Provence, a well regarded Orange County eatery located in the hotel, is open for breakfast, lunch, and dinner. The Westin has partnered with many local restaurants where you are given signing privileges allowing you to put the tab on your room bill. A walk through a nearby park leads to the Orange County Theater District, and a stroll across the Unity pedestrian bridge puts you practically at the front doors of South Coast Plaza.

Garden Grove

HYATT REGENCY ORANGE COUNTY $$
11999 Harbor Blvd.
(714) 750-1234
www.orangecounty.hyatt.com

Technically, this 654-room hotel is located in Garden Grove, but it borders the city of Anaheim and is just down the road from Disneyland. A glass atrium grounds this semi-high-rise hotel where the 87 Kids Suites, separated from parents' rooms by French doors, offer a few added amenities including bunk beds, an activity table, and a second television. The hotel also features a restaurant and lounge plus two pools, an equal number of Jacuzzis, a fitness center, tennis courts, basketball hoop, and free shuttle service to Disneyland. There are some restaurants within walking distance and the hotel sits midway between the 22 and 5 Freeways.

City of Orange

DOUBLETREE RESORT $$
100 The City Dr.
(714) 634-4500
www.doubletree1hilton.com

This clean, centrally located hotel sits next-door to the Block of Orange, which provides plenty of shopping and entertainment. It's also close to the 5 and 22 Freeways as well as Disneyland, which is a few miles north via surface streets. Armed with a AAA Three Diamond rating, the linear hotel features three categories of rooms, including standard, suites, and an executive floor, plus accommodations for disabled guests. There is an on-site fitness center, tennis court, basketball hoops, and a swimming pool. The hotel also features an all-day, upscale dining restaurant plus a casual cafe serving Starbucks coffee. Happy hour takes place in the hotel's atrium lobby bar, which also offers casual dining and a pub-like setting.

RUTA'S OLD TOWN INN $
274 North Glassell St.
(714) 628-1818
www.rutasoldtowninnca.com

Set among the leafy streets and bungalows from a bygone era is this standout bed and breakfast inn, one of the few you'll find in The OC. An original Sears Craftsman home built in 1910, the inn has been restored to its early 20th-century splendor. With just three rooms, bedecked in Victorian charm, it feels as if you almost have the run of the house because the inn can only accommodate a maximum of six guests—one of which is you. Each room has a queen bed and private bathroom, and the nightly rate includes a full continental breakfast each morning. Enjoy a glass of wine from a wicker chair on the cozy front porch, stroll to the quaint shops that dot the town center, or head to a local sidewalk cafe for an evening meal. You're rather close to Angel Stadium and the Honda Center. Disneyland is also just a short drive with Knott's Berry Farm being just a few miles further. You can also hop on the freeway and be at the beach in 20 minutes.

COASTAL ORANGE COUNTY

Dana Point

BLUE LANTERN INN $$
34343 Street of the Blue Lantern
(949) 661-1304
www.bluelanterninn.com

One of Orange County's few bed and breakfast inns, this three-story hideaway, part of the Four Sisters Inn portfolio, teeters high above a coastal bluff and looks as if it belongs on the Eastern seaboard. Tapped as a Top U.S. Seaside Inn by the editors of *Travel + Leisure*, the Blue Lantern Inn features just 29 rooms with varying appointments, such as fireplaces and jetted tubs, and most have mini-fridges stocked with complimentary soft drinks. A handful of rooms also boast private decks. The nightly rate includes a full breakfast plus afternoon wine and hors d'oeuvres, all-day refreshments, turndown service, pet-friendly rooms, and a snug spa for massage and body treatments. Children are welcome. The inn is located within walking distance to restaurants and shops.

**LAGUNA CLIFFS MARRIOTT
RESORT & SPA** $$
25135 Park Lantern
(949) 661-5000
www.lagunacliffs.com

Perched on an ocean bluff in the southern coastal town of Dana Point, this full-service resort is extremely family friendly while managing to retain a luxurious feel. A veil of fog often hangs above the hotel in the early morning hours, but once the vapor dissipates there are spectacular views of the ocean and harbor. The nearly 400 rooms and suites are divided into a pair of arch-shaped wings and each wing has its own pool. The rooms, which are light and airy with seaside influences, are on the small side but each has a balcony and, in most instances, a view. The hotel offers two restaurants including an all-day dining eatery with indoor and outdoor seating. In addition, there is a full-service spa and lobby lounge.

**THE RITZ-CARLTON,
LAGUNA NIGUEL** $$$$
One Ritz-Carlton Dr.
(949) 240-2000
www.ritzcarlton.com/resorts/laguna_niguel

The Ritz-Carlton, which bills itself as a Laguna Beach property but actually rests atop a bluff in Dana Point, has the distinction of being the very first oceanfront luxury resort to grace the Orange County coastline. Opened during the 1980s, the 393-room hotel looks as good as it did when it made its debut all those years ago. A recent renovation has resulted in a more casual and relaxed ambience. The rooms have a color palette reflecting the coastal setting and most of the public spaces have spectacular ocean views. There are also hidden, outdoor nooks where Adirondack chairs are positioned along the ocean bluff for guests to enjoy the views or get lost in a good book. The Ritz-Carlton has a signature restaurant and bar, both with ocean views; a wine and chocolate bar; luxury spa; pair of swimming pools; and an adjacent golf course. A stay at this isolated resort requires a vehicle as it's not really within walking distance to any commercial outlets.

Huntington Beach

**HILTON WATERFRONT
BEACH RESORT** $$
21100 Pacific Coast Hwy.
(714) 845-8000
www.waterfrontresorts.com

Before the Hilton came along, Huntington Beach was fraught with cheap motels stretched along Pacific Coast Highway. But the Hilton spawned interest from other hoteliers, and now there are three rather spectacular properties all within a mile of one another.

Located across from the beach and featuring 290 recently renovated guestrooms with full or partial ocean views and private balconies, plus an additional 24 suites displaying full ocean views, the Hilton Waterfront Beach Resort features pet-friendly amenities, an ocean view restaurant and bar, heated swimming pool, and lighted tennis courts. For a nominal fee, the hotel will provide guests with beach bonfire necessities, including marshmallows and firewood.

HYATT REGENCY HUNTINGTON BEACH RESORT & SPA $$
21500 Pacific Coast Hwy.
(714) 698-1234
www.huntingtonbeach.hyatt.com
Located at the corner of Beach Boulevard and Pacific Coast Highway is this lovely Spanish-style resort punctuated with meandering pathways and outdoor fireplaces. Cool ocean breezes sweep across the central plaza and the private balconies belonging to the 517 rooms and suites. Its location, across from the surf and sand, makes it easily accessible to the beach via an elevated bridge, and downtown Huntington Beach is a lengthy jaunt, but still within walking distance. The resort has a lagoon-style swimming pool complete with cabanas and recently added waterslides that kids will find appealing. There is also a full-service spa on the premises, as well as a collection of casual-to-elegant restaurants including a lounge. Mankota's Grill, positioned poolside with views of the Pacific Ocean, ignites its fire pit each evening, providing a cozy spot for cocktails and s'mores.

SHOREBREAK HOTEL $$
500 Pacific Coast Hwy.
(714) 861-4470
www.shorebreakhotel.com
Huntington Beach's newest and only lifestyle hotel has finally opened. The four-star and fabulous Shorebreak Hotel, part of the San Francisco–based Joie de Vivre portfolio of properties, is situated in downtown Huntington Beach with Pacific Coast Highway separating the building from the sand. With a surf chic motif showcasing a modern, streamlined design, the hotel still manages to exude a laidback and inviting vibe. The newly built hotel, which is just a year old, features rooms with ocean views, contemporary furnishings, and step-out balconies. Onsite is the Zimzala Restaurant and Bar offering Mediterranean fare, a surf-inspired décor, and plenty of spirits. Room service is offered 24/7. The hotel has a fitness center with a yoga studio and a deck that includes a private courtyard

with a fleet of fire pits. There are bath and beach butler services available upon request, pet-friendly rooms, and a 24-hour business center. Best of all, step outside the front door and you're near just about everything: the beach, Main Street's restaurants and pubs, and shopping.

Renting Cottages

Orange County has plenty of splashy resorts, but not many opportunities to rent a cottage. Laguna Beach has a few options, including **Laguna Magical Cottages** (949-494-4554 or www.lagunamagicalcottages.com) near the estates of Bill Gates, Bette Midler, Heather Locklear, and Nicole Simpson. There are just two batten-board cottages that sleep up to four with ocean views and full kitchens, which can be reserved for a minimum of two nights or by the month. **Arabella Laguna** (949-376-5744 or www.arabellalaguna.com) also offers historic cottages, studios, and suites housed in four buildings that can sleep up to six guests. They, too, come with full kitchens and plenty of plush appointments. The **Manzanita Cottages** (877-661-2533 or www.manzanitacottages.com) include four enchanting cottages plus a studio apartment. Built in 1927 by film producer Harry Reed as a private getaway for his celebrity friends, these abodes include full kitchens, lovely sitting areas, and a common courtyard. They are so secluded that many longtime residents of Laguna Beach don't know they exist, even though they're just four blocks from the village.

Laguna Beach

CASA LAGUNA INN $$
2510 South Coast Hwy.
(949) 494-2996
www.casalaguna.com

While the mega resorts have their oceanfront settings as one of their big draws, Casa Laguna Inn, separated from the beach by Pacific Coast Highway, is all about charm. An enchanting, 20-room terraced retreat with a staggering layout, this 1930s Mediterranean-style bed and breakfast is housed in an historic structure complete with its own bell tower. Music from the big band era is heard throughout the lobby and pool deck area, and an array of complimentary beverages is available throughout the day. A few times a year the inn hosts local artists on-site who create plein air masterpieces as guests go about their business. Behind each guestroom door is a magnificent retreat with fireplaces, aged wood floors, and magnificent views, with no two rooms alike. The emphasis at Casa Laguna Inn is placed on the service, which includes a full gourmet breakfast, informal evening wine and cheese, pet-friendly accommodations, spa treatments, and extra added touches. The inn is not suited for young children.

MONTAGE LAGUNA BEACH $$$$
30801 South Coast Hwy.
(949) 715-6000
www.montagelagunabeach.com

When money is no object, Montage Laguna Beach rises to the top of anyone's list. Located on 30 waterfront acres and built to resemble a vintage California Craftsman retreat, a popular architectural style of the early 1920s, the Montage has a terraced design with the entry level being the top floor and the guestrooms located below. Many of the rooms feature views overlooking the main swimming pool and ocean with spa-like bathrooms, plein air artwork, aromatherapy candles, ample-size tubs, and balconies. There are two restaurants, the freestanding, bungalow-style Studio, which has won every major culinary award, and the all-day dining Loft, located in the main building. There is also a seasonal, casual eatery located off the main pool. The oceanfront Spa Montage is a mini oasis of luxury offering every imaginable body therapy, from signature massage to soothing facials. Guests of Montage also enjoy privileges at local golf courses and, in addition to the main swimming pool, the resort has two other pools on the premises. As one would expect, the service at the Montage is unbelievably attentive.

SURF AND SAND RESORT $$$
1555 South Coast Hwy.
(949) 497-4477
www.surfandsandresort.com

This oceanfront hotel, with its boxy 1950s-style architecture, may not look like much from the outside, but looks can be deceiving. Rising four floors atop a modest ocean bluff, Surf and Sand almost seems one with the sea—especially when you're standing on one of the jutting balconies. The 165 rooms and suites, best described as beach chic with plantation shutters and a crisp color scheme, are housed in five mid-century towers. There is a small, oceanfront pool and a pathway that trails down to the sand. The Surf and Sand also has a lovely spa, intimate all-day dining restaurant located just feet above the pounding surf, and a delightful open-air lounge that also boasts million-dollar views.

Newport Beach

BALBOA BAY CLUB & RESORT $$$
1221 West Coast Hwy.
(949) 645-5000
www.balboabayclub.com

The 60-year-old Balboa Bay Club & Resort, once a private club attracting such luminaries as John Wayne, Ronald and Nancy Reagan, Humphrey Bogart, and Natalie Wood, entered a new era when it opened to the public in 2003 after a multimillion-dollar expansion that resulted in the addition of a 160-room hotel. Located on a 15-acre waterfront sprawl, guestrooms take on a residential feel behind the Italian villa façade with chaise lounge-laden patios and sunken tubs. The

Home Away from Home

Staying in a hotel isn't for everyone. Some people prefer the comforts of home, and that's where Home Away (www.homeaway.com) can be of help. The company connects homeowners and property managers with travelers seeking space, value, and amenities that a hotel may not be able to offer. It's especially ideal for multi-family getaways or generational travel where large groups need to be housed under one roof with common rooms. The site is free to use and provides property descriptions from location, to the square footage, to the number of bedrooms and more. Many of the listings for Orange County are beachfront properties that can be rented by the night, but more often by the week and month. You'll find everything from charming clapboard cottages and modern townhomes to sprawling estates that can sleep up to 16 people.

oped as a South Seas movie set in the 1920s, and eventually became part of a seaside colony. All the original abodes, with many returned to their original splendor, are still standing thanks to the efforts of the Crystal Cove Alliance, which worked diligently to save the cottages from the hands of developers. Aside from the rustic cottages, which include kitchens and breathtaking ocean views, there are also dorm-style cottages where guests enjoy private rooms but share common areas including bathrooms in most cases. Unlike at a typical resort, daily maid service isn't available and, if you're staying multiple days, your linens and towels are replaced after four days. But taking into consideration that oceanfront cottages start at $121 per night, it's an incredible bargain to say the least. For added convenience, there are two casual restaurants available and many more eateries in the nearby village of Laguna Beach. In addition, there are often educational opportunities, such as plein air painting and junior ranger programs. The cottages are extremely popular with a sometimes long wait list, especially in the summer months. Reservations are taken all year long and must be made in advance.

FAIRMONT NEWPORT BEACH $$
4500 MacArthur Blvd.
(949) 476-2001
www.fairmont.com
Located a bit inland, close to John Wayne Airport, this 440-room hotel features a modern design and luxurious experience as only the Fairmont can deliver. Its freeway-close location makes it a snap to reach Orange County's theme parks, shopping destinations, and coastline. The average guestroom spans more than 300 square feet and features a rich palette of chocolate and gold. There is a restaurant and lounge plus an ample-size swimming pool with private cabanas housing flat screen TVs. Other amenities include a health club and full-service spa.

casually elegant suites have a bit more room and include fireplaces. The resort also features a private beach, an Olympic-size swimming pool, and a 17,000-square-foot luxury spa, plus restaurants and lounges.

CRYSTAL COVE BEACH COTTAGES $
Crystal Cove State Park
(800) 444-7275
www.crystalcovebeachcottages.org
Once reserved for privileged families, these formerly land-leased seaside bungalows are now available to the public for overnight stays and longer getaways. Located in Crystal Cove State Park, the clapboard cottages were first devel-

HYATT REGENCY NEWPORT BEACH $$
1107 Jamboree Rd.
(949) 729-1234
www.newportbeach.hyatt.com

For years the Hyatt Regency was the place to stay when visiting Newport Beach. In recent years the competition for this hotel has gotten fierce, but the resort has managed to retain a very contemporary feel with the passing of time. The Spanish-style property features 403 guestrooms and suites with private balconies, tropical motifs, bay views, seating areas, and mini-fridges. There are three swimming pools, including the cabana-laden Lido pool where Dive-in Movies are shown during the summer months. Other amenities include a 24-hour fitness center, a par 3 golf course, lighted tennis courts, and plenty of activities for the kids, including shuffleboard, table tennis, and volleyball. Bikes are also available for a nominal rental fee. While the hotel doesn't have its own spa, hotel guests can arrange for a massage or facial at Spa Gregorie's located in Fashion Island. The Hyatt also has a restaurant and lounge.

i A consortium of high-end resorts has formed The OCeanfront, a one-stop Web site for accessing information about Orange County's coastal properties. With a simple click of the mouse, guests are linked to the resort Web sites and can also make online reservations. Information about the individual beach communities, such as shopping destinations and golfing opportunities, is also readily available at www.theoceanfrontca.com.

THE ISLAND HOTEL $$$
690 Newport Center Dr.
(949) 759-0808
www.theislandhotel.com
Rising from the pavement adjacent to Fashion Island, Orange County's premier shopping experience, is The Island Hotel. This former Four Seasons property continues the tradition of its predecessor by offering four-star accommodations, services, and amenities. An attractive weekday hotel for business types and appealing to leisure travelers on weekends, the hotel is just a short drive from the beach. The spacious rooms are divided into three categories with 64 Executive Suites, 19 Luxury Suites, and 300 well-appointed Guest Rooms.

Rooms feature step-out balconies and/or furnished patios and views of either Newport Harbor or the Pacific Ocean. Bathrooms are cloaked in marble and refrigerated private bars are fully stocked with beverages and edibles. The hotel is home to the Palm Terrace Restaurant and the more informal Palm Terrace Lounge plus a 4,000-square-foot spa and an expansive swimming pool. Fashion Island, home to Neiman Marcus, Bloomingdale's, and a soon-to-open Nordstrom, shares the same acreage and is within walking distance. The seaside villages of Corona del Mar, Laguna Beach, and Balboa Island are easily accessible by car.

MARRIOTT NEWPORT BEACH
HOTEL & SPA $$
900 Newport Center Dr.
(949) 729-3500
A parking lot separates this 532-room hotel from Fashion Island. While not as posh as its neighbor, The Island Hotel, the Marriott has done an incredible job transforming this particular property into a luxurious retreat after a pricey $70 million renovation. The contemporary, two-tower hotel features rooms with bold color schemes, with some offering ocean views and others eyeing the comings and goings of fashionistas. There is a freeform swimming pool near the bar and another hidden place to plunge tucked a bit out of sight. Pure Blu, the hotel's full-service spa, offers an array of signature treatments for men and women, including the innovative Hot Seashell Massage. The hotel is home to Sam & Harry's, a contemporary American-style eatery with outdoor dining and fire pits plus a new lobby lounge with a menu of sushi, fresh seafood, and cocktails. There is also a Starbucks on site with grab and go items, but if none of these options are appealing, there are some 40 restaurants within walking distance. Another bonus, an Edwards Cinema with multiple screens, is also within the Fashion Island enclave.

NEWPORT DUNES $
1131 Back Bay Dr.
(949) 729-3863 or (800) 765-7661
www.newportdunes.com

This RV resort has an upscale feel and is located adjacent to Fashion Island, up the road from Balboa Island, and a few miles from Laguna Beach. There are 394 RV sites, 12 cottages, a private 10-acre beach encircling the wave-free swim lagoon, and a 405-slip marina. There are also a swimming pool, convenient market, and restaurant on the premises. During the summer they have an outdoor movie night creating a community-like atmosphere for guests. The complex also orchestrates many fun activities, including basketball tournaments, ice cream socials, and kayak tours.

THE RESORT AT PELICAN HILL $$$$
22701 Pelican Hill Rd. South
(949) 467-6800 or (800) 315-8214
www.pelicanhill.com

Joining the ranks of Orange County's extremely plush coastal resorts is the newest edition, The Resort at Pelican Hill. The much anticipated opening took place in late 2008 and has added an entirely new level of luxury to the region. The resort, located atop a hillside with expansive Pacific Ocean views, features 204 spectacular bungalows and 128 multi-room villas with every amenity imaginable, including wet bars, deep marble soaking tubs, and fireplaces, ranging in size from 847 square feet to a little more than 3,500 square feet. Fashioned after a seaside village, the 504-acre resort boasts an iconic Coliseum-style pool, one of the largest circular pools with tiered decks and spacious cabanas, a Tom Fazio–designed 36-hole golf course with panoramic ocean views, a spacious spa with 22 treatment salons and a menu of therapies, and a collection of casual-to-elegant restaurants. The Resort at Pelican Hill embraces the absence of ordinary by offering extraordinary surroundings, amenities, and services.

Seal Beach

AYRES HOTEL $
12850 Seal Beach Blvd.
(562) 596-8330 or (800) 706-4890
www.ayreshotel.com

This family-owned chain of Southern California hotels offers comfortable rooms and personal service. This particular location was built to serve the employees of nearby Boeing, but shouldn't be overlooked by leisure travelers. Located right off the 405 Freeway at the Seal Beach Boulevard exit, the hotel is just feet away from the Los Angeles County line. The living room-style lobby has an intimate feel, and there are 102 guestrooms, classified as studio suites, plus a pair of one-bedroom suites featuring king- and queen-size beds, refrigerators and microwaves, coffee makers, and writing desks. Guests enjoy a complimentary breakfast and an afternoon

Renaissance ClubSport

If you're traveling to Orange County on vacation and also want to experience San Diego and Los Angeles, consider the Renaissance ClubSport in Aliso Viejo (949-643-6700 or www.marriott.com). While there isn't much to do in Aliso Viejo, its position, near I-5, provides a good home base for extended stays. Travel south for about 70 minutes and you'll be in downtown San Diego; head the other way for about the same amount of time and you're in Los Angeles. In addition, the hotel, which is relatively new, is full-service with a collection of nicely appointed guestrooms, a spa, a 74,000-square-foot fitness facility, a restaurant and bar, child-care services, and much more. It also has a wellness element with nutritional seminars and weight management counselors. The hotel is located off the 73 Toll Road, which merges with I-5 near Mission Viejo. Rates are extremely reasonable, too.

hospitality reception Monday through Thursday. A heated swimming pool adds a bit of recreation to your stay while on-site washers and dryers provide convenience. Within walking distance are several restaurants and shops, and downtown Seal Beach, along with the sand, is just a couple of miles south. Nearby attractions include Los Alamitos Race Track, Disneyland, and Knott's Berry Farm.

HAMPTON INN SEAL BEACH $
2401 Seal Beach Blvd.
(562) 594-3939
www.hamptoninn.hilton.com
The Hampton Inn delivers a dependable room for the budget-minded. This particular hotel is also close to the beach—about a three-minute drive. It, too, is close to the Los Angeles County line, about a mile or so from the freeway, and sits right outside of Boeing. With 110 rooms, including standard and what Hampton defines as a suite, which is basically a standard room with more space, the Hampton Inn is an easy-in/easy-out hotel with self-parking and a few added amenities, such as complimentary breakfast and beverages. There is also a swimming pool and fitness room. While there isn't a restaurant on the premises, next door is a fast food eatery and within a mile or two are several individual and chain restaurants.

RESTAURANTS

If there is one thing Orange County isn't lacking, it is an abundance of restaurants with one to fit every craving, occasion, and, most importantly, budget. There are a handful of landmark restaurants, but it's a culinary merry-go-round trying to stay on top of the competition. Today's line cook could very well be tomorrow's celebrity chef, and the restaurant of the moment, the one where it's almost impossible to get a reservation on a Saturday night, can be quickly relegated to the number two spot as soon as the next best thing opens its doors.

But Orange County isn't all that fickle when it comes to matters of the palate. Mexican influences have longed played an instrumental role on menus across the county. Giant-size burritos filled with an array of beans, cheese, and meats can be ordered "wet," with zesty sauce, fresh-made guacamole, and dollops of sour cream crowning the edible work of art. Even restaurants that specialize in some other type of cuisine will have one or two items that speak to the Mexican culture by using spices or condiments typically found in Mexican cooking. With a majority of the county fronting the coast, fresh seafood restaurants and sushi bars are equally popular with restaurant goers.

Orange County is also home to Little Saigon, the nation's oldest and largest community of Vietnamese Americans. This prominent enclave, located in Westminster and Garden Grove, has an abundance of Vietnamese restaurants and markets. Those who enjoy sampling ethnic fare will also find Persian, Thai, Korean, Brazilian, Indian, Peruvian, Caribbean, Cuban, and Japanese restaurants scattered throughout the county. Of course, Orange County is also rich with Cal-cuisine bistros, intimate wine bars, vegetarian eateries, Spanish tapas, and brew pubs.

OVERVIEW

Traveling can be an adventure, but once in a while, it's comforting to seek out the familiar when on the road. This is especially true when it comes to dining. Those chain restaurants, the Cheesecake Factories, PF Chang's, and California Pizza Kitchens, are all decent restaurants with little surprise as to what's on the menu or how it will taste. We've decided to omit the chain restaurants because we're confident that you'll be able to locate these without our guidance. However, local chains, those found only within Orange County or Southern California, have been included.

While we've recommended what we consider to be great dining choices, from casual to elegant, the best indication of an exceptional restaurant is whether or not it's crowded. If you're walking by an eatery and see most every table full and a queue of people waiting to be seated, chances are it's where the locals go and it's good. Nothing says "great meal" like the clatter of forks and knives resonating from the inside of a restaurant. While we've certainly rounded up an impressive and lengthy roster of places to please your palate, it's impossible to describe each and every restaurant within the confines of Orange County. But we have selected the best based on a number of criteria, including cuisine, location, and service. Some are selected for their convenience, such as those within the Disneyland Resort, while others boast spectacular ocean views that only add to the overall experience. We've also plucked out a few landmark restaurants as well as a few that are new to the Orange County dining scene. Keep in mind that restaurants often change their hours and the kitchen door can also become one that revolves when it comes to the comings and goings of chefs. We purposely did not include information such as days of operation and the mastermind under toque unless the chef also happens to be the owner. But we did note in most instances whether a restaurant is open for dinner only, offers all-day dining, or is open on weekends for brunch. Still, it's best to call ahead and confirm that such information is still the most current and up-to-date.

TO BRING THE KIDS OR NOT TO BRING THE KIDS? THAT IS THE QUESTION

We've also noted when a restaurant is simply not appropriate for children due to the menu offerings or the ambiance and, at the same time, we've called attention to those establishments that truly cater to families. You'll also find a couple of themed restaurants in our Kidstuff chapter that will be especially appealing to young diners and their adult companions.

HOW TO NAVIGATE THIS CHAPTER

Restaurants are listed in alphabetical order by location, then by cuisine. Unless you're staying in a walkable area, such as downtown Huntington Beach or Laguna Beach, chances are you'll need a car to reach your dining destination. Orange County, while nearly not as big as Los Angeles County, is still a sprawling region that usually requires four wheels. The finer restaurants and trendier bistros, especially those in congested areas where parking is limited, will more than likely provide valet parking, which costs a few extra dollars for the convenience. When possible, especially on weekend evenings or celebratory nights, such as Valentine's Day, be sure to make advance reservations. Otherwise you may arrive only to find out that the restaurant is full or that the wait could take up to an hour or more.

DRESS UP OR DRESS DOWN?

Orange County, as well as most of Southern California, has a very casual, laid-back vibe where shorts, sandals, and T-shirts are perfectly accept-able at most restaurants. However, the more trendy eateries and wine bars may not have a specific dress code, but the clientele is more likely to ditch the board shorts and flip flops and opt for something a bit dressier but a style that is still considered casual. Guys might wear jeans and a polo shirt, while those of the female persuasion could very well be clad in a little black dress and strappy heels. A few restaurants have strict dress codes, and we've been sure to note which ones require more appropriate attire. And, keep in mind, region often dictates dress. For example, the restaurants at Disneyland Resort, including the more upscale eateries, are fine with guests arriving in shorts and sandals because, after all, the setting is in the midst of a theme park. The beach cities vary as well. Huntington Beach, which is a bona fide surf ghetto with patrons spilling out onto the sidewalk just blocks from the beach, not only tolerates ultra-casual clothing but embraces it. Surf wear, manufactured by the likes of Quicksilver, Hurley, and others, is considered couture in these parts. But travel a bit further south, say to Newport Beach or Laguna Beach, and people tend to wear trendy, more label- and designer-centric clothing.

PAY UP

Most restaurants nowadays accept major credit cards or debit cards and, if policy calls for cash only, we've been sure to make note of it. Again, even payment policies can change. The restaurant that took American Express last week may now only accept MasterCard or Visa. When in doubt, inquire before you arrive or are seated. As for personal checks, there are very few, if any, dining establishments in Orange County that will allow you to write a check for a meal with the exception of markets that also sells prepared food.

HOW TO STRETCH YOUR BUDGET

If you're on a budget or simply want to save a little money when eating out, some of Orange County's local publications often advertise restaurant happy hours and dining promotions. One such publication is *OC Weekly*, a free weekly publication found throughout the county. Many of the community newspapers, which are free and typically publish on a weekly basis, will run advertisements that also feature local restaurant promotions, such as two-for-one offers, free appetizer with entree, etc. If you're planning on spending an extended amount of time in the region, the *Entertainment Book*'s Orange County edition, which is valid for one year starting November 1, features a number of dining discounts for both casual eateries and fine dining restaurants. You can visit their Web site at www .entertainmentbook.com for more information.

Per Person (excluding beverages)
$.................... Under $10
$$ $10–30
$$$ $31–75
$$$$ .... $76 and above

ANAHEIM

American

JT SCHMID'S RESTAURANT & BREWERY   **$$**
2610 East Katella Ave.
(714) 634-9200
www.jtschmids.com
With a convenient location across from the Honda Center, a short jaunt from Anaheim Stadium, and a few miles from Disneyland, JT Schmid's is a casual brew pub featuring a contemporary, but informal, menu including wood-fired pizzas, salads, sandwiches, and thick Angus steaks. The setting is a mix of tables, booths, and bar-style seating for optimum viewing of sporting events on one of the wide screen televisions. There is also a full bar and outdoor patio, which features live entertainment from late spring to early fall.

German

BIERSTUBE   **$**
1340 South Sanderson Ave.
(714) 563-4166
www.thephoenixclub.com

Located within the Phoenix Club, a social venue for German ex-pats, is this traditional hofbrau-style pub. Completely authentic, since it is run by Germans, the menu features traditional German fare such as goulash, bratwurst, marinated herring, and fresh-baked pretzels. Spirits, which run the gamut from draft beer and wine, are also from the Old Country but you'll find a few domestic offerings as well. Bierstube is across the freeway from Angel Stadium and just down the road from the Honda Center. Disneyland is nearby as well. If you want a more traditional dining experience, the Phoenix Club is also home to the Loreley Restaurant, which offers hearty German fare such as wienerschnitzel and sauerbraten as well as fine steaks and seafood.

Italian

ANAHEIM WHITE HOUSE   **$$$**
887 South Anaheim Blvd.
(714) 772-1382
www.anaheimwhitehouse.com
Located in a 1909 historic landmark and featuring a dozen private rooms, the Anaheim White House first came on The OC dining scene in 1987 and has since garnered a loyal following. Though the name doesn't really speak to the Italian cuisine, the owner is a native of Verona, Italy, the selection of entrees is authentic, and the wine list features more than 200 labels. This upscale ristorante, not far from Anaheim Stadium, is often a culinary stop for those in town performing at the Big A. Madonna and many others have enjoyed a meal at the Anaheim White House.

Wine Bar

POP THE CORK   **$$**
321 West Katella Ave.
(714) 408-1678
www.pop-the-cork.com
In recent years wine bars have found a niche among restaurant goers who want to do a little wine tasting and a little noshing, but don't really want a heavy meal. Pop the Cork, located near Disneyland in the new Anaheim Garden Walk outdoor complex, is one of the newest such

places to open in The OC and features 40 to 50 wines available by the taste, flight, or glass, plus an additional 150 labels by the bottle. The menu is somewhat communal and designed to be shared, from plates of fine meat and artisan cheeses to a variety of olives and breads. There are also individual pizzas, grilled sandwiches, and salads. A retail area carries bottles of wine and wine-related accessories.

Dining at Disney

If you're staying at one of the hotels located at the Disneyland Resort, there are so many places to dine right on the premises that there really is no need to stray from the Magic Kingdom. Avoid the restaurants inside either park, which are mostly expensive, fast food stops; instead, head to Downtown Disney. Mixed among the storefronts are **La Brea Bakery** featuring salads and sandwiches, **Catal Restaurant** and **Uva Bar,** part of the Patina empire offering balcony seating and a sophisticated menu of Mediterranean favorites, and **Napa Rose,** the award-winning and critically acclaimed fine dining restaurant inside Disney's Grand Californian Hotel. Downtown Disney also features **Naples Ristorante e Pizzeria,** another Patina-owned restaurant, plus recognizable chains including **Rainforest Café, ESPN Zone,** and **House of Blues. Napolini,** a postage stamp–size market and deli, is great for inexpensive, grab and go sandwiches, salads, and pizza.

BALBOA ISLAND

Italian

AMELIA'S ON BALBOA ISLAND $$
311 Marine Ave.
(949) 673-6580
www.ameliasbalboaisland.com
For nearly 50 years Amelia's, a charming and intimate bistro, has been serving a menu of fresh seafood and innovative pasta dishes. As if ripped from the streets of some quaint European village, but looking perfectly in place on Balboa's main drag, Amelia's serves up such dishes as fresh bay scallops, filet mignon, and linguini tossed with calamari. A decent wine list enhances the experience.

BREA

French

LA VIE EN ROSE $$$$
240 South State College Blvd.
(714) 529-8333
www.lavnrose.com
This classic French restaurant, located across from the Brea Mall and just a few miles from Cal State Fullerton, has a mostly French staff. Replicated from a farmhouse in Normandy, the main dining room has several alcoves for enjoying an intimate meal and there is also a patio for dining al fresco. The lunch menu offer more casual fare, such as soup, salad, and sandwiches along with some heavier entrees. Dinner is strictly a dining experience and features an array of appetizers ranging from pâté to caviar with many main courses incorporating classic French sauces. Not to be missed are the French onion soup or any of the homemade desserts. The prix fixe menu, which includes three courses, is quite a bargain at lunch. The wine list is equally impressive and the restaurant often hosts wine dinners. It's doubtful that tiny taste buds will find much to their liking here, so it's best to go with grown ups.

CORONA DEL MAR (NEWPORT BEACH)

Continental

FIVE CROWNS $$$$
3801 East Coast Hwy.
(949) 760-0331
www.lawrysonline.com

Reminiscent of an English country inn, complete with ivy-covered façade and a red London phone booth outside its entrance, the bi-level Five Crowns has been the backdrop for many special occasions celebrated by Orange County families. Illuminated by candlelight and crackling fireplaces, the restaurant, part of the Lawry's family of fine dining, has been serving traditional meals and exceptional service for more than four decades. Guests dine amid rich wood paneling and antique furnishings while grazing on a menu of prime rib, top-grade beef, and poultry dishes along with seasonal seafood all elegantly presented. Crème brûlée and English trifle are some of the classic desserts offered here. Brunch is served every Sunday and features an array of classic, substantial dishes. You will find an excellent wine list as well. While many California restaurants have loosened up on their dress codes to accommodate a generation of casually clad guests, Five Crowns still enforces its dress code excluding jeans, tank tops, and T-shirts. Put on a pair of slacks and collared shirt if you plan on crossing the Five Crowns threshold.

Steaks

LANDMARK $$$
3520 East Coast Hwy.
(949) 675-5556
www.landmarknewport.com

With a patio decorated with throw pillows, roomy booths, and chairs divided among a trio of dining areas, Landmark is not your father's steakhouse. Hip with offerings that only a carnivore could love, the menu features a selection of juicy steaks and chops that include bone-in or blackened rib eye, filet mignon, and double breasted airline chicken stuffed with goat cheese and pancetta.

A further look at the menu reveals a number of seafood dishes as well, including Chilean sea bass and crispy New Zealand king salmon. There is even an artisan cheese platter and Kobe beef sliders. Pair your meal with a draft beer or glass of wine, or belly up to the U-shaped bar for a martini or gin and tonic. The crème brûlée is the perfect ending to a meal.

DANA POINT

Mexican

TACO SURF $
34195 Pacific Coast Hwy.
(949) 661-5754
www.tacosurf.com

This local chain, which also has locations in Seal Beach and Sunset Beach, has good, cheap food. A heaping basket of tortilla chips and homemade salsa arrives to the table as you mull over the menu of tacos, burritos, fish, quesadillas, and tostadas. The décor is ultra casual, consisting of booths, tables, and cement floors. Draft and bottled beers, wine, and margaritas crafted from wine rather than the more commonly used tequila, are also available. On weekdays Taco Surf has a great happy hour from 3 to 6 p.m. where street tacos, which consist of a small tortilla, choice of meat, cilantro, and salsa, are just $1 each and select beer is drastically reduced. There is also a menu for kids.

Wine Bar

ENO—WINE, CHEESE AND CHOCOLATE $$
One Ritz-Carlton Dr.
(949) 240-2000
www.ritzcarlton.com

With only 36 seats and more than 300 vintages, Eno, located inside the Ritz-Carlton Hotel, offers a truly exceptional experience for gourmands and those interested in learning about the nuances of wine, cheese, and chocolate. The sommelier brings guests and grapes together with the introduction of new and unusual wines. Guests can graze on international cheeses, charcuterie, and silky chocolates while enjoying flights of wine or wine by the glass. Bottles of wine, glassware, and wine-inspired accessories are available for sale, too. Open evenings only, Eno often hosts epicurean outings inviting chocolatiers, vintners, and fromage experts to share their knowledge and passion with guests through tastings and pairings. Considering the setting and menu selection, Eno is strictly an adults-only venue.

FULLERTON

French

THE CELLAR $$$
305 North Harbor Blvd.
(714) 525-5682
www.cellardining.com
For nearly 40 years The Cellar in downtown Fullerton has been welcoming guests to its basement location in the historic Villa del Sol building. Built by the imagineers who constructed the Pirates of the Caribbean at Disneyland, the restaurant has the feel of an elegant cellar with its soft glow cast from dangling chandeliers, graceful arches, walls with a cave-like quality, and pair of fireplaces. The menu of traditional French cuisine includes escargot, bacon-wrapped scallops, French onion soup, and herb roasted rack of lamb. The Chateaubriand Bouquetiere serves two people and is accompanied by an array of fresh vegetables and traditional bearnaise sauce. A restaurant of this caliber, especially one named The Cellar, boasts a wonderful, far reaching wine list.

Italian

ANGELO'S AND VINCI'S RISTORANTE $
550 North Harbor Blvd.
(657) 879-4022
www.angelosandvincis.com
This downtown Fullerton restaurant, located next to the historic Fox Fullerton Theatre, is a visually intriguing eatery reminiscent of an Italian town. The décor is a mix of bric-a-brac and photos of famous faces gracing the restaurant's walls. The restaurant was established by the late Steven Peck, a veteran actor and dancer of stage

and screen. Angelo's and Vinci's does a superb job behind the kitchen door stuffing their own pastas, rolling the tortellini, creating an array of Sicilian sauces, and baking their own bread. The cannoli is a house favorite and the perfect way to conclude your meal.

MULBERRY STREET RISTORANTE $$
114 West Wilshire Ave.
(657) 525-1056
www.mulberry-st.com
For more than a quarter century the family-run Mulberry Street has been dazzling diners with its mix of Italian fare and fresh seafood. Infused with inspiration from New York's Little Italy, where the real Mulberry Street is found, this trattoria is also spot-on when it comes to its incredible selection of desserts and features a full bar and nice selection of wine. Located less than 15 minutes from Disneyland and Knott's Berry Farm in downtown Fullerton, Mulberry Street is perfectly suited for family meals.

Vegetarian

RUTABEGORZ $
211 Pomona Ave.
(714) 738-9339
www.rutabegorz.com
Long before espresso made its way to the mainstream, this bohemian-style restaurant, founded in 1971 by a quartet of long-haired college kids, was making "coffee and clouds" for its loyal following. Nearly 40 years later they're still brewing coffee and making an array of veggie-style dishes in a charming little building in downtown Fullerton. Soups, salads, and sandwiches are cleverly prepared and include such combos as pepperoni, cream cheese, olives, and tomatoes on squaw bread. Fondue is also on the menu, as are a lot of dishes that begin with the word "veggie." Ah, but it's not all carrots and cucumbers, either. Vegetarians and carnivores can dine side by side as there are plenty of dishes containing meat and chicken. Wine, beer, and cocktails also play a prominent role, as does a long list of coffee concoctions. Kids have their own menu, too.

HUNTINGTON BEACH

Bistro

SHADES $$

21100 Pacific Coast Hwy.

(714) 845-8000

www.waterfrontresort.com

Located poolside at the Waterfront Hilton in Huntington Beach, this upscale bistro features a small dining room and an inviting outdoor area with umbrellas and an oversized fire pit surrounded by comfy chairs. The hybrid setting is ideal for a romantic dinner, but also lends itself well to families with children. The limited menu features a small selection of seafood and steak plus sandwiches, salads, artisan cheeses, pâtés, and charcuterie. Tapas include deviled eggs and Kobe meatball sliders, while breakfast consists of smoothies, eggs, and griddle items.

IRVINE

Deli

LUCCA CAFÉ $

6507 Quail Hill Parkway

(949) 725-1773

www.luccacafe.net

Part deli, part wine bar, Lucca Café is a hip urban eatery trapped in a suburban location. The menu is a mix of gourmet sandwiches, pasta, and salads for lunch with an artisan cheese plate, honey-grilled salmon, and a generous crab salad, plus a long list of other specialties including grilled meat and fowl. The wine list is lengthy with many selections offered by the glass. There is a children's menu, too.

Indian

CHAKRA INDIAN CUISINE $$

4143 Campus Dr.

(949) 854-0009

www.chakracuisine.com

Bucking tradition and opting for a hipper, somewhat seductive ambiance, Chakra takes the flavors of India and adds a contemporary twist. The

Cali Favorites

Some of Orange County's best restaurants have multiple locations throughout the region, but are not considered to be national chains. A few worthy of your time and tasting include:

Chronic Taco: First opened in Newport Beach in 2002, Chronic Taco now has several OC locations. What you'll find on the menu is good, cheap Mexican food for breakfast, lunch, and dinner. The founders have created an offshoot, Chronic Cantina, which has a party atmosphere. www.eatchronictacos.com.

In-N-Out Burger: Until recent years, In-N-Out was only found in Los Angeles and Orange Counties, but now they've expanded to many other regions. The menu, which features the quintessential California burger, also offers fries, sodas, shakes, and nothing more. Established more than 50 years ago, the company is still privately owned by the founding family. www.in-n-out.com.

Wahoo's Fish Tacos: Founded in 1988 in Costa Mesa with satellite locations in Huntington Beach and Laguna Beach, Wahoo's has greatly expanded to other markets. This casual, cantina-like restaurant is known for its fish tacos and other Mexican fare. www.wahoos.com.

Yard House: Featuring a menu of American fusion plus one of the world's largest selections of draft beers. There are weekday and late-night happy hours, plus a kids' menu, too. The selection of music, everything from '60s rock to old-school '80s, adds to the energetic vibe. www.yardhouse.com.

setting is like eye candy for the epicurean—sexy dining room, stylish bar, and a pair of outdoor patios for supping under the stars. The soft glow of candles, coupled with original murals and rich fabrics, adds a sensual touch. The menu is a mix of complex tastes and traditional flavors with the aroma of curry wafting through the air. The calicut crab biscuit and tandoori salmon are must-trys, and the outdoor fire pit is an ideal place to gather around to do a little grazing while enjoying a signature chakratini.

LAGUNA BEACH

American

THE BEACH HOUSE $$
619 Sleepy Hollow Lane
(949) 494-9707
www.thebeachhouse.com
Located off Coast Highway at the end of a narrow road sits the Beach House. Housed in a delightful 1920s beachfront cottage, which once belonged to Hollywood film star Slim Summerville who appeared in such films as *Jesse James* and *Rebecca of Sunnybrook Farm*, the Beach House is the quintessential seaside restaurant. The dining room, with its bank of windows, offers a delightful backdrop for enjoying breakfast, lunch, or dinner. But some of the best tables are the handful along the narrow outside deck, which have breathtaking views of the ocean. Signature dishes include blackened ahi salad, lobster quesadilla, macadamia crusted mahi mahi, and a lobster clubhouse sandwich. Breakfast items include seafood crepes and a crab, avocado, and lobster omelet, and a weekend brunch offers an even more extensive menu.

SPLASHES $$
1555 South Coast Hwy.
(949) 497-4477
www.surfandsandresort.com
Located just above sea level on the ground floor of the remarkable Surf and Sand Hotel is the intimate Splashes restaurant. Open for breakfast, lunch, and dinner, each table is positioned to make the most of the ocean views with an outdoor terrace completing the picture. For breakfast it's a variety of egg dishes and smoked salmon. Lunch features a medley of salads and artisan sandwiches. As for dinner, expect a cheese plate or dayboat scallops for starters, followed by a selection of fresh seafood, beef, or poultry. A full bar and delightful wine list round out the dining experience, or you could just stop in for a dessert of a warm flourless chocolate pyramid and a cordial.

230 FOREST AVENUE $$
230 Forest Ave.
(949) 494-2545
www.230forestavenue.com
Named for its location in the heart of Laguna Beach's enchanting village, 230 Forest Avenue is equal parts art gallery, bistro, and lounge. The intimate space, just a block from the beach, features exposed brick walls, a rotating collection of local art, and a few sidewalk tables. The menu highlights a selection of entrees with produce provided by local purveyors. There are fresh seafood and dry aged steaks, plus some lighter fare including salads, sandwiches, and pasta. Stop in for a full meal or nothing more than drinks and appetizers. The restaurant also sees its share of celebrities in town for a weekend getaway.

Asian Fusion

FIVE FEET $$$
328 Glenneyre St.
(949) 497-4955
www.fivefeetrestaurants.com
Owner/Chef Michael Kang pioneered Asian fusion when he opened his signature restaurant 25 years ago. It's an explosion of flavor when east meets west behind the kitchen door. Szechaun spices are combined with delicate French sauces resulting in innovative flavors and innovative dishes, such as fresh Maryland soft-shell crab topped with mango ginger coulis and tropical salsa. The hoisin barbecue beef short ribs are also popular and are accompanied by garlic mashed potatoes and Maui onion rings. Five Feet also

offers a chef's tasting menu, a decent wine list, innovative presentations, and a great Laguna Beach location.

Bistro

THE LOFT $$$

30801 South Coast Hwy.

(949) 715-6000

www.montagelagunabeach.com

The Montage Resort & Spa is home to two critically acclaimed restaurants, one of which is the Loft, located on the hotel's fourth floor with sweeping ocean views. The menu is a mix of seasonal American fare with items ranging from breakfast favorites to gourmet sandwiches and savory soups for lunch. Dinner is an added treat with fresh seafood and prime cuts of beef. The Loft also has a bistro menu and a very reasonably priced children's menu. The décor is inviting with an airy feel coupled with a bistro-style bar, six-foot wood-burning rotisserie, and an interactive cheese gallery.

Breakfast/Lunch

CAFÉ ZINC & MARKET $

350 Ocean Ave.

(949) 494-6302

www.cafezinc.com

This popular eatery is best known for its healthy dishes and frothy cappuccinos, not to mention its loyal following that includes the likes of Julia Louis-Dreyfus, Bette Midler, and Heather Locklear. Open for breakfast and lunch, the menu is a mix of omelets, quiche, and handcrafted soups. Grab and go items, such as savory scones and gourmet sandwiches, are also available and the market, with its shelves of delightful edibles, allows you to recreate the Café Zinc experience at home.

THE COTTAGE RESTAURANT $

308 North Coast Hwy.

(949) 494-3023

www.thecottagerestaurant.com

Open daily for lunch and dinner, it's the breakfast that garners the longest lines outside this vintage California bungalow. Morning meals are traditional plates of eggs and bacon, pancakes and waffles, omelettes and scrambles, and pots of fresh coffee. Lunch and dinner features a medley of home-style California cuisine. The cottage itself offers a cozy setting, but there is also a garden patio for taking meals. Beer and wine are the only alcohol served.

Continental

DIZZ AS IS $$$

2794 South Coast Hwy.

(949) 494-5250

Housed in a shingled abode with red awning accents, Dizz's is filled with relics from the 1920s coupled with images of Marilyn Monroe and other starlets from decades past. Admittedly kitschy, this dimly lit eatery also offers an outdoor patio and fire pit for those who enjoy eating al fresco. Dizz's serves an array of fish, marinated meats, chicken, and lamb. There are also pâté, salads, and soups. Feel free to stop in for just a drink, but note that the bar has only a handful of stools to offer. If you ask for a restaurant recommendation while in Laguna Beach, chances are Dizz as Is will be among the top ten—it's simply a favorite even if the décor is a little dated. As for the kids, leave them at home as this is strictly geared toward adult palates.

Thai

ROYAL THAI CUISINE $$$

1750 South Pacific Coast Hwy.

(949) 494-THAI

www.royalthaicuisine.com

With two Orange County coastal locations, including Newport Beach, Royal Thai Cuisine has garnered a loyal following with its offerings of pad Thai, tom kah soup, and mee krob. The dishes are spicy, but the chefs will gladly increase the level to make it even spicier. For those with less than iron stomachs, the intensity can be toned down. For the culinary-inclined, Royal Thai Cuisine also offers cooking classes.

friendly place about 15 miles east of Disneyland and just a few miles inland from Seal Beach.

Best Brews

If you're looking for a place to get your beer on, The OC has a number of destinations to quench your thirst with an ale, lager, or stout.

- **Alcatraz Brewing Co.,** The Block at Orange, 20 City Blvd., Orange, (714) 939-8686
- **The Auld Dubliner,** 2497 Park Ave., Tustin, (714) 259-1562
- **The Goat Hill Tavern,** 1830 Newport Blvd., Costa Mesa, (949) 548-1109
- **Huntington Beach Beer Co.,** 201 Main St., Huntington Beach, (714) 960-5343
- **Ocean Brewing Co.,** 237 Ocean Ave., Laguna Beach, (949) 497-3381
- **Steelhead Brewing Co.,** 4175 Campus Dr., Irvine, (949) 856-2227
- **Tustin Brewing Co.,** 13011 Newport Ave., Tustin, (714) 665-2337
- **Yard House,** multiple locations including Irvine Spectrum and Fashion Island, (949) 727-0959

LOS ALAMITOS

Deli

KATELLA DELI $
4470 Katella Ave.
(562) 594-8611
Located across the street from the Los Alamitos Race Track, this is one of Orange County's few Jewish delis, offering great blintzes, bagels and lox, mile-high sandwiches, and endless desserts. Open for breakfast, lunch, and dinner, most of the menu items are traditional Jewish fare (but not kosher), such as the matzo soup, and the portions are very generous. This is also an extremely family-

NEWPORT BEACH

American

THE DOCK $
2816 Lafayette Ave.
(949) 673-9463
www.eatatthedock.com
This location has been the home of several failed restaurants, but it seems that The Dock may have all the right ingredients for success. Located on the Rhine Channel in Newport Beach's Cannery Village, The Dock is a casual but stylish dining destination with an eclectic menu of seafood, salads, beef, and weekends-only breakfast specialties. Equally appetizing is the view, which overlooks the water, and the wine list is incredibly long and includes an array of vintages by the glass.

Gourmet Markets

PASCAL EPICERIE & WINE $
1000 North Bristol
(949) 263-9400 ext. 2
www.pascalnpb.com
For the epicurean, Pascal's is like paradise. Grab and go items, such as scones and paninis, offer convenience, but this lovely French market also has take-out dinners, complete picnic hampers for summer concerts, and a varied list of salads, sandwiches, quiche, side dishes, croissants, breads, and more. The wine cellar carries a variety of vintages to complement your edible acquisition. Continental breakfast is also available.

Italian/American

THE OLD SPAGHETTI FACTORY $
2110 Newport Blvd.
(949) 675-8654
www.osf.com
This family-friendly restaurant has long waits, but if you can time it right you'll be seated quickly. The dining room is filled with antiques including a street car outfitted with tables and chairs. The

⊙ Close-up

Sink Your Teeth into Something Created—Or Perfected— in The OC

The Balboa Bar, found at Dad's on Balboa Island in Newport Beach, is nothing more than a square vanilla ice-cream treat on a stick, dipped in a vat of chocolate, and rolled around in a pan of sprinkles or nuts. Oh, but it's so good.

The roadside Crystal Cove Shake Shack, a 1946 landmark now owned by Ruby's Diner and located along the south side of Pacific Coast Highway halfway between Newport Beach and Laguna Beach in Crystal Cove, is home to the date shake, a blended drink of dates and ice-cream.

What could be a better pairing than a million-dollar view and a chilled martini? At The Montage Resort & Spa in Laguna Beach you get both. Their OC-tini, a mélange of Bacardi 'O' Rum, Cointreau, and fresh orange juice, is best enjoyed in the ocean view lobby at sunset.

Rudolph Boysen created the boysenberry, but Walter Knott commercially cultivated it, and every boysenberry in the entire world can trace its roots back to Knott's Berry Farm. The juicy berry, a cross between a blackberry, red raspberry, and loganberry, makes a fabulous pie, and Mrs. Knott's Chicken Dinner Restaurant is the best place to sample a slice.

menu is mostly pasta coupled with your choice of sauces plus salads and a few other selections. This location has a full bar, too.

Mediterranean

ZOV'S NEIGHBORHOOD CAFÉ & BAR $$
21123 Newport Coast Dr.
(949) 760-9687
www.zovs.com

The original Zov's Bistro, which has gained national acclaim, is located in Tustin, but chef/owner Zov Karamardian has branched out in recent years adding two additional Orange County locations to her portfolio. The dining room, with its scattering of tables and stylish counter seating, is lofty in design with ambient lighting. The menu, which includes lunch and dinner, features starters such as hummus and baba ghanoush. There is also Moroccan salad, grilled lamb, and chicken kabobs alongside Zov's signature meatloaf and blackened spicy ahi. Breakfast, served weekends only, is a bit more traditional with omelets, griddle specialties, oatmeal, and bagels and lox. There is also a nightly happy hour and full bar.

Seafood

THE CANNERY $$
3010 Lafayette Rd.
(949) 566-0060
www.cannerynewport.com

Tucked away in Cannery Village overlooking the water is The Cannery, housed in a once-bustling tuna canning plant. This is more than just a seafood restaurant. Upstairs is an Asian dining room where Japanese specialties are served from the sushi bar. The water-level Grill Room is more of a chophouse offering succulent steaks and poultry. The Jellyfish Bar is a great gathering spot for drinks and appetizers. The Cannery feels like many restaurants at one spectacular location. The best tables are those outside overlooking the Rhine Channel.

THE CRAB COOKER $
2200 Newport Blvd.
(949) 673-0100
www.crabcooker.com

Newport Beach is full of fancy seafood restaurants, but if you don't mind communal dining and food served on paper plates you'll pay half the price for an excellent seafood meal. The Crab Cooker, opened in 1951 and housed in a red shack just a crab-toss from the pier, catches its own fish daily and uses three important criteria: smell, sight, and touch. If it smells fishy, the experts at The Crab Cooker claim it will taste fishy and, therefore, is low quality. The restaurant only stocks and serves quality fish and shellfish that are odorless with a firm, solid texture. Clam chowder and a chunk of fresh fisherman's bread will run you $4, while lobster is less than $30. You can also order oysters on the half shell, crab cakes, or king crab claws. All entrees come with sauce and fresh lemon plus a choice of Romano potatoes or rice pilaf and cole slaw or fresh tomatoes. The menu has nothing to offer landlubbers—it's strictly fish, fish, and more fish. Wine and beer are also available.

21 OCEANFRONT   **$$$**
2100 West Oceanfront
(949) 673-2100
www.21oceanfront.com
This strictly surf and turf restaurant, located below the Doryman Inn near the Newport pier, has the feel of an exclusive club with its three dining rooms plus patio with its Pacific Ocean backdrop. The menu is classic cuisine that includes filet mignon, steak Diane, succulent crab legs, and colossal tiger prawns. The wine list features an extraordinary selection of vintages and is a serial winner of *Wine Spectator*'s Award of Excellence. You can also bring your own bottle, but why bother with a selection of 300 labels hailing from France, Italy, Napa, Portugal, and Spain? The restaurant features live entertainment nightly, too. For a fine dining experience, 21 Oceanfront delivers.

Sushi

BLUEFIN   **$$$**
7592 East Coast Hwy.
(949) 715-7373
Guests have two dining options—either at the sushi bar or at a long row of banquettes positioned against the wall. Dim lighting and mini-

Mariner Mile

Newport Beach's automotive and nautical hub is found along a stretch of Pacific Coast Highway known as Mariner Mile. Mixed among the fleet of luxury cars and multimillion-dollar yachts are a number of restaurants. There are some names you will recognize, like **Joe's Crab Shack**, but there are many others that offer a one-of-a-kind experience. **Villa Nova** recalls the Italian waterfront with its hand-painted murals and traditional menu of pasta, veal, and seafood. The **Alley Restaurant** is a 21-year-old local landmark serving aged steaks, fresh seafood, and pasta with a full bar reminiscent of a San Francisco saloon at the turn of the century. The casual **Cappy's Café** is an American-style roadhouse known for its generous portions and delicious breakfasts. There is also **China Palace, Duke's Place** and **First Cabin** both located at the Balboa Bay Club Resort, **Royal Thai Cuisine, Jack Shrimp, Charthouse**, and many others. Those located on the harbor offer dock and dine valet service. During the annual Newport Beach Christmas Boat Parade, held for five consecutive nights in December, reservations are hard to come by because those restaurants on the water offer a front row seat and the best parade viewing coupled with creative holiday menus.

malist décor add to the hipness, and the menu of hot and cold appetizers, fresh fish, and teeth-sinking sushi do wonders for the palate as well.

Electric martinis, warm sake, and ice-cold Japanese beer are ideal menu pairings. Bluefin is a great date night, but families are also present with chopsticks in hand.

ORANGE

American

PJ'S ABBEY $$
182 South Orange St.
(714) 771-8556
www.pjsabbey.com
Housed in an 1891 Gothic-style church, with its original stained-glass windows and polished wood furnishings in tact, is PJ's Abbey. The original pulpit can be found near the front door as guests enter, and a few leftover pews even provide a place to sit while waiting for a table. The restaurant, open for lunch, dinner, and weekend brunch, serves classic American fare coupled with a few unexpected finds. The weighty list of entrees includes a club sandwich, grilled meatloaf, and a sampling of pasta dishes, plus fresh seafood, grilled Angus rib eye, and rack of lamb. Weekend brunch is a mix of omelets, huevos rancheros, steel cut Irish oatmeal, and mimosas. Live jazz is enjoyed every Saturday night. PJ's usually introduces a special menu for holidays, such as Easter and Valentine's Day, and often hosts winemaker and beer dinners.

Mexican

MORENO'S $
4328 East Chapman Ave.
(714) 639-2189
www.morenosrestaurant.com
An evening at Moreno's feels like a trip south of the border. The ivy-laden building, a reconfigured church and meeting hall that dates back to the late 1800s, features an open-air courtyard that is ideal on warm summer evenings. A woman making corn tortillas by hand along with strolling mariachis add to the festivities. The menu, be it lunch, dinner, or weekend brunch, features classic Mexican dishes that are ample in size and flavor. Children are embraced and the menu features a list of kid-friendly dishes. Moreno's blended salt-rimmed margaritas are a house specialty.

ORANGE HILL $$
6410 East Chapman Ave.
(714) 997-2910
www.theorangehillrestaurant.com
Clinging to a hillside high above The OC sits this large, terraced restaurant with cascading waterfalls and koi ponds. A popular spot for post-nuptial celebrations and prom dates, this dinner-only restaurant takes American classics and adds a contemporary twist. There are crab cakes, lobster bisque, and salads that are ideally paired with the extensive menu of seafood, prime rib, free-range chicken, and vegetarian offerings. A weekend brunch buffet is ideal for the entire family and includes made-to-order omelets and pasta, plus a carving station and more. Orange Hill is also known for its extensive wine list and fabulous views.

SAN CLEMENTE

Desserts/Crepes

LA GALETTE CREPERIE $
612 Avenida Victoria
(949) 498-5335
www.lagalettecreperie.com
Located at the San Clemente Pier and open from breakfast through dinner, La Galette Creperie brings Breton-style crepes to coastal Orange County. These soft, wafer-thin shells are filled and folded with an array of fresh and decadent ingredients, from rich, silky chocolate and fresh quartered strawberries to ripe pears poached in red wine. A rosette of whipped cream or drizzling of chocolate adds the crowning touch to this French dessert. Fresh coffee, espresso, Italian sodas, and blended teas are also available. For those who want something more substantial, La Galette Creperie also offers crepes filled with

seafood, meats, and cheeses, as well as salads and sandwiches prepared in full view at the exhibition kitchen.

SAN JUAN CAPISTRANO

Fondue

SIMPLY FONDUE $$$
31761 Camino Capistrano
(949) 240-0300
www.simplyfondueorangecounty.com
As of late, fondue is making a comeback and Simply Fondue is leading the way. The restaurant, with its colorful décor, makes dining fun because those at the table have to participate in creating their meals. Melting pot dishes include an array of meat, seafood, and poultry with a trio of cooking styles including the tableside fondue grill. Devoted dippers can also select from the traditional Swiss Chalet offering, which is a cheese fondue using Gruyere and Emmenthaler cheeses, beer, and spices. Chocolate fondue ranks right up there for those just wanting dessert. Simply Fondue also has a selection of salads, prix fixe meals, and a menu that children will find appealing. In addition to its vast wine selection, Simply Fondue also has a refreshing list of martinis as well as a full bar.

Mexican

EL ADOBE DE CAPISTRANO $$
31891 Camino Capistrano
(949) 493-1163
www.eladobedecapistrano.com
Located a few short blocks from the Mission and recognized by the state as an historical landmark, El Adobe de Capistrano was a favorite dining destination of Richard Nixon. The building was originally two separate structures with one being an original adobe home owned by Miguel Yorba and built in 1797 while the other, built in 1812, housed the court and jails. The walls of the restaurant's cocktail lounge belonged to the original adobe, and it's easy to visualize the jailbirds that were once holed up in what is now the wine cellar. In addition to the main dining room and patio, there are also private rooms for events and special occasions. The menu features traditional Mexican fare along with steaks and seafood plus the best salt-rimmed margaritas blended at the bar. The restaurant, which features a reasonably priced kids' menu, is open for lunch, dinner, and Sunday brunch.

SEAL BEACH

Barbecue

BEACHWOOD BBQ $$
131 ½ Main St.
(562) 493-4500
www.beachwoodbbq.com
With a slogan that reads, "Where the fork meets the pork," it's hard to go wrong at this seaside barbecue eatery. Beachwood takes a low and slow approach with their meats, which are slowly smoked, dry rubbed, and thoughtfully flavored, allowing the taste of the meat to stand on its own without a thick coating of sauce. The menu is a bit of a surprise and offers so much more than baby backs. For example, there are fried green tomatoes, deviled eggs, and BBQ fondue for two featuring grilled sausage, meatballs, hush puppies, assorted breads, and veggies accompanied by a spicy beer cheese sauce. More traditional offerings include short ribs, brisket, and pulled pork. There are also salads, seafood, and meatloaf made with wild boar plus plenty of side dishes to select. As for barbecue sauce, it's sitting right there on the table for diners to apply as they see fit.

Seafood

WALT'S WHARF $$
201 Main St.
(562) 375-0286
www.waltswharf.com
The only fish fresher than the selection at Walt's are those found swimming in the nearby ocean. This two-story institution, located in the Old Town section of Seal Beach, specializes in oak-grilled seafood, such as Alaskan king crab legs

and swordfish. Crab cakes, clam chowder, and halibut also play an instrumental role on the daily menu. While Walt's Wharf certainly appeals to seafood lovers, there are also a number of dishes on the menu that have not been pulled from the ocean, including beef and pasta selections. This is an extremely popular dining destination, one that is appropriate for kids, and it's not unusual to wait an hour or more to be seated. Walt's Wharf is open for lunch and dinner.

SOUTH COAST PLAZA AREA (SANTA ANA/COSTA MESA)

American

LEATHERBY'S CAFÉ ROUGE   **$$$**
615 Town Center Dr.
(714) 429-7640
www.patinagroup.com
From the Patina Restaurant Group empire, headed by celeb chef Joachim Splichal, comes the dinner-only Leatherby's Rouge Café located inside the Renee and Henry Segerstrom Concert Hall near South Coast Plaza. The minimalist décor coupled with the exceptional modern American dishes result in a celebration of flavors. Starters include duck confit, a fromage plate, and seared foie gras. Signature dishes range from a half-pound elk burger to braised rabbit to a 10-ounce pork porterhouse. There is a three-course prix fixe menu available as well. Tuesday through Friday from 5 to 7 p.m. it's happy hour, featuring many dishes found on the main menu coupled with a variety of drink specials. This may be the ideal way to combine a pre-show meal with an evening at the Segerstrom Concert Hall. Leatherby's also hosts holiday dinners, such as Thanksgiving and Easter, for those who want an elegant meal but have no time to pull it together.

French

MARCHÉ MODERNE   **$$**
3333 Bristol St. (South Coast Plaza—Level 3 next to Nordstrom)
(714) 434-7900
www.marchemoderne.net

Located in the most unlikely of places, the penthouse level at South Coast Plaza, Marché Moderne, which translates to modern market, is *tres magnifique*. Even the *LA Times* restaurant critic, who rarely gives a restaurant more than a single star, lauded Marché Moderne, giving it three-star status (four-star is the highest). This hip French bistro is ideal for an après-shopping lunch, as well as dinner, and offers artisan-made cheese and charcuterie plates, foie gras coupled with boutique-style sandwiches, and wood-burning oven tarts. A three-course menu, which changes daily, is also offered. Duck and pork shanks are accompanied by pommes frites, while a succulent roasted chicken breast gets a bit dressed up with truffle-scented pommes puree. The wine list won't disappoint either. Not a lot on the menu for children except for perhaps the cheese plate, but even those are geared towards more sophisticated palates.

Italian

ANTONELLO RISTORANTE   **$$$**
1611 Sunflower Ave.
(714) 751-7153
www.antonello.com
On the radar of every OC foodie, Antonello is a favorite of restaurant critics, too. With its long list of antipasti, soups, salads, and pasta specialties, plus fresh seafood, poultry, and beef, finding a bottle of wine to complement your meal won't be difficult considering the restaurant stocks some 700-plus foreign and domestic labels. Antonello is located near South Coast Plaza, has a dress code, and is not suited for children.

Persian

DARYA   **$$**
3800 South Plaza Dr.
(714) 557-6600
www.daryasouthcoastplaza.com
For the past 20 years Darya has been a magnet for those who savor Persian fare. Enjoyed amid an ornate dining room, replete with sleek marble columns and dangling chandeliers, Darya's menu features a selection of traditional appetizers and

entrees along with a full bar. The menu is thick and infused with yogurt, eggplant, garlic, herbs, and onions, and chicken, seafood, beef, lamb, and vegetarian dishes are all well represented. Darya's signature dish, Naderi Kebab, is a medley of succulent center cut filet mignon that is marinated and cut into chunks. The boiled chicken is served with fried walnut pomegranate sauce. You'll find an extensive wine list as well. Some of the best seats are located on the patio.

SUNSET BEACH

Sushi

DAIMONS $$
16232 Pacific Coast Hwy.
(562) 592-4852
For those who want a little sound with their sushi, this hole-in-the-wall delivers. A resident DJ gets the party going as diners nosh on teppan specialties and sip sake to the beat. The sushi chef does a spectacular job creating California rolls and has also been known to take beer breaks with guests. Located on a lonely stretch of Pacific Coast Highway, Daimons is a favorite of locals.

NIGHTLIFE

Because Orange County is a sprawling region, nightlife, or anything else for that matter, isn't contained to one specific area. It tends to be spread around, which can be a good thing, since no matter where you are, you won't have to travel far to find some sort of evening fun. And the term *nightlife* is subjective, although it's usually assumed to include drinking, dancing, and late nights. But in Orange County, nightlife can mean many things. Sure, there are the usual suspects—the high-energy clubs and watering holes where people stand elbow to elbow simply because it's the *place du jour*. And these places tend to appeal to a younger crowd where anybody over 30 is considered over the hill. But by just broadening the spectrum, nightlife can also include wine bars, jazz clubs, neighborhood pubs and sports bars, comedy clubs, or billiard halls. Even bowling has gotten hip inside some local alleys.

The inland areas, which for the most part are bedroom communities, have fewer options than those by the coast. Huntington Beach has a laidback vibe along Main Street, where people spill out onto the sidewalk from surf-centric bars and pubs. Newport Beach has more swanky venues, especially at some of the resort lounges, and the same could be said for Laguna Beach, although it has a nice collection of places in the village to enjoy live music and evening gallery receptions that wouldn't be considered high brow. Seal Beach is a bit quieter, catering mostly to locals, and the same can be said for Dana Point and San Clemente. There are also entertainment centers, such as Irvine Spectrum and The Block of Orange, where you can park your car and wander the open-air walkways until you happen upon something that piques your interest.

OVERVIEW

Those who live behind the Orange Curtain, a term used to describe the dividing line between the more conservative Orange County and left-leaning Los Angeles County, can be fickle when it comes to nightlife. The newest bar, club or watering hole to open its doors, especially if its located along the coast, is *the* place to see and be seen—that is, until a newer, more trendy place enters the race. It's a never-ending cycle where loyalty rarely wins, and today's crowded clubs are tomorrow's vacant storefronts.

Unlike Los Angeles, there are no velvet ropes to cross, doormen to bribe, or red carpets to walk. Typically Orange County nightclubs and bars are rather low-key. For starters, things get going around 9 p.m. on weekends, which is early by most city standards. Second, the party is over by 2 a.m. with the last call for alcohol

at 1:30 a.m.; alcohol cannot be sold between 2 a.m. and 6 a.m. in the state of California. Finally, while everyone likes to get their groove on, the people of Orange County, and most of Southern California, enjoy taking advantage of the region's flawless weather, which means serious workouts on most mornings. It's only the determined barfly that needs a little push out the door long after the last dance has been danced and the last drink has been drunk. As for after-hours joints, you'd be hard pressed to find anything open, except for a 24-hour diner (and even those are scarce), since the sale of alcohol after 2 a.m. is prohibited.

Most nightclubs will have a cover charge on weekends and, where alcohol is served, a 21-and-over policy is usually in place, although there are exceptions. The legal drinking age in California, as well as the rest of the United States, is 21, and anyone who looks under 40 will likely be asked to produce identification, either a driver's license, state ID card, or a passport. California law enforcement has a very low tolerance for drinking and driving, so driver beware. Anyone with a blood alcohol level of 0.08 or higher is considered legally intoxicated and, if pulled over by the police or California Highway Patrol, will be asked to take a sobriety or breathalyzer test if the attending officer suspects any alcohol has been consumed. Occasionally, the police will set up sobriety check points, stopping cars at random to see if drivers are under the influence. These are usually noted in the newspaper with just a few sentences. Don't put your life—or others—in danger by getting behind the wheel after downing a few drinks. Always appoint a designated driver and, if you feel the least bit hesitant as to whether you should climb behind the steering wheel, reconsider and ask the bartender to call you a taxi or check into a nearby hotel to sleep it off.

i The smoking laws have gotten extremely strict not only in Orange County, but throughout the state of California. You are not allowed to light up in a restaurant, bar, or most public areas, as well as all workplace areas and, in some instances, public beaches. You'll notice there are no ashtrays lying around on tables or atop bars because smoking in these establishments is strictly prohibited.

Nightclubs, comedy clubs, bars, lounges, pubs, and anything else considered an after-dark destination are known to change their hours, formats, and dress codes, or close their doors altogether without the least bit of warning. The club that once required a collared shirt may now cater to a T-shirt and ripped jeans crowd. And the all-'80s Wednesday night that was so fun last week is now hip-hop Hump Night with a much different clientele. Pick up a copy of *OC Weekly*, which is a free publication distributed weekly and found in newsstands and retail shops throughout Orange County. The free monthly *944 Magazine* is another great source, as are the Thursday and Sunday editions of the *LA Times*

and the Thursday edition of the *Orange County Register*. *GreersOC.com*, a free online subscription newsletter, reports on happenings daily, and the Web site also tracks the comings and goings of life in The OC.

BARS AND PUBS

Costa Mesa

GOAT HILL TAVERN
1830 Newport Blvd.
(949) 548-8428
This OC institution has survived every trend and has transcended generations with a clientele that remains steadfast. Devotees of all ages still consider the Goat Hill Tavern, named for the goats that once roamed freely in these parts, to be the best bar in the county, and for good reason. There are endless beers on tap all reasonably priced, baskets brimming with peanuts, and, as a result, a floor full of discarded peanut shells. It doesn't cost a dime to play a game of shuffle board, and the Goat Hill Tavern also has plenty of pool tables. The covered patio is great for sipping ice-cold beer on a warm Southern California evening.

KITSCH BAR
891 Baker St.
(714) 546-8580
www.kitschbar.com
Promoting itself as an intimate full liquor lounge and one that has no cover charge, the Kitsch Bar also offers no food, shows, no televised sports, and doesn't encourage dancing. There is no sign displayed on the building to let you know it's even there, a practice that is more typical of LA clubs, and the staff doesn't bother to answer the phone. So, what's the appeal of the Kitsch Bar? It's quirky and a departure from the typical Orange County club scene. The mood is mellow, the lighting dim, the décor minimal and hip. Obscure films are projected on the wall behind the bar and each night there is something to look forward to. Ask to be a guest bartender on Sunday nights, watch a movie and enjoy free popcorn

on Mondays, and the rest of the week pop in to enjoy a mix of music spun by a variety of DJs. Just don't get carried away with any dancing.

Fullerton

BRIAN'S BEER AND BILLIARDS
1944 North Placentia Ave.
(714) 993-1401
www.briansbeer.com
Right around the time Ronald Reagan took office, Brian's Beer and Billiards, simply known as Brian's, was born. The cheap beer and low-key vibe were an immediate hit with the students at nearby Cal State Fullerton. A couple of years later the owner opened up a Laundromat a few doors down, and in between cycles people would pass the time inside Brian's, which cleverly ran lights into the bar to let patrons know when their clothes were dry. Its strip mall location is obscure, but people manage to find this legendary joint.

OLDE SHIP BRITISH PUB
709 North Harbor Blvd.
(714) 871-7447
www.theoldeship.com
English ex-pats are sure to feel right at home inside this British-owned pub. It truly embraces the public house mentality that has been a tradition on the other side of the pond for centuries. On tap are 20 British draft beers, but if you fancy a gin and tonic or frothy margarita, the mixologist behind the bar will be more than happy to accommodate. The menu is traditional as well, listing bangers and mash along with other English food. But crab cakes, garlic prawns, and smoked salmon with capers make an appearance on the menu as well. Their slogan, "You'll Be a Stranger Here But Once," must ring true because the Olde Ship British Pub has a loyal following of locals.

Huntington Beach

KILLARNEY PUB & GRILL
209 Main St.
(714) 536-7887
www.killarneypubandgrill.com

Touted as the only Irish pub on Huntington Beach's Main Street, Killarney's pays homage to the motherland by pairing Irish ales, stouts, and lagers with food you're likely to find in a Dublin cafe. Wraps and salads add a California touch.

Laguna Beach

MARINE ROOM TAVERN
214 Ocean Ave.
(949) 494-3027
With its name emblazoned on a green awning draped over the entrance to the building, it's hard to miss the Marine Room Tavern. A rebel among Laguna Beach's wine bars and bistros, this funky find, with wood carved sailfish and marlin adorning outdated paneled walls, proves to be a welcome departure from the more yuppified establishments. The interiors are a mix of hardwood floors, cozy furnishings, and a well-stocked bar proving to be the ideal backdrop for throwing back a pint or two. On Thursday night and Sunday afternoon there is live entertainment.

Newport Beach

BALBOA SALOON
700 East Bay Ave.
(949) 673-9783
www.balboasaloon.com
Flying darts, friendly billiard games, sounds of clinking glasses—this is what you can expect when you walk inside the Balboa Saloon. The big screen television displays major sporting events and there are some smaller screens strategically placed as well. The saloon's bank of windows lets you take in the beach scene from the comfort of a bar stool. There's even free Wi-Fi, but this Balboa Peninsula dive bar really doesn't attract a "have computer, will travel" crowd.

THE BEACH BALL
2116 West Oceanfront
(949) 675-8041
www.beachballbar.com
As far as dive bars go, The Beach Ball in tony Newport Beach near the pier does a good job with its no-frills ambiance. The bar is small, but

manages to fit a few pool tables inside. There is a long list of drinks and music sans the dance floor, but patrons still like to do a little impromptu dancing—especially after a few drinks. With the beach just across the way, the views at sunset are spectacular.

BLACKIE'S BY THE SEA
2118 West Oceanfront
(949) 675-1074
www.blackiesbythesea.com

A couple of doors down from The Beach Ball on the same side of the boardwalk is this competing dive bar. It, too, offers ice-cold beer on tap, scantily clad women spilling out the door, televisions positioned at every turn for optimum viewing, and a few munchies, sandwiches, and snacks to chase the beer. Blackie's is popular because it's cheap, from the beer to the pool tables in the back. Well-heeled patrons bypass the entrance to Blackie's for one of the more upscale Newport Beach watering holes. That suits the loyal clientele just fine. It just means more beer to go around.

CROW BAR AND KITCHEN
2325 East Coast Hwy.
(949) 675-0070
www.crowbarcdm.com

This Corona del Mar gastropub attracts a polo shirt and khakis kind of crowd. The small bar is usually two people deep and a pair of large communal tables creates a sense of camaraderie. The Crow Bar has quite a few beers on tap, and, as for the menu, you'll find Irish stew right alongside haughtier fare such as blue crab deviled eggs. Even though this is a pub, which typically translates to pints of ale, don't overlook the Crow Bar's long list of wines by the glass.

MALARKEY'S IRISH PUB
3011 Newport Blvd.
(949) 675-2340

Orange County really likes its Irish pubs, and Malarkey's in Newport Beach is among the more popular. It doesn't really try to be anything other than what it is—a pub that caters to a beer guz-

zling crowd. There's no chi-chi menu or martini glasses dangling from the hands of the well manicured; instead, people gather around at the copper-topped square bar holding their pints and chatting it up.

THE QUIET WOMAN
3224 East Coast Hwy.
(949) 640-7440
www.quietwoman.com

This pub's logo, displayed prominently at its entrance, is every man's dream. It depicts a headless lass—hence the name "The Quiet Woman." The moniker is quite common on pub signs throughout England. The Quiet Woman is a hybrid of sorts, being part restaurant and part bar. The bar is more upscale than the traditional pub, which coalesces nicely with similar establishments found in the seaside village of Corona del Mar. Patrons tend to favor electric-colored martinis rather than amber-hued beer, and students from nearby UCI are often the guilty culprits enjoying the funny-named libations. Five nights a week The Quiet Woman features live entertainment and the restaurant area is extremely family friendly.

WOODY'S WHARF
2318 Newport Blvd.
(949) 675-0474
www.woodyswharf.com

What was once a place used to store and repair boats is now Woody's Wharf, a favorite Newport Beach watering hole sporting a rusty rowboat on its roof and a landmark blue whale sign out front. Opened in 1965 along the waterfront, the likes of John Wayne, Cary Grant and Mickey Mantle have all warmed the bar stools at Woody's. At one time actor and karate champ Chuck Norris was the proprietor and his doorman was an undiscovered Jean-Claude Van Damme. Woody's Wharf is a bit tattered at the edges, but that's what makes it so desirable. Sailors and yachtsmen fresh from the sea often make Woody's their first terra firma stop, but there is also a dockside menu for those who prefer to dine and splash. On weekends the house rocks with live music until the 2 a.m. closing, when everyone is then asked to drink up and get out.

Orange

HAVEN GASTROPUB
190 South Glassell St.
(714) 221-0680
www.havengastropub.com
Micro brews and an impressive selection of Scotch and whiskey are sure to catch the attention of any pub crawler. Perhaps that's why the newly opened Haven Gastropub in the Old Towne section of Orange has been an instant success. Its menu is best described as comfort food, only with some added panache. A few things you're likely to find are a glazed pork sandwich, house-cured pickles, traditional fish and chips served with coleslaw, and an Irish stew that outdoes the Emerald Isle.

Gastropub

Leave it to the Brits to come up with a hipper way to say "pub." The gastropub is an English term that originated around 1990, blending the words *gastronomy* and *pub*. It's used to describe a public house specializing in high-quality food rather than the run-of-the-mill fare typically served in a pub. The gastropub is catching on in Orange County, even if the word "gastropub" isn't part of the name. The gastropub concept actually strikes a nice balance where people can enjoy the friendly atmosphere of a pub but also reap from it a good meal.

O'HARE'S PUB
150 North Glassell St.
(714) 532-9264
Locals and coeds from Chapman University, located just down the street, like to gather inside this Old Towne Orange hole in the wall. Irish to the core, students especially like O'Hare's because the drinks are cheap, there are pool tables, and a friendly game of darts can add a bit of escapism during finals week. O'Hare's isn't very big—in fact, it's small—but what it lacks in square footage it makes up for in fun.

San Clemente

MOLLY BLOOM'S IRISH BAR
2391 South El Camino Real
(949) 218-0120
www.mollybloomsirishbar.com
The locals gather near the fireplace at Molly's to listen to live music, sample the beer, and sip wine. And, unlike other pubs that claim to be Irish, Molly Bloom's actually plays authentic Irish music with local musicians doing the honors. On occasion, talents from Ireland make their way to this neighborhood pub to perform. The bar menu, for the most part, is traditional Irish grub, from the spinach and cheese pie to the corned beef and cabbage. Every day is St. Patrick's Day at this seaside watering hole.

THE SWALLOW'S INN
31786 Camino Capistrano
(949) 493-3188
www.swallowsinn.com
It's hard to pigeonhole the clientele of this honky tonk. All walks of life are represented, from surfers and bikers to business types and construction workers. This makes for some colorful demographics, but when everyone is in flip flops and jeans it works. Each night of the week features some sort of entertainment, from live music and karaoke to beer pong competitions. The menu is limited, but people don't come to the Swallow's Inn for the food. For a buck a bag you can graze on roasted peanuts, salted pretzels, or popcorn drizzled with butter.

Seal Beach

THE ABBEY
306 Main St.
(562) 799-4246

Main Street in Seal Beach is the ideal backdrop for a neighborhood pub, and The Abbey, with its snug size and handful of taps, is a great place to pop into after seeing a movie at the vintage Bay Theater a few storefronts down. If The Abbey is too crowded, you can always head to the much larger O'Malley's on the same side of the street only closer to the beach.

Sunset Beach

MOTHER'S TAVERN
16701 Pacific Coast Hwy.
(562) 592-2111
Those speeding along Pacific Coast Highway could easily miss the tiny red building belonging to Mother's Tavern, unless the fleet of pricey Harleys catches their eye. This inviting neighborhood bar isn't shy about asking first-time visitors to donate their bras, underwear, or socks to display alongside other discarded garments that cling to the ceiling. Rumor has it that the building that now houses Mother's was a ticket station for the Pacific Electric Railway many decades ago and, judging by its petite size, it's very possible. Guests belly up to the cozy bar to enjoy a beer and, on some weekends, live local bands. If there is no band in the house, the selection from the jukebox will have to do.

NADINE'S IRISH MIST
16655 Pacific Coast Hwy.
(562) 592-7000
www.nadinesirishmist.com
This roadhouse, owned by an Irish lad and lass, was a rundown restaurant and bar before the owners bought the one-story building and transformed it into a destination. The beautiful wood bar and inviting staff are why people choose to imbibe here. During happy hour, which is Monday through Friday from noon until 7 p.m., the prices are dirt cheap and on weekends there is usually live entertainment. Of course, the menu is a tribute to Irish fare and there is always plenty of Guinness to go around.

LIVE MUSIC

Anaheim

CHAIN REACTION
1652 West Lincoln Ave.
(714) 635-6067
www.allages.com
One of the few clubs with no age limit—and no alcohol—is centrally located off I-5 in Anaheim. Chain Reaction rocks with a mix of ska, punk, rock, alternative, and heavy metal thrown in for good measure. Most of the bands that take to the tiny stage are homegrown in Orange County with a local following. But today's no-label lyricist could be tomorrow's Grammy nominee. Most shows hover between $8 and $20 per person, so you won't break the bank spending a night here either.

THE GROVE OF ANAHEIM
2200 East Katella Ave.
(714) 712-2750
www.grove-of-anaheim.com
Built in the late 1990s Tinseltown Studios, an attraction where guests were made to feel like movie stars with a red carpet welcome and faux paparazzi, enjoyed about 15 minutes of fame before it closed its doors. It then was converted into the Sun Theatre, a concert venue that was eventually renamed The Grove of Anaheim and operated by the very successful Nederlander concert promoters. Located just down the road from Disneyland and even closer to Angel Stadium and the Honda Center, The Grove of Anaheim has a 1,700-person capacity. Recent performances include Snoop Dogg, Three Dog Night, and Ice Cube. During the daytime the venue doubles as a stop for children's entertainers with the likes of The Wiggles, Doodlebops, and others doing what they do best.

HOUSE OF BLUES
1530 South Disneyland Dr.
(714) 778-2583
www.houseofblues.com
Located in Downtown Disney, this House of Blues location opened in 2001 and gets its share of

headlining acts that are passing through Orange County. Recent performances by Joe Perry of Aerosmith and teen queen Selena Gomez have been well received, and the House of Blues weekly Gospel Brunch on Sunday is a show in itself.

Costa Mesa

DETROIT BAR
843 West 19th St.
(949) 642-0600
www.detroitbar.com
It would seem a nondescript strip mall would be a most unlikely place for a cool joint that serves up some attitude along with live music, but the Detroit Bar is all that and more. Its eclectic mix of live performances includes well-known touring acts and emerging indie-rock bands as well as a weekly line-up of DJs that spin a wide range of music.

San Juan Capistrano

THE COACH HOUSE
33157 Camino Capistrano
(949) 496-8930
www.thecoachhouse.com
The Coach House is one of those places you could easily pass by without giving it a second glance. But you would be amazed at the acts that have graced this club's stage through its history. In addition to musical acts and cover bands like Dread Zeppelin, there are also comedy nights that include acts that normally play at larger, more urban venues. Half the seats are reserved for those coming for dinner and a show, who get the better seats, with non-dining guests placed at smaller cocktail-style tables.

Santa Ana

GALAXY CONCERT THEATRE
3503 South Harbor Blvd.
(714) 957-0600
www.galaxytheatre.com
Run by the same people who manage the Coach House, this Vegas-style theater, with its dinner offerings and shaken and stirred drinks, may

look a bit vintage but it offers an electrifying mix of pop, punk, and rock. The monthly line-up includes mostly local talent and those bands on the brink of making a name for themselves, but occasionally a well-known act sweeps in and dominates the stage. For the most part, the big name acts, like English Beat and the Smithereens, still have a fan base but aren't really producing new music these days.

SPORTS BARS

Anaheim

ESPN ZONE
1500 South Disneyland Dr.
(714) 300-3776
www.espnzone.com
When it comes to sports bars, this chainlet offers the ultimate viewing experience with more than 150 monitors including a high definition big screen housed in more than 10,000 square feet of space with interactive games and attractions. Best of all, it's located at Downtown Disney, a no-admission, open-air entertainment center at Disneyland Resort, and is designed for the entire family to experience. Diehard fans can perhaps sneak away to catch the big game while the rest of the family roams the theme park. The American menu of grilled food appeals to both adults and pint-size diners.

LOFFLER SPORTS BAR & GRILL, ANAHEIM
8901 Katella Ave.
(714) 826-2040
This casual bar, located on the fringes of a middle-class neighborhood, has a typical 1960s façade and is a bit on the drab side from an outsider's perspective. Inside is an entirely different story. This is a local hangout enjoyed by college students and retirees alike. During NFL season the fans arrive to catch all the pigskin action, enjoy one of the many beers on tap, shoot a game of pool, or play a friendly game of darts. At night Loffler's turns into more of a dive bar with live bands and a modest cover charge. Admission is free Sunday through Thursday.

THROWBACKS SPORTS BAR & GRILL
1759 South Claudina Way
(714) 533-3813
www.throwbackssportsbar.com

Located right off I-5 and less than a mile from Disneyland, Throwbacks has it all: flat screen televisions, a pair of billiards tables, dart boards, karaoke, a jukebox, and plenty of draft beer. When you can't get a good seat at Angel Stadium or the Honda Center, one of the classic black stools that line the bar feels almost like you're at the game. Throwbacks Sports Bar & Grill televises all Angel, Ducks, Dodgers, and Lakers games plus Ultimate Fighting and many other major sporting events. On Friday nights there is live music as well.

Costa Mesa

CORNER OFFICE
580 Anton Blvd.
(714) 979-9922

The Corner Office, with its white-collar crowd and Internet access, wears its name well. Located among the high-rise buildings near South Coast Plaza, everywhere you turn there is another oversized television monitor displaying the latest sporting event. Beers flow freely and pair nicely with the pub menu of wings and steaks. During basketball season this is where Orange County Lakers fans come for televised games.

GARF'S SPORTS LOUNGE
3046 Bristol St.
(714) 435-4070
www.garfsbar.com

Located in Costa Mesa, but removed from the tony South Coast Plaza area, it is a never-ending party at Garf's where the beer is cold and the crowd is loud. Every day brings with it a new special, and if you want to watch the latest college game, keep track of the handicaps on the PGA Tour, slip away from the house for Monday Night Football, or catch all the ESPN action, then you need to program Garf's into your Blackberry. The menu is rather straightforward—burgers, sandwiches, tacos—and, in addition to beer, there is also a full bar.

Fountain Valley

SILKY SULLIVAN'S
10201 Slater Ave.
(714) 963-2718
www.silkysullivans.com

Fans of the sport of kings will immediately connect this bar's name with the greatest "come from behind" horse—Silky Sullivan—who won the 1958 Santa Anita Derby after trailing far behind the other horses for most of the race. Silky Sullivan's, the bar, has managed to keep a steady pace for 25 years serving tap beer, pub-style food, and a place to watch sports. Located in a former post office, Silky Sullivan's embraces that Irish pub spirit with a décor of dark wood and a never ending supply of Guinness.

Los Alamitos

STARTING GATE
5052 Katella Ave.
(562) 598-8957

Tucked away in a low-slung strip center near the Los Alamitos Race Track, the Starting Gate takes you back a few decades with a décor that looks as if it were pulled from a 1970s catalogue. Locals come to catch the latest sporting events, but a different crowd flocks here at night to belly up to one of three bars and do a little dancing on the oversized dance floor.

Newport Beach

RUDY'S PUB AND GRILL
3110 Newport Blvd.
(949) 723-0293
www.rudyspubandgrill.com

Ensconced in the heart of Newport Beach in a building that once housed an upper crust pie shop and, eventually, a French bistro, Rudy's opened in 1999 and transformed the refined interior into a casual sports bar that now contains 32 high definition plasma screen TVs, a retractable roof to make the most of the cool ocean breezes, a menu that appeals to most palates, and a neighborhood that now has its own place to enjoy televised sports. Rudy's gets packed whenever the Angels, Lakers,

Clippers, or Anaheim Ducks are playing. For the most part, Rudy's is a family friendly spot where parents can dine with their kids at high top tables or lower dining tables that seat larger parties.

Orange

OC SPORTS GRILL
450 North State College Blvd.
(714) 935-0300
www.ocsportsgrill.com
With a name like OC Sports Grill there is no mistaking what type of place this is. With a fleet of some 50 high definition televisions, enjoying any game or tournament is a no-brainer. The Blizzard Beer system keeps the kegs of golden liquid chilled to a cool 29 degrees. There are also two bars, which cuts down on wait time; eight pool tables; a menu of decent food; and the only place in Orange County that offers 100-ounce frosty beer tappers at the table. OC Sports Grill also shows all UFC and PPV boxing events, which is the next best thing to having a ringside seat. A cover charge sometimes applies.

Yorba Linda

CANYON INN
6821 Fairlynn Blvd.
(714) 779-0880
www.canyoninnsportsbar.com
Since the mid 1960s, North Orange County residents have been keeping this haunt hopping. There are a dozen televisions including nine flat screens and a 72-inch high-definition big screen. A pair of pool tables, 300,000-song online jukebox, a full menu, and daily happy hour helps to lure in the crowds. On Tuesday and Thursday there is a resident DJ in the house and dancing by a mostly 40-plus crowd.

WINE BARS

Anaheim

POP THE CORK
321 West Katella Ave.
(714) 408-1678
www.pop-the-cork.com

This tasteful wine bar is a nice addition to the Disneyland area and is located in the new Anaheim GardenWalk, an open-air dining and entertainment center. Wine snobs will enjoy the selection by the glass, which numbers approximately 50. Those who prefer to have a bottle will be pleased with the 150-label cellar. There are also tastings and wine flights, and selections can be paired with artisan cheese, tapenades, bread, and panini sandwiches. If you're doing multiple days at Disneyland, this is a nice reprieve.

Dana Point

ENO—WINE, CHEESE AND CHOCOLATE
One Ritz-Carlton Dr. (Lobby Level, Ritz-Carlton Hotel)
(949) 240-2000
www.ritzcarlton.com
This adults-only destination just off the lobby at the tony Ritz-Carlton Hotel offers the ultimate epicurean experience. With just three dozen seats and some 300 vintages, guests receive a crash course in wine, cheese, and chocolate tasting, learning to distinguish subtleties as well as how to best pair these indulgences. Open evenings only, the setting has no ocean view but after you've finished at Eno you can stroll to the lobby bar to enjoy an aperitif where the large picture window frames breathtaking seascapes.

Newport Beach

WINE GALLERY
2411 East Coast Hwy., Suite 250
Corona del Mar
(949) 675-3410
www.cdmwinegallery.com
Surrounded by bottles and bottles of wine, the wine bar inside the Wine Gallery's tasting room is an ideal opportunity to sample new releases from specific vineyards, taste varietals from obscure regions, conduct comparisons, and take notes, but it's not just for the serious wine collector. The Wine Gallery is as much a retail shop as it is a tasting destination and if you enjoy what you've sampled, you can purchase a bottle and be on your way.

The Wine Artist

Fashioned after a Tuscan winery, the Wine Artist (949-675-3410, www.thewineartist.com) in Laguna Niguel is a boutique winery that opens its doors for special events. Private wine tasting events can include selections from Tijeras Creek Winery, produced on the premises. Hosts and hostesses can also make and bottle their own wines with guests, too. But oenophiles will especially enjoy designing their own custom wine label, which can run the gamut from a photo and original artwork to special messages and is an innovative way to announce such milestones as the birth of a baby or engagement.

WINE LAB NEWPORT
2901 West Coast Hwy., Suite 100
(949) 515-8466
www.winelabnewport.com
This cellar-like wine bar and wine boutique is a place to go when you want to learn about and have fun with wine. The staff carefully selects its wines, which can be ordered in flights or by the glass starting at just $4, plus there are more than 150 vintages under $20 a bottle. Many of the wines found at Wine Lab Newport are produced in small batches and not readily available at national retailers, so it's like visiting a remote winery without having to travel. These wines, according to the experts who work here, are far more interesting and provide better value. In addition to wine, there is a small but impressive pairing menu including small plates, artisan cheeses, and Italian cured meats.

San Clemente

THE CELLAR
156 Del Mar
(949) 492-3663
www.thecellarsite.com
The Cellar, not to be confused with the downtown Fullerton restaurant of the same name, is housed in a lofty space and features an appetizing selection of food and wine. The décor is spacious and tastefully styled with sculptures made to look like wine bottles, window frames pulled from New York City's Cooper Unions Science building, and furniture crafted from poured concrete and recycled wood. The soft lighting certainly sets the tone for an evening of grazing from the small-plates menu of tapenade and flat bread. Adding to all this is the pianist who helps to give this hip find a jazzy touch. On your way out be sure to visit the cheese shop where a rich selection of fromage, wine, and chocolates is available to go.

VINE WINE COUNTRY CUISINE
211 North El Camino Real
(949) 361-3079
www.vinesanclemente.com
The crisp white exterior of this restaurant has the look and feel of a tasting room. Guests can sneak into the rustic wine bar with its roaring fire and counter-height tables that are actually wine barrels and watch the chef work his magic from within the exhibition kitchen. Their thoughtful wine list includes an array of mostly California varietals along with some vintages from Washington and Oregon, but there is a nice selection of international labels, too, from the wine producing regions of Italy, France, Spain, Portugal, Argentina, Chile, and Canada. Wines can be paired with a selection of cheeses and small plates or full-size entrees. Wednesdays are educational tasting nights when guests can sample four wines paired with a selection of edibles.

San Juan Capistrano

NAPA VALLEY WINE BAR
31781 Camino Capistrano
(949) 493-6272
www.napavalleywinebar.com
The name may not be all that unique and San Juan Capistrano is a long way from the Napa Valley, but this smart little wine bar, with its crimson-colored walls and hanging blackboard with hand-written suggestions, works great in this seaside community. Guests can sit at high top tables enjoying wine, conversation, the sound of the nearby mission bells, and, on occasion, live entertainment. A menu of tapas, cheese, cured meats, and desserts is nicely paired with featured wines.

TANNINS RESTAURANT AND WINE BAR
27211 Ortega Hwy.
(949) 661-8466
www.tanninsrestaurant.com
Tannins takes a different approach when it comes to wine bars. Ibiza at Tannins is a wine lounge with a Euro feel. There are several areas to imbibe and converse including living room–style seating with plush sofas and clubby chairs, cocktail tables for no more than four, an outdoor area with additional seating, and a row of chairs lining the bar. This is actually a destination within a destination and features a retro-mod design, a mix of jazz and soul music, innovative fare, and a selection of wines as well as bottle service. Its energy level is definitely a few decibels above the traditional wine bar. If Ibiza isn't quite your style, Tannins offers regular wine tastings and pairings.

Sunset Beach

BRIX
16635 Pacific Coast Hwy.
(562) 612-0413
www.brix4wine.com
From the outside, Brix doesn't look any different from the many other buildings lining busy Pacific Coast Highway, but this casual wine cave has an interesting collection of worldly wines that are available to taste each and every day. If they don't

have a particular wine, they can do a little detective work and find what you're looking for, then have it shipped to your front door. Tasters can enjoy a selection of tapas, and this is one of the few wine bars that has a full-time, certified sommelier on staff to enhance your overall experience.

Tustin

THE WINERY RESTAURANT
2647 Park Ave.
(714) 258-7600
www.thewineryrestaurant.net
With a wine list that climbs above a 650-bottle selection plus impromptu tours of its 800-square-foot wine cellar and a name that says it all, this award-winning destination, located at The District at Tustin, is for both the novice and the connoisseur. The bar, cloaked in cool marble and made to look like a dried, pressed grape leaf, is flanked with velvety stools for optimum comfort. The Winery also has a 1,000-square-foot limestone patio with a fireplace and retractable awning. The menu is equally pleasing and designed to complement the many vintages and varietals. Crush Hour is a real bargain with wines by the glass starting at just $6 and select appetizers, such as the artisan cheese plate, all offered at $7. Those who enjoy drinking their beverage from a pilsner glass can take advantage of the selection of $4 beers that are also offered during Crush Hour.

Yorba Linda

VERSAI THE WINE BAR
18248 Imperial Hwy.
(714) 993-3676
www.versaithewinebar.com
This two-year-old vino destination is a welcome addition to the North Orange County culinary scene. Located down the road from the Richard Nixon Library, Versai has filled a niche with its selection of fine wines, innovative fare, and monthly wine tours. Soft lighting in the shape of delicate grape vines twinkles from above and the glow of candles adds to the mellow mood. Happy hour gets high marks with its selection of

$5 appetizers and wines by the glass, as do the $3 beers. From the expansive bar crafted from cherry wood to the vintage look of a French wine cellar, Versai is worth toasting.

Wine Bars

Wine bars have certainly come into fashion in recent years. Could it be Hollywood's influence with the 2004 sleeper film *Sideways* that inspired a new breed of oenophiles? Most people working behind the bar are eager to educate the novice taster on the nuances of wine. For example, an *appellation* is the geographic region where the grapes are grown to make that particular wine. A *sommelier* is a wine expert with extensive training, and a *varietal* is a type of wine whose name is taken from the grape from which it's made. The person behind the bar at any of these Orange County wine bars should be able to educate their guests by explaining how to read a wine label as well as the best way to store wine acquisitions so that they maintain taste and quality. Don't be shy to ask questions, as most wine hosts are more than eager to share their knowledge.

GAY AND LESBIAN

While Orange County's nightlife for gays and lesbians is decent, it's definitely not nearly as vibrant as what's taking place in Los Angeles. West Hollywood and Silverlake are two very gay-centric neighborhoods where many businesses are gay-owned and nightclubs cater to a gay crowd. But Orange County has no such specific neighborhood or district, although Laguna Beach comes close and has a larger gay population. For the most part Orange County's gay bars and clubs represent a small percentage compared to clubs for straight people and are dispersed throughout the region.

Costa Mesa

TIN LIZZIE SALOON
752 Saint Clair
(714) 966-2029
www.tinlizziesaloon.com
There's no dance floor or gyrating guests, but Tin Lizzie Saloon is more of an upscale retreat with plush pin-and-tuck banquettes cloaked in a rich red hue coupled with velvet drapes and avant-garde photography displayed on the walls. A selection of premium wines by the glass is available, as well as a handful of signature martinis. Guests can stake claim to one of the stools that front the long wooden bar or engage in a game of pool at one of the tables. While Tin Lizzie caters to OC's gay and lesbian community, it's mostly men that find their way through the doors.

Garden Grove

THE FRAT HOUSE
8112 Garden Grove Blvd.
(714) 373-3728
www.frathouseniteclub.com
It's definitely a place where the boys can hang out, but perhaps it should have "and Sorority Mixer" in its name too because there are many lesbians who also frequent The Frat House. Transgenders and bisexuals enjoy the scene here as well. Catering to a more mature crowd, The Frat House is open late 365 days a year, including Christmas. In addition to great music and dancing, there is also a selection of video games, pool tables, a digital jukebox, and free Wi-Fi for those who need the connection. Almost every day of the week has some hook to attract guests, such as Fiesta Latina or rousing drag shows. There are plenty of spirits, beers both on tap and bottled, and drink specials during the week before 8 p.m.

Laguna Beach

CLUB BOUNCE
1460 South Coast Hwy.
(949) 494-0056

A magnet for those wanting a good time, Club Bounce is jumping most every night of the week. Gay and lesbian patrons, along with a few straight guests, mingle with one another at the bar or upstairs where the dance floor is located. While Club Bounce attracts a hip, young crowd, there is no shortage of older club goers. And if the age median seems to be all over the board, so are the guests. There are fresh, young college boys, lipstick lesbians, the occasional transvestite, a straight couple checking things out—just about anyone, and they're all inside mixing and mingling with one another beautifully.

Newport Beach

LUCKY SUNDAYS (INSIDE RED)
4647 MacArthur Blvd.
(714) 855-6189
www.luckysundays.com

Located inside Red, a swank Newport Beach club, Lucky Sundays is a weekly gathering of OC's beautiful males and requires its guests to be 18 or older. Every Sunday this über popular club kicks it into high gear with its somewhat naughty set of female impersonators who start performing soon after the doors are open and begin what will inevitably be a high octane evening. In addition, Lucky Sundays has two rooms, DJs spinning all night long, a fully stocked bar for the 21 and older crowd with well drinks just $5 from open to close (soft drinks for those 18 to 20), bottle service, and sexy go-go boys shaking things up. There is also a variety of lounges including a VIP room and outdoor area with its own bar. It seems that if you're over 30 you're too old to be at Lucky Sundays. Club Lucky, which is part of Lucky Sundays, also hosts bi-monthly dance parties at the House of Blues in Downtown Disney.

COMEDY CLUBS

Irvine

THE IMPROV
71 Fortune Dr., Irvine Spectrum
(949) 854-8455
www.symfonee.com

The original Improv has been a long-time fixture on LA's Melrose Avenue, but in the last decade or so The Improv has spawned many locations including two in Orange County, one at the Irvine Spectrum, and another in Downtown Brea (120 South Brea Boulevard, 714-482-0700). Headlining acts make their way to the stage, with recent performances that have included *Saturday Night Live* alums Jay Mohr, better known for his role as the backstabbing agent in *Jerry Maguire*, and Jim Breuer. Dinner and a show is an option, or you can reserve a seat for just the show. Those who book dinner reservations enjoy priority seating.

DANCE CLUBS

Anaheim

HEAT ULTRA LOUNGE
321 West Katella Ave.
(714) 776-4328
www.heatultraloungeoc.com

One of the newest clubs to debut in The OC, Heat Ultra Lounge is situated at the new Anaheim GardenWalk near Disneyland. But, rest assured, this is no Mickey Mouse operation. The club's interior, with its living room–style vibe, innovative lighting, impromptu laser show, and state-of-the-art sound system, adds a new dimension to Orange County's nightlife. Upscale and extremely spacious, Heat Ultra Lounge features a dance floor, trio of bars, a pair of DJs manning their own stations, and bottle service for those willing to shell out the money. There are also VIP sections, which seem to be the standard these days for any club that wants to offer its guests an exclusive experience. Heat Ultra Lounge also has an indoor smoking patio, something that is almost unheard of these days.

Costa Mesa

SUTRA LOUNGE
1870 Harbor Blvd.
(949) 722-7103
www.sutrabar.com
Located on the top floor of the open-air Triangle Square, Sutra Lounge has managed to remain one of Orange County's top nightclubs. With its seductive interiors and pricey bottle service, not to mention a bouncer who at times cherry picks those who get to cross the threshold, Sutra Lounge seems more LA than OC. The women tend to be barely 21 and arrive wearing skimpy dresses and lots of makeup, while the guys try to look cool in hopes of getting inside. There are many bars and a VIP area for those who warrant such status. Security is often plentiful.

Irvine

iLOUNGE
18912 MacArthur Blvd.
(949) 833-1900
www.iloungeoc.com
Not a lot happens in Irvine after 10 p.m., but with the addition of iLounge outsiders are finding their way into this planned community. Nightly DJs spin tunes while the ladies and gents take to the dance floor. A young crowd, mostly from nearby Newport Beach, swarm the swank lounge and supper club, pose on the outside patio, and cross their fingers that they'll be granted entry into one of the themed VIP areas, including the Penthouse Room with its vaulted ceilings.

Laguna Beach

CLUB M
680 South Coast Hwy.
www.club.mosunclubm.com
This weekend-only spot is a sophisticated space and a place to mingle after sundown. With a decent size dance floor and a DJ spinning everything from techno and hip hop to Top 40 hits, Club M also hosts some live acts to add to the pulsation. Currently, this is one of The OC's "got to get to" clubs for the young, fit, and 21-plus

crowd. A full bar manned by mixologists helps to quench the thirst of club goers. Below Club M is Mosun, a sushi bar that stays open late to satisfy any cravings. Both share the same owner.

BILLIARDS AND BOWLING

Newport Beach

CLASSIC Q BILLIARDS
4250 Martingale Way
(949) 261-9458
www.theclassicq.com
For nearly 20 years players have headed to the Classic Q in Newport Beach to play pool—there are nine tables in all—or try their skill at the dart boards and watch sports on the plasma screens. When fresh air is needed, there is an inviting patio for dining or having an ice-cold beer or cocktail. Classic rock and Top 40 hits can constantly be heard in the background as well. Happy hour is Monday through Friday from 4 to 6 p.m.

Orange

DANNY K'S BILLIARD CAFÉ
1096 North Main St.
(714) 771-9706
www.dannyks.com
This old-fashioned pool hall offers no gimmicks, fancy food, or live entertainment. What it can do is pour beer from some 30 taps and present a straightforward menu prepared not by some chef, but by a regular cook. There is foosball and plenty of pool tables. Several large televisions are positioned throughout for those watching sports. Danny K's is an old-fashioned pool hall that isn't influenced by the latest trends.

LUCKY STRIKE
20 City Blvd.
(714) 937-5263
www.bowlluckystrike.com
When the landmark Hollywood Star Lanes, where *The Big Lebowski* was filmed, closed its doors after 43 years the void was filled with the opening of Lucky Strike Lanes. Now there are locations

across the United States, including at The Block of Orange. Lucky Strike is a hybrid bowling alley and nightclub with flashing lights, a soundtrack of cool tunes, and a menu that has taken bowling alley food to new heights. This location may not have the cachet of its LA counterpart, which attracts an A-list Hollywood crowd, but The OC draws a good looking bunch of bowlers to its lanes.

Tustin

STRIKE OC
2405 Park Ave.
(714) 258-2695
www.bowlmor.com
This is definitely not your father's bowling alley. Part of a small chainlet, Strike OC, located at The District at Tustin Legacy, has made bowling hip once again. Its glow-in-the-dark lanes, coupled with big screen video walls and a pounding sound system, gives bowlers a clubby experience even when tossing out gutter balls. You can dine and drink here as well. And, cool mom and dads can bring the entire family to this place for a high-energy evening. Bowling takes place until midnight most nights; 2 a.m. on weekends.

JAZZ BARS

Fullerton

STEAMERS JAZZ CLUB AND CAFÉ
138 West Commonwealth Ave.
(714) 871-8800
www.steamersjazz.com
Located in the heart of downtown Fullerton, Steamers is one of North Orange County's long-standing and only jazz venues. While all ages are welcome, this sultry escape isn't really appropriate for kids. The strains of jazz and big band music are heard seven nights a week and are accompanied by a full menu of eclectic edibles as well as libations. But having dinner isn't a requirement; you can come in for just a drink and the live entertainment.

Newport Beach

OYSTERS
2515 East Coast Hwy.
(949) 675-0810
www.oystersrestaurant.com
Located on Pacific Coast Highway and housed in a brick corner building emblazoned with a neon sign, Oysters is still going strong after 20 years. Its lounge, a destination for jazz lovers, features some great local and well-known talents. While you're enjoying the music, order a hand-shaken cocktail, glass of wine, or chilled beer. While their menu offers many dishes made with such fine ingredients as black truffles and Asian pear chutney, it's not above serving something as simple as an old-fashioned hamburger with American cheese. This in itself is refreshing, especially for Newport Beach/Corona del Mar where image is everything.

Seal Beach

SPAGHETTINI GRILL AND JAZZ CLUB
3005 Old Ranch Rd.
(562) 596-2199
www.spaghettini.com
This established venue, which is known for its Northern Italian cuisine and live jazz, sits on the edge of Orange County just over the LA/OC dividing line. The owners are also co-hosts of *The Sweet Life* on MyJAzzNetwork.com and are able to lure some great names in jazz to their establishment, including David Benoit, Dave Koz, and Freddie Ravel. Sundays the restaurant and club host Smooth Jazz Sunday Brunch sponsored by LA's top jazz station, KTWV The Wave.

OCEANFRONT BARS AND LOUNGES

Orange County may not be the party capital of the world, but it certainly has something that most urban destinations can't match—the ocean. If you're going to stay in The OC, then make the most of the coast by slipping into a lounge where the music is occasionally muffled by the sound of pounding surf. The following are just a few of the top oceanfront bars and lounges.

Laguna Beach

15FIFTYFIVE AT THE SURF AND SAND RESORT AND SPA
1555 South Coast Hwy.
(949) 376-3779
www.surfandsandresort.com

This snug, open-air bar, with its outdoor patio and transparent glass balustrade, is mostly frequented by hotel guests of the Surf and Sand Resort who only have to take the elevator to enjoy a cocktail under the stars. It's the ideal situation for others, too, because the lounge is rarely overcrowded. The furniture, a gathering of teak loveseats with oversize cushions and plenty of throw pillows, adds intimacy to this already intimate space. There are fire pits to take the chill off a cool night and the sound of the surf is always present.

LAS BRISAS
361 Cliff Dr.
(949) 597-5434
www.lasbrislaslagunabeach.com

This restaurant is legendary for its location—a seaside cliff overlooking the Pacific in lovely Laguna Beach. Opened in 1938 as the Victor Hugo Inn, it was transformed into its present state 30 years ago. The menu is an abundance of Mexican-style seafood, but you can stop into Las Brisas just for a salt-rimmed margarita and to watch a most spectacular sunset from practically any seat in the house or on the patio.

MONTAGE RESORT & SPA
30801 Coast Hwy.
(949) 715-6000
www.montagelagunabeach.com

The Lobby Lounge inside the Montage Resort & Spa is an experience that shouldn't be missed. The crowd is well dressed and the cocktails, while pricey, are always mixed just right. You can get a drink anywhere, but you won't find better ocean views than from this vantage point. You can sit at the tiny bar or on one of the oversized sofas that face the floor-to-ceiling window.

Newport Beach

DUKE'S PLACE AT THE BALBOA BAY CLUB & RESORT
1221 Coast Hwy.
(949) 645-5000
www.balboabayclub.com

Duke's Place is named for Newport Beach's most cherished resident, John Wayne. Guests are privy to the talents of jazz musicians, light meals, signature drinks, and those fabulous harbor views.

SUNSET AND WINE CRUISES

Newport Beach

GONDOLA ROMANCE
3400 Via Oporto, Suite 202
(949) 675-4730
www.gondolaromance.com

Gondolas were first introduced to the region in 1984 when Gondola Getaway opened in nearby Long Beach. Now there are more companies offering gondola rides including Gondola Romance, which can ferry from two to six passengers in gondolas fashioned after those found on the Venice canals, only these gondolas are powered by electricity and feature canopies that can be fully enclosed. The two-hour experience takes you along the calm waters of Newport Bay with a gondolier to guide the vessel. All cruises include a beverage of your choice (you can also bring your own bottle of wine), fruit, chocolates, cheese, and crackers. Blankets and music are also provided along with a keepsake Polaroid photo of you and your party aboard the gondola. Dinner cruises are also available.

HORNBLOWER CRUISES AND EVENTS
2431 West Coast Hwy.
(949) 646-0155
www.hornbloweryachts.com

One of the many benefits of being near the ocean is enjoying an evening dinner cruise. Hornblower Cruises has been hosting such events for 25 years, and their evening weekend cruises, with Friday and Saturday night bon voyages at 7:30 p.m. returning to the dock at 10:30 p.m., are extremely popular with out-of-towners. While on board, passengers enjoy a welcome cocktail before settling down for a three-course dinner. Afterwards, singles and couples can take to the dance floor or sit on the outdoor deck and enjoy the harbor views. Hornblower has a Sunday brunch cruise as well.

PACIFIC AVALON
2901 West Coast Hwy.
(949) 673-8545
www.pacificavalon.com

On the last Thursday of every month Pacific Avalon hosts a floating sunset wine tasting while cruising Newport Harbor. Guests board one of three luxury yachts, 100 feet to 150 feet in size, and cruise for three hours. Each month a new, specialty wine produced by a well-known winery is introduced and paired with an assortment of imported cheeses, artisan breads, fresh grapes, and plump olives. On board is a cheese sommelier whose role is to educate and explain which cheeses complement which wines the best. There is also a wine professional to explain how the featured wines were created as well as their nuances.

PERFORMING ARTS

Orange County has no core theater district and you won't find the ballyhoo of Broadway here either, but The OC can certainly take a bow when it comes to the performing arts. Within the county's neat boundaries you will find classical orchestras, repertory theater, ballet, community theater, and much more. Orange County's performing arts entered a new era of progress in 2006 as the Orange County Performing Arts Center completed a major and much welcomed expansion. The new and improved arts campus now includes the 3,000-seat Segerstrom Hall; the 2,000-seat Renée and Henry Segerstrom Concert Hall; the intimate 500-seat Samueli Theater; and a 46,000-square-foot, al fresco arts plaza where special events are staged. Heralded for its striking design and flawless acoustics, the Orange County Performing Arts Center presents a breadth of year-round entertainment including award-winning ballet companies and national tours of leading Broadway productions plus ovation-worthy chamber ensembles, soloists, classical and pop vocalists, jazz entertainers, cabaret artists and many noteworthy events.

BALLET

FESTIVAL BALLET THEATRE
Irvine Barclay Theater, UC Irvine Campus
4255 Campus Drive
(949) 851-9930
www.festivalballet.org
Formerly known as Ballet Pacifica, a recent name change and milestone anniversary marks a new day for this talented dance troupe. Presenting an outstanding mix of classical and contemporary ballet, many fabled stories are brought to life through dance which help to introduce children to both the concept of ballet as well as the performing arts. Recent productions have included *Puss & Boots* and *Little Red Riding Hood*, just to name a few.

MUSICAL PERFORMANCES

MOZART CLASSICAL ORCHESTRA
Inside the Renée and Henry Segerstrom Concert Hall at the Orange County Peforming Arts Center
Dedicated to bringing quality performances of chamber orchestra works from the classical rep-

ertoire, the Mozart Classical Orchestra, founded in 1985, is lead by its Founding Music Director Ami Porat. Performances are a marriage of rarely heard works and classic orchestral composures resulting in a balanced performance that is often thematic.

ORANGE COUNTY PERFORMING ARTS CENTER
600 Town Center Drive, Costa Mesa
(714) 556-2121
www.ocpac.org
The following performing arts ensembles take to the stages beneath the roof of the Orange County Performing Arts Center. Segerstrom Hall is home to presentations of dance and Broadway spectaculars; Renée and Henry Segerstrom Concert Hall is the backdrop for the Pacific Symphony, Pacific Chorale, and the Philharmonic Society of Orange County; and the intimate Samueli Theater, which offers a variety of seating configurations, is the setting for the Family and Concert Series as well as cabaret and jazz productions where the venue is transformed into club-style seating with tables of four scattered about.

PACIFIC CHORALE
Inside the Renée and Henry Segerstrom Concert Hall at the Orange County Peforming Arts Center

For more than 40 years, this group of sopranos, altos, and tenors has amazed audiences with their vocal range and body of work. Under the direction of John Alexander and touted as one of the nation's finest choral ensembles, Pacific Chorale often performs with the region's leading orchestras including the Hollywood Bowl Orchestra. The singing ensemble takes to the stage inside the 2,000-seat Renee and Henry Segerstrom Concert Hall.

PACIFIC SYMPHONY
Inside the Renée and Henry Segerstrom Concert Hall at the Orange County Peforming Arts Center

Under the musical direction of Carl St. Clair, the Pacific Symphony also performs inside the 2,000-seat Rene and Henry Segerstrom Concert Hall. Founded in 1978, this is one of the largest orchestras to form in the United States since the late 1960s. An outstanding ensemble, the symphony entertains with an array of musical genres, from classical music and pops to the commissioning of leading composers. The Pacific Symphony recently embarked on a new genre of multimedia concerts entitled "Music Unwound," which features visual elements and varied formats highlighting great masterworks. The symphony, on average, produces more than 100 concerts a year as well as a diverse array of educational and community programs.

PHILHARMONIC SOCIETY OF ORANGE COUNTY
(949) 553-2422
www.philharmonicsociety.org

Recognized as a world leader in the presentation and education of fine music, the Philharmonic Society of Orange County is a collective organization whose members include renowned symphony orchestras, chamber ensembles, and soloists with music education programs offered to children from kindergarten to high school at no charge. Performances take place at the Irvine Barclay Theatre, the Orange County Performing Arts Center, and the Orange County Museum of Art.

THEATER

CAMINO REAL PLAYHOUSE
1776 El Camino Real, San Juan Capistrano
(949) 489-8082
www.caminorealplayhouse.org

Located in south Orange County and celebrating two outstanding decades, the Camino Real Playhouse has produced some 140-plus full-scale theatrical productions including a dozen or more playwriting festivals. During the summer Shakespearian dramas and comedies unfold beneath the stars at the Historic Town Center Park adjacent to the playhouse.

FULLERTON CIVIC LIGHT OPERA
Plummer Auditorium
218 West Commonwealth Ave., Fullerton
(714) 879-1732
www.fclo.com

For nearly four decades the Fullerton Civic Light Opera, a recipient of countless Drama-Logue awards, has been producing an array of musical performances within the confines of the historic Plummer Auditorium near the campus of Fullerton Community College. Recent productions include *Ring of Fire*, which chronicles the life of the legendary Johnny Cash, and the classic *Brigadoon*. Because of its close proximity to downtown Fullerton, you can easily make a night of it with dinner, a show, and a post-theater cocktail.

LAGUNA PLAYHOUSE
Moulton Theater
606 Laguna Canyon Rd., Laguna Beach
(949) 497-ARTS
www.lagunaplayhouse.org

With a long and successful history the Laguna Playhouse has been the toast of the coast since 1920. It began when a group of residents offered readings and performances in local homes and storefronts before blossoming into a full-fledged troupe. During the 1965 production of Stephen Vincent Benet's *John Brown's Body* an unknown Harrison Ford caught the attention of the audience, giving a stellar and memorable performance. The playhouse produces an array of classical and contemporary dramas as well as comedies, musicals, and youth-oriented productions. Nearby are several restaurants and lounges for a pre- or post-theater outing.

THE OC PAVILION
801 North Main St., Santa Ana
(714) 550-0880
www.ocpavilion.com
This building, which once served as the Western Regional Headquarters for Bank of America, was transformed into a stylish destination where residents can enjoy an array of theater, live musical performances, and more. The OC Pavilion's opulent lobby sets the stage for an extraordinary experience with its dangling chandeliers, rich leather furniture, conversational nooks, and antiques. The OC Pavilion features The Vault VIP Lounge, named for its original use as a bank vault and an ideal place to enjoy live jazz and cocktails before or after the show, and the elegant Ambrosia, offering fine dining, a private wine cellar for intimate dinners, and a convenient destination for a post-production dinner. The intimate 500-seat main theater guarantees a good view from most any vantage point and the state-of-the-art sound system is equally dynamic. Recent productions have included the classic tale of *Peter Pan* plus *Hotel California—A Salute to the Eagles*, and a two-night engagement with Bill Medley of the Righteous Brothers.

SOUTH COAST REPERTORY
655 Town Center Dr., Costa Mesa
(714) 957-2602
www.scr.org

Since its founding in 1964, South Coast Repertory has been regarded as one of the nation's leading producers of new plays as well as a venue for classics and thought-provoking dramas. Its home, the Folino Theatre Center, features the 507-seat main Segerstrom Stage and the more intimate Argyros Stage, which has just 161 seats. A typical season boasts 11 original productions including the classic holiday story of *A Christmas Carol*. South Coast Repertory also offers plays for young audiences as well as educational and outreach programs.

LA's Nearby Art Scene

Orange County's close proximity to downtown Los Angeles provides visitors and residents with additional opportunities to enjoy the arts. The **Music Center**, located at 135 North Grand Ave. (213-972-7211, www.musiccenter.org), is home to four internationally acclaimed resident companies that include the Los Angeles Philharmonic (which performs at the Hollywood Bowl during the summer), Center Theatre Group, the Los Angeles Opera, and the Los Angeles Master Chorale. The Music Center features an equal number of venues, including the state-of-the-art Walt Disney Concert Hall, the Dorothy Chandler Pavilion, the Ahmanson Theatre, and the Mark Taper Forum. In addition, there are a handful of open-air theaters, plazas, and garden settings where more informal afternoon concerts are staged.

ATTRACTIONS

Southern California is rich with amusement parks, and two of the largest are located in Orange County within minutes of one another. But in addition to roller coasters, water parks, and Mickey Mouse, the region has some alternative attractions that don't necessarily cost a lot of money or require your entire day to enjoy. Some may be surprised to learn that Orange County, with its reputation for designer shopping and waterfront homes, has some rather down to earth offerings. The Balboa Peninsula and its vintage Fun Zone are just a swagger from the former estate of John Wayne and overlook the bay where million-dollar yachts bob year-round.

This chapter is categorized by interest and alphabetical order. We don't list hours of operation or admission prices, as these are subject to change. If you're planning on spending consecutive days enjoying Disneyland Resort, we do recommend that you consider staying at one of the Disney hotel properties or a nearby hotel to maximize your time. The park also offers multi-day passes and Hopper Passes, which allow you to go back and forth between Disneyland and Disney's California Adventure.

AMUSEMENTS

BALBOA PENINSULA/BALBOA FUN ZONE
600 East Bay Ave., Newport Beach
(949) 673-0408
www.balboafunzone.com

When it comes to old-fashioned entertainment, it's hard to beat the Balboa Fun Zone located on a bay front boardwalk in Newport Beach. This is one of the few coastal amusement areas still operating in Southern California and is also one of the oldest. There are now only two rides left, a carousel and a Ferris wheel that has served as a beacon since 1936. The boardwalk also features a couple of vintage arcades with old-fashioned Skee-Ball and black and white photo booths that compete with hi-tech video games. There are snack kiosks here as well where you can grab ice cream cones, cotton candy, and other amusement-style fare. At Balboa Boat Rental (949-673-7200) you can take to the seas in a kayak, paddle board, pedal boat, wave runner, sail boat, or power boat. Perhaps the easiest and most enjoyable watercraft is the canopied Duffy electric boat, which operates on electricity and is an ideal way to putt around the

bay. Across the water is Balboa Island, where a narrow main street is lined with individual shops and restaurants.

The easiest way to reach Balboa Island from the Balboa Peninsula is to take the auto ferry located right next to the Fun Zone. Since 1919, the ferry has provided continuous service between the two lands, which are separated by 0.25 miles and divided by the bay. A maximum of three cars are allowed on the barge and those on foot or bike can get a lift as well. The ferry operates weekdays until midnight and on weekends until 2 a.m. and is as much an attraction as the Ferris wheel or carousel.

EXTREME ADVENTURE

AIR COMBAT USA
230 North Dale Place, Fullerton
(714) 522-7590
www.aircombatusa.com

On a wing and a prayer, visitors to Orange County can have a true fighter pilot experience. By all accounts, participants assume the role of pilots as they engage in actual air combat aboard an

SoCal CityPass

If while staying in Orange County you plan to visit all the big-name attractions, including those in neighboring Los Angeles and San Diego counties, purchasing a Southern California CityPass (888-330-5008, www.citypass.com) will save you up to 30 percent off admissions. The concept is simple and includes a booklet containing admission tickets to all the top theme parks and attractions for one low price. Once you visit your first attraction, you have 14 days to access the remaining destinations. Included is a three-day Disneyland Resort Hopper Bonus Pass valid at both the original Disneyland and Disney's California Adventure. This pass allows you to move freely back and forth between the two venues and also includes one Magic Morning, which gives you early access to the park before it opens to the general public. Magic Morning access is available only on Saturday, Sunday, Tuesday, or Thursday, so if this perk is important to you you'll want to plan your trip to the Magic Kingdom accordingly. The Southern California CityPass also includes general admission to Universal Studios Hollywood; SeaWorld San Diego; the world-famous San Diego Zoo with unlimited use of the Guided Bus Tour, Express Bus, and Skyfari Aerial Tram; or admission to San Diego's Wild Animal Park which includes Journey into Africa Tour, Conservation Carousel Ride, and all the daily shows and exhibits. Each booklet contains directions, park hours, insider tips, and theme park information as well as transportation alternatives between the Disneyland Resort area and Los Angeles as well as between Disneyland Resort and San Diego. Southern California CityPass has both adult-priced booklets and a separate booklet priced for children three to nine years of age. Kids under three years of age are free and pay no admission to any of the above attractions.

authentic aircraft—not a simulator. Everything is real sans the bullets, and no pilot license is required. Air Combat USA has been featured on *Good Morning America* as well as *The Apprentice* and is an ideal way to spend an afternoon for the competitive-minded individual. An onboard camera captures the entire experience and pilots are given a keepsake DVD at the end of their flight.

Air Combat USA also offers stunt biplane rides that put visitors in the pilot seat with no experience required. Harkening back to the days of the barnstormer, the fun takes place in a classic 1935 open-cockpit biplane. With speeds exceeding 200 miles per hour, four times the force of gravity, and stunts that include loops, rolls, hammerheads, and spins above the Pacific Ocean, this flight experience is not for the faint of heart.

FLIGHT DECK AIR COMBAT CENTER
1601 South Sunkist St., Suite A, Anaheim
(714) 937-1511
www.flightdeck1.com
Like Air Combat USA, this combat center provides an equal amount of thrills. The difference is that Flight Deck Air Combat Center stays grounded using a military flight simulator instead of actual aircraft. "Pilots" get a flight briefing before take off and, soon after, find themselves engaged in combat, performing aerial maneuvers and other in-flight antics before coming to a safe landing. Flight Deck Air Combat Center is ideal for an individual challenge or for company team building. It's also a popular destination for bachelor parties.

Close-up

Orange County Piers

California is known for its piers, those long structures that jut out into the ocean. Most every beach city has one and many are recognized as historic landmarks, having been fortunate enough to withstand countless lashings from Mother Nature's hurricane-like winds, rainstorms, fires, and raging surf. Some, such as the Huntington Beach Pier, had to be completely rebuilt but are stronger and sturdier than ever. Orange County has several significant piers as well as a collection of small fishing piers. A walk along the pier makes for a great date or family outing and a place to spot migrating grey whales, too. Best of all, an afternoon or evening visit to any of the piers costs absolutely nothing except maybe a few quarters for metered parking.

A stroll along the pier is actually an enjoyable way to spend an afternoon, and many piers have restaurants that anchor one end or the other. The **Seal Beach Pier** is an ideal spot for fishermen. At the base of the pier is a fenced-in playground and at the very end of the pier is a Ruby's Diner with its sweeping ocean views. The **Huntington Beach Pier,** at the foot of Main Street, was originally built in 1914 but a major storm in 1988 caused the waves to swell some 20 feet, destroying approximately 50 feet of the pier. In 1992, the new pier, stretching more than 1,800 feet, opened and is one of the longest municipal piers in the state. Surfing competitions are held beneath the sturdy structure and a weekly farmers' market takes place near its entrance as well. Just like the Seal Beach Pier, a red-roofed Ruby's Diner sits at the very end of the Huntington Beach Pier and boasts incredible views and a kid-friendly menu of American favorites.

Newport Beach has two major piers including the **Newport Pier,** also known as McFadden's Wharf, and the **Balboa Pier.** The Newport Pier is a wooden structure and a gathering spot for fishermen arriving after a day at sea to sell their catch to the public. The pier has a lifeguard station and a two-story restaurant with shops and additional dining opportunities along the neighboring boardwalk. The Balboa Pier, located on the Balboa Peninsula a few miles down the road, was built in 1906 as a complement to the Balboa Pavilion and is a popular place for anglers. It, too, was heavily damaged by severe storms and, as a result, the wooden posts called for steel sheathing and braces as reinforcement. At the end of the pier is the original Ruby's Diner, a former bait shop turned 45-seat eatery, which opened in 1982, spawning a national chain.

Between Newport Beach and San Clemente there are small fishing piers but nothing really notable until you reach the **San Clemente Pier.** The original wooden pier was erected in the late 1920s and measured some 1,200 feet before a hurricane destroyed it in 1939. It was eventually rebuilt and thrived for several decades until 1983 when a major storm wreaked havoc on Southern California, taking with it 400 feet from the end of the pier and almost 100 feet more from its mid-section. The pier reopened in the mid 1980s, this time nearly 1,300 feet long with polyethylene-coated steel pylons and an elevated end. At the foot of the pier is the landmark Fisherman's Restaurant, where locals go for breakfast, lunch, dinner, and sunset cocktails as well as to enjoy the amazing views.

K1 SPEED RACE
1000 North Edward Court, Anaheim
(714) 632-6999
www.k1speed.com
It rarely rains in Southern California, but when it does K1 Speed Race offers a nice diversion with its indoor kart racing. Drivers must be at least 4'11" tall, under 300 pounds, and 18 or older; those under 18 who meet the height and weight requirements must be accompanied by a driving adult. Drivers race against one another in speedy electric carts with a track that includes a pair of tunnels that pass beneath a 3,000-square-foot mezzanine. Speed demons will also enjoy the series of tight and challenging hairpin turns, the long front straightaway, and the overall thrill of

the race. At night racing takes on a party quality with an after dark light show, high energy music, and illuminated tunnels. K1's Arrive and Drive program is geared toward drivers of all levels, novices to pros, who want to race against the clock and each other for 14 adrenalin-inducing laps. Scores and performance feedbacks are given to drivers via a detailed printout that records lap times, positions, and ranking.

THEME PARKS

DISNEYLAND RESORT
1313 Harbor Blvd., Anaheim
(714) 781-4565
www.disneyland.com

Entire travel guides have been dedicated to the Disney empire, but we're able to break it down for you in just a few paragraphs. Disneyland Resort, touted as the Happiest Place on Earth, consists of two theme parks plus a pseudo downtown esplanade that has no admission charge and offers open-air dining and entertainment. The original Disneyland still has a magical feel that begins when you step through the gates. Main Street, USA, is near the point of entry and the only "avenue" that leads to the various themed areas. The street is flanked with shops, restaurants, and some entertainment and is framed by the presence of Sleeping Beauty's Castle in the background. Near the castle there are various footpaths that branch out and lead to the different themed lands, including Fantasyland, Adventureland, Tomorrowland, New Orleans Square, Frontierland, Critter Country, and Mickey's Toontown. Disney has gotten very savvy in terms of how it markets its merchandise, too. After disembarking from most rides, at least those that are extremely popular or where a Disney character is part of the ride, guests typically have to exit through a well-stocked store full of themed merchandise. Throughout the day and evening there are parades, shows, live music, and more. There are plenty of places to eat in the park, though most are quick-service fast-food outlets. There is a better selection of restaurants at Downtown Disney. Just be sure that when exit-

Disney Passes

Disney offers a Hopper Pass, which includes admission to both Disneyland and Disney's California Adventure. Some passes are restricted to one day, meaning that you must visit both parks on the same day while other passes allow you to enjoy one park per day. If you will only be at Disneyland Resort for a day and are a first-time visitor, we recommend that you skip Disney's California Adventure and spend your time at Disneyland instead. The original park has so much to offer and you're unlikely to run out of things to do. Disney's California Adventure on the other hand is entertaining, but after a few hours—even if there is no construction taking place due to the renovation—there simply isn't enough to see and do. Regardless of which park you visit, be sure to take advantage of Fast Pass for the most popular rides. Instead of waiting hours to board a ride, you can save time using this convenient system. Look for the Fast Pass sign near an attraction (only the most popular rides offer this convenience) and slide your admission ticket into the machine. The machine will then return your ticket along with a Fast Pass ticket indicating a specific time frame in which to return to the ride. This sometimes can be hours later, but in the meantime you're free to roam the park, grab a bite to eat, or catch a show. When you return to the ride at your specified time, you bypass the queue and are immediately ushered onto the attraction.

Close-up

A Few Fun and Interesting Facts About Disneyland

The official Tom Sawyer and Becky Thatcher made the trek from Hannibal, Missouri, to dedicate Tom Sawyer Island in 1956.

Disneyland's famous "E" ticket was introduced in 1959, entitling the bearer admission to selected attractions.

The first major motion picture to cast Disneyland in the role of its principal shooting location was the 1963 film *40 Pounds of Trouble* starring Tony Curtis and Suzanne Pleshette.

In 1964 Walt Disney hosted all the Olympic teams, more than 400 athletes, on their way to the Summer Olympics in Japan. Each was treated to an entire day at Disneyland, and comedian Bob Hope joined Walt and a cast of Hollywood stars to entertain the Olympians in a spectacular show along the banks of the park's Rivers of America.

The Main Street Electrical Parade made its debut in 1972.

When the Disneyland Hotel opened the 13-story Bonita Tower in 1978, it was the first hotel building in the nation with a solar heating system—not to mention Anaheim's tallest structure.

Not only have dignitaries and movie stars graced the gates of Disneyland, but the stork has been known to make deliveries as well. Disneyland welcomed its first birth in 1979 when Teresa Salcedo was born near Main Street, USA, on a busy Fourth of July.

Did you know the park's 250 millionth visitor on August 24, 1985, was the recipient of a brand-new Cadillac and lifetime Disneyland pass? The only problem was that the winner from Anchorage, Alaska, was just three years old!

Ronald Reagan, Art Linkletter, and Bob Cummings were the co-hosts of the Disneyland opening day TV special in 1955. The trio returned for the park's 35th anniversary in 1990 to lead a parade down Main Street, USA, joined by Disney CEO Michael Eisner and Vice Chairman Roy E. Disney.

The legendary Elizabeth Taylor took over the park on February 27, 1992 for a "private" 60th birthday party with 1,000 of her closest friends.

Disney's Fast Pass was introduced in 1999 and provided guests with time-saving virtual queuing using computers to issue advance reservations for the park's most popular rides.

For the second time in its history, Disneyland played a starring role in 1996 as the location for a major motion picture, *That Thing You Do*, starring Tom Hanks.

Disneyland welcomed its 2 billionth guest in 2006, a number nearly equal to the populations of China and India combined.

Downtown Disney, a free outdoor attraction consisting of shops, restaurants, and a multiplex movie theater, is located outside the entrance to both theme parks. Dining options include a mix of national chains, such as Rain Forest Café, as well as local eateries, such as La Brea Bakery. Shops are also a mélange of well-known retailers—Build A Bear and LEGO—and one-of-a-kind-shops. The World of Disney is perhaps the largest of the lot and filled with dress-up clothes, collectibles, and every Disney logo item imaginable.

ing the park you get your hand stamped as you exit the main gate. This will allow you to reenter the park on the same day. During Halloween and the Christmas season Disney goes all out with décor, entertainment, and a few ride transformations that reflect the given holiday.

Disney's other theme park, Disney's California Adventure, opened a decade ago and never quite reached its potential as far as admission goes. Some say it's because its theme, which pays homage to the Golden State, was ill conceived considering that visitors to the park are already in California and, for the most part, can visit places like Hollywood in person if they so desire. So Disney announced it will update and expand Disney's California Adventure, replacing some of its attractions with newer, more appealing rides, including the World of Color, an after-dark show taking place in the lagoon and featuring a choreographed performance of fountains and hi-tech lasers with images appearing on a screen of water. A 12-acre addition will include Cars Land, opening in 2012 and featuring themed attractions from the movie *Cars*. Under the Sea: Journey of the Little Mermaid will be another new addition to the retooled theme park. In the meantime, Disney's California Adventure will remain open. A few signature rides include The Twilight Zone Tower of Terror, a ride not for those with a weak stomach, as well as Soarin' Over California, which takes you on a flight above the state's notable cities, landmarks, and parks. In the spirit of Disney, Disney's California Adventure also features parades, strolling characters (Mickey Mouse is dressed like a tourist), and seasonal fireworks shows.

KNOTT'S BERRY FARM
8039 Beach Blvd., Buena Park
(714) 220-5200
www.knotts.com
While Disneyland is Orange County's star attraction, Knott's Berry Farm is billed as America's first theme park. Walter Knott and his wife Virginia owned a 20-acre berry farm and roadside chicken restaurant during the Great Depression. Lines would encircle the building, which served more than 4,000 dinners on Sunday evenings. In order to keep his customers entertained as their hunger mounted, Walter developed his Ghost Town, which became the first of Knott's Berry Farm's themed areas. During the next several decades the Knott family expanded its theme park, attracting quite a following from local residents as well as visitors to Southern California. The theme park remained in the family, passing from Walter and Virginia to their children. Finally, in 1997 the family put the business up for sale and it was acquired by Cedar Fair, L.P.

With new operators at the helm, Knott's Berry Farm became a destination for thrill seekers who have a penchant for extreme rides. In addition to the original Ghost Town, which still exists, Knott's Berry Farm has several themed areas that offer rides from mild to wild, including The Boardwalk, Wild Water Wilderness, and Fiesta Village, which contain a mix of mellow and extreme attractions. Camp Snoopy is geared toward younger children and offers rides that keep them entertained but not frightened. Knott's Berry Farm also has its own marketplace, a free area located adjacent to the park with shops, Mrs. Knott's Chicken Dinner Restaurant, and a replica of Independence Hall where historic reenactments take place.

Knott's Scary Farm

While Disneyland trumps Knott's Berry Farm in terms of ambiance and attractions, there is one thing on which Knott's Berry Farm has managed to corner the market, and that's its annual Halloween event, Knott's Scary Farm. Every October for the past 30-plus years the park has put on one of the biggest Halloween Haunts in Southern California. During the day it's business as usual, but come dusk attendants clear out the park in order to transform it into a frightening place where lifelike monsters, ghouls, and mummies roam the park and unexpectedly appear on rides. Knott's Scary Farm's Halloween Haunt typically takes place for the entire month of October and requires a separate admission price. The event often sells out weeks in advance and is not recommended for young children or those who frighten easily.

(Q) Close-up

A Look Back at Disney History

The year was 1955, the height of the Fabulous Fifties. It had been a decade since World War II had ended, but the world was feeling a chill from the Cold War. World leaders Winston Churchill and USSR Premier Malenkov resigned, Tennessee Williams won the Pulitzer Prize for *Cat on a Hot Tin Roof*, the Academy Award for Best Picture went to *Marty*, and people mourned the passing of Albert Einstein and James Dean. The year also marked the debut of the hovercraft and MG convertible. And, on July 17, Walt Disney made the biggest splash of the year—if not the entire decade—with the opening of Disneyland, dubbed the Happiest Place on Earth.

As luck would have it, July 17, 1955, proved to be the hottest day of the summer in Southern California, both in terms of weather and A-list gatherings. It was the opening of Disneyland, an event attended by the era's most revered celebrities—Frank Sinatra, Jerry Lewis, Sammy Davis Jr., and Debbie Reynolds, just to name a few. Opening day ushered in a new era of amusement as Disneyland presented 18 major ride-through adventures and shows with $1 general admission and ride tickets ranging from 10 to 50 cents.

Throughout that first year Disneyland received a parade of VIP visitors, among them vice president and California native Richard Nixon, comedian Milton Berle and actor Jimmy Stewart and, of course, the famed Mickey Mouse Club Mouseketeers. And, where to house all these famous folk? The Disneyland Hotel, of course. Built by actress Bonita Granville and her husband, oil tycoon Jack Wrather, who were close friends of Walt's, the hotel only had seven rooms ready on opening day. It officially opened on October 5 of that year and was designated the "Official Hotel of the Magic Kingdom."

Fewer than five years later Disneyland welcomed its 20 millionth guest in April of 1960. In 1965, Disneyland celebrated its 10th anniversary with a spectacular, year-long Tencennial Celebration with Walt Disney presiding over the opening of It's a Small World with waters from all seven continents poured into its River of the World. New Orleans Square was the first new "land" to open in a decade and, sadly, this colorful mid-summer dedication was the last over which Walt Disney would preside before his untimely death in December.

The 1970s opened with a summer-long 15th anniversary celebration attended by more than five million people. Some 130 members of Disneyland's original 1955 cast gathered for a special ceremony on July 17 to mark the occasion. Disneyland's 20th anniversary in 1975 marked the beginning of a 15-month salute to the nation's bicentennial with the most elaborate parade in the park's two-decade history—America on Parade. In 1977 five *Mercury* astronauts were instrumental in the opening ceremonies for Space Mountain. This new light-speed, white-knuckle race through space featured a spectacular cone-shaped structure creating a space shuttle experience for guests as they traveled through the darkness of outer space. The next year the original Mouseketeers, including Annette Funicello, gathered at the park for the worldwide celebration of Mickey Mouse's 50th birthday. The Matterhorn Bobsleds excelled with new speed sensations, ice crystals, sharp bends, quick plunges, and a resident Abominable Snowman. And by the end of the decade the Disneyland Hotel had opened the 319-room Marina Tower, a state-of-the-art convention center, the 13-story Bonita Tower, and a hotel marina—the first for an inland hotel—complete with a "Dancing Waters Show" first seen at Radio City Music Hall in 1953.

The 1980s began with a year-long Silver Anniversary celebration complete with a pre-parade show at the 92nd Pasadena Tournament of Roses Parade on New Year's Day. The highlight of the 12-month celebration came about on the park's actual birthday, July 17, when it stayed open for a record 24 hours. In 1982 the park officially retired the famed alphabet-style attraction coupons—which required an "E" ticket for the best rides, a term still used by locals when referring to the best of the best—in favor of a single all-access Passport that provided visitors admission to all adventures and shows. Many rides were revamped during this decade, too. Snow White's Scary Adventures got a bit scarier; Mr. Toad's Wild Ride was even wilder; and the Mad Tea Party was even madder than before. For its 30th birthday in 1985, Disneyland turned the tables on guests by giving every 30th visitor through the turnstile a gift. The Gift-Giver Extraordinaire computer presented its top prize, a new Cadillac and lifetime pass, to the park's 250 millionth visitor on August 24. The recipient? A three-year-old from Anchorage, Alaska, who was assisted with accepting the prize by his joyful parents.

Big Thunder Ranch, a two-acre area that replicated an 1880s working ranch complete with draft horses, petting barnyard, and Big Thunder Barbeque Restaurant were added, and *Captain EO,* a 3-D film produced by George Lucas and directed by Francis Ford Coppola, opened in the Magic Eye Theater. It starred the gloved one, Michael Jackson, and was an instant success. Star Tours, a flight-simulator journey to the Moon of Endor and beyond, was also launched. The decade ended at Disneyland with quite a splash as Splash Mountain, a towering 87-foot flume ride, opened beside Critter Country in 1989.

Disney underwent many changes during the 1990s. Nobody's a bigger or more beloved star than Mickey Mouse, and in 1993 Mickey's Toontown opened. It was the largest new land in more than two decades and was designed as the official "residence" of Mickey Mouse and all the favorite Disney characters. The land of vivid colors, free-swinging motion, and cartoon-like settings became an instant hit with children of all ages. There were talking manhole covers, dancing dishes, and spinning flowers. Best of all, the Disney characters were always at their homes to greet young visitors.

Indiana Jones Adventure—Temple of the Forbidden Eye, also made its debut. Enjoyed from behind the wheel of a safari-style Jeep, guests race and rollick through crags and caverns— much like the movie hero—while attempting to ward off danger. Disney's animated movies played a role in the development of new attractions, including the addition of Triton Gardens, a playground with jumping waters, and an Ariel statue from *The Little Mermaid.* Tomorrowland followed suit with Toy Story Fun House, while Tarzan's Treehouse, inspired by the animated film *Tarzan,* opened in Adventureland replacing the Swiss Family Treehouse.

The new millennium brought many changes for Disneyland as it made the transition from theme park to bona fide resort. In 2001 the greatest expansion in the park's 46-year history came on January 12 with the opening of Downtown Disney, a lifestyle destination center replete with dining, shopping, and nighttime entertainment. Less than a month later, Disney's Grand Californian Hotel, a Craftsman-style lodge, and Disney's California Adventure, a theme park paying homage to the Golden State, opened as well.

Walt Disney promised on opening day that "Disneyland will continue to grow, to add new things, as long as there is imagination left in the world." Still, no matter how many changes Disneyland undergoes, from new rides and landscapes to the most cutting-edge entertainment, the sense one gets upon entering the park's gates hasn't changed since opening day. It's a feeling that blends excitement with magic and pure fantasy. It's knowing all the words to "A Pirate's Life" and "It's A Small World," and singing along with enthusiasm. It's the anticipation of waiting in line to board a favorite ride, and the thrill of encountering a beloved Disney character at an unexpected moment. It's that fabulous—yet often forgotten—feeling of being a kid once again.

MUSEUMS

A museum, at least in Orange County, isn't defined by four walls or its collection of artifacts. A museum exists to enhance guests' visits by exposing them to something new, offering an educational element, or simply welcoming visitors to a venue that is architecturally significant. Orange County's museums consist of the usual suspects, as well as a few offbeat venues that are both innovative and interesting. There is a presidential library to explore as well as historic homes, beautiful gardens, works of art by renowned California artists, and even some ocean-inspired venues.

This chapter has been organized by category: art museums, historic venues, and those places that are a little unconventional but interesting nonetheless. At the end of this chapter you will find museums that offer free admission on various days of the month.

Because admission and hours are subject to change, we have omitted such details and suggest you call ahead or visit individual Web sites. Under each heading, museums are listed in alphabetical order.

ART MUSEUMS

BOWERS MUSEUM
2002 North Main St., Santa Ana
(714) 567-3600
www.bowers.org
Situated near downtown Santa Ana is Bowers Museum, an internationally celebrated institution of art and culture. The museum, founded in 1936, celebrates world cultures through their art, which explains why its permanent collection includes tribal beauty, plein air paintings from renowned California artists, Native American artifacts, and pre-Columbian art. In 2007 the museum added a new 30,000-square-foot wing, which doubled exhibit space adding two new galleries and many other amenities. The Bowers Kidseum, located on the premises, is the only cultural art-based center in Orange County with a focus on children's art education that is fun and intriguing. Kids are exposed to artifacts and exhibits enhanced by hands-on and interactive activities including art classes, creative projects, and storytelling. Visitors to either museum should plan to lunch at Tangata, the elegant 160-seat restaurant located on the premises with wonderful al fresco dining.

IRVINE MUSEUM
18881 Von Karman Ave., Ground Floor, Irvine
(949) 476-2565
www.irvinemuseum.org
Founded in 1992 by Joan Irvine Smith and her mother, Athalie R. Clarke, this is the only California museum solely dedicated to the preservation and display of California Impressionism, a style of art also known as plein air that defined the California art scene from 1890 to 1930. Many plein air works captured California landscapes before the state was subjected to its population growth and mass urbanization. The museum installs new exhibitions every four months and houses a bookstore that carries catalogues, books, and note cards featuring paintings that depict this style of art. Docent-led tours can also be arranged in advance.

LAGUNA ART MUSEUM
307 Cliff Dr., Laguna Beach
(949) 494-8971
www.lagunaartmuseum.org
With a focus on American art, mainly of the California persuasion, Laguna Art Museum's exhibitions, catalogues, and educational com-

ponents examine unconventional and regionally significant themes, such as auto and surf culture, through the eyes and brush strokes of California artists. Recent exhibits have included the cutting-edge *Shag: The Flesh is Willing* featuring the artist's pictorial interests, nudes and purgatory, in an investigation of the 1950s cocktail culture and notion of sin. The museum's permanent collection, which includes more than 3,500 works of art from the early 19th century to present, are less controversial but interesting nonetheless. A recent exhibition, Collecting California: Selections from Laguna Art Museum, included 85 works from the permanent collection and some of the most noteworthy pieces created in California during the past 150 years. Every October the museum hosts its annual Plein Air Painting Invitational, a weeklong celebration that unites artists with collectors who have an opportunity to add to their collection by purchasing original pieces.

MUZEO MUSEUM
241 South Anaheim Blvd., Anaheim
(714) 956-8936
www.muzeo.org
Less than three years old, Orange County's newest museum is dedicated to the arts, knowledge, entertainment, and culture. There are some 20,000 square feet of exhibition and educational space including the historic 1908 Carnegie Library, which houses the museum's Program Building displaying regional history and themed exhibitions. In addition to its permanent collection, The Muzeo hosts an average of three traveling exhibitions a year that would not otherwise make their way to The OC. Each exhibit, whether permanent or traveling, is enhanced with special programs, events, and activities.

ORANGE COUNTY CENTER FOR CONTEMPORARY ARTS
117 North Sycamore St., Santa Ana
(714) 667-1517
www.occca.org
For three decades the Orange County Center for Contemporary Arts (OCCCA) has provided emerging and established artists, as well as guest artists, an environment for exploring and developing expression in the arts. This artist-operated compound is located in the Santa Ana Artist Village, and presents a variety of programs at no charge, from films and forums to first Saturday artist receptions. Exhibitions tend to be thought provoking, unconventional, and a bit edgy, which is what sets OCCCA apart from the region's other artistic venues.

Plan Ahead for Some Free Time

Timing is everything, and on certain days of the month many of Orange County's museums open their doors and invite the public at no cost.

Bowers Museum: Visitors enjoy free access both to the main museum, Kidseum, and to all activities the first Sunday of every month.

Irvine Museum: The museum offers free admission year-round, and on Friday docents lead visitors on free walking tours.

Orange County Museum of Art: Those planning a trip to the Orange County Museum of Art can enjoy free admission the second Sunday of the month.

Fullerton Arboretum: Located on the campus of Cal State Fullerton, this sprawling haven offers free admission year-round.

HISTORY MUSEUMS

CASA ROMANTICA
415 Avenida Granada, San Clemente
(949) 428-2139
www.casaromantica.org

Casa Romantica's architecture is as interesting as the events and programs that take place beneath its storied roof. Built in 1927 by Ole Hanson, a co-founder of San Clemente, as his family home and designed by Carl Lindbom, who was also responsible for the design of Casa Pacifica, Richard Nixon's nearby Western White House, the home features seven bedrooms and an equal number of baths. It has had many owners and many names over the years and even served as a home for senior citizens as well as a venue for special events. Listed on the National Register of Historic Places, Casa Romantica, which teeters atop an ocean bluff, began a new lease on life at the dawn of the new millennium. It now offers a broad range of artistic and educational programs to the public, collaborating with such organizations as the Orange County Library and San Clemente Historical Society. Programs include a poetry series, speakers' series, and artist workshops, which take place in an ample-size studio with hands-on activities that include lessons in gardening, arts and crafts, and the creative arts. A satellite public library includes a special collection of books chronicling the region's history, culture, and ecology and can be viewed by appointment. Every Wednesday at 10 a.m. children gather around for Casa Kids Story Time, a free event geared towards children ages three to five years.

HERITAGE MUSEUM OF ORANGE COUNTY
3101 West Harvard St., Santa Ana
(714) 540-0404
www.heritagemuseumoc.org
Located on 12 acres punctuated with flora and citrus groves, the Heritage Museum of Orange County is like a mini compound with an historic plaza and several buildings dating from the 1890. One of these noted buildings is the 1898 Kellogg House, where three generations of native Californians lived before the Victorian gem was donated and moved to the museum grounds in 1981. Santa Ana's last surviving freshwater marsh, a reminder of the once extensive wetlands that existed throughout lowland Orange County, is also located on the premises. Throughout the year the museum hosts a number of annual events, including the Great Pumpkin Weigh-Off in October and a Victorian Holiday Tea in December. Mind Your Manners is geared towards children ages seven to nine and is a fun etiquette class held in the dining room of the Kellogg house. It includes a proper Victorian tea party where children learn the setting of a formal table, making introductions, and using proper telephone etiquette. There is an abundance of enrichment classes for school groups, too.

MISSION SAN JUAN CAPISTRANO
26801 Ortega Hwy., San Juan Capistrano
(949) 234-1300
www.missionsjc.com
No visit to California, be it north or south, should exclude a trip to one of the 21 missions established by Father Junípero Serra. Mission San Juan Capistrano was founded on November 1, 1776 and was the seventh mission established. As

Swallows Festival

The romance and folklore of the mission is revisited each spring with the return of the swallows. Legend has it that the birds originally sought sanctuary at the mission from an innkeeper who destroyed their nests elsewhere. The explanation for their annual return is so the young can nest safely within the confines of the mission walls. Mythology aside, the swallows arrive in groups to build their nests, made from a mixture of saliva and mud, which can be found along the area's rocky cliffs, caves, and under the eaves of the mission's edifice. The annual Swallows Festival is held every March and visitors from all over descend on Mission San Juan Capistrano to partake in the revelry.

Close-up

Presidential Tour of a Lifetime

If you're going to visit the Richard Nixon Library and Birthplace, you can embark on an entire tour of Nixon's early life. About 20 minutes from the library is the town of Whittier where a young Richard Nixon courted Patricia Ryan. Nixon attended Whittier Union High School, located at the corner of Philadelphia Street and Pierce Avenue, earning his diploma in 1930. Patricia Ryan, the future Mrs. Nixon, taught here as well during the late 1930s. Richard Nixon was also an alumnus of nearby Whittier College where he was elected student body president. The house where Pat Ryan lived when she met the future president still stands at 13513 Terrace Place. The couple married at the Mission Inn in neighboring Riverside in 1940 and moved to a modest home in Whittier at 14033 Honeysuckle Lane after Nixon was elected to Congress. The Whittier Museum and Historical Society at 6755 Newline Ave. has exhibits chronicling Nixon's life. To reach Whittier from Yorba Linda, take Imperial Highway west for about 9 miles and turn right on Beach Boulevard. Travel a half mile, turn left on Lambert Road, and travel to 1st Avenue. Take 1st Avenue to Whittier Boulevard and turn left, making a slight right onto Pickering Avenue. Next, make a left on Philadelphia Street—you are in the general vicinity of both the college and high school attended by Richard Nixon.

with all of the missions, it was the Indians that were responsible, not by choice, to construct the buildings. The sound of the centuries-old bells guides you to the grounds where fabled arches, Moorish Fountains, Indian burial grounds, ruins of a stone church, soldiers' barracks, and a 10-acre garden are all found behind the cloistered wall. All of these historic relics are open to the public and, on the last Saturday of each month, the mission hosts Living History Days where costumed docents reenact forgotten skills, such as wool spinning and panning for gold. Audio tours are available for both kids and adults.

THE RICHARD NIXON LIBRARY
AND BIRTHPLACE
18001 Yorba Linda Blvd., Yorba Linda
(714) 993-5075
www.nixonlibraryfoundation.org
Southern California is home to two presidential libraries, the Reagan Library in Simi Valley and the Richard Nixon Library and Birthplace in Yorba Linda. The nine-acre complex is the only presidential library in the United States that was built and maintained exclusively through private funds. What makes it even more interesting is that President Nixon's fully restored birthplace,

which was also his childhood home, is still positioned in its original place and was built by the president's father a year before his birth. Nearby are the flower-circlet memorial sites of both the President and Mrs. Nixon. The library itself has been described as a 52,000-square-foot, three-dimensional walk-through memoir featuring 22 state-of-the-art galleries, movie and interactive video theaters, and a First Lady's Garden. The museum also hosts a number of special events and speaker forums throughout the year.

SPECIAL INTEREST MUSEUMS

FULLERTON ARBORETUM
1900 Associated Rd., Cal State Fullerton campus, Fullerton
(657) 278-3407
www.fullertonarboretum.org
Located on the campus of Cal State Fullerton, this verdant 26-acre plot features a collection of more than 4,000 unique plants that are divided into tidy geographical sections. Also located on these grounds is the Nikkei Museum, which highlights the agricultural impact and contributions the Japanese American community made to the development of Orange County. The

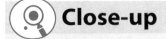 **Close-up**

The *Queen Mary*

Just over the Orange County line is a ship of magnificent proportions—the *Queen Mary*. The *Queen Mary*'s transatlantic career began with Cunard in May of 1936 when she set sail on her maiden voyage from Southampton, England, to New York City. For the next 31 years she would ferry countless passengers across the high seas, including some 600,000 soldiers during her stint as a World War II troop ship. Following the war, the *Queen Mary* embarked on "Operation Diaper," reuniting thousands of war brides and their bouncing babies with their heroic husbands. In 1947 the *Queen Mary* returned to civilian service as a passenger liner and resumed her reign along the North Atlantic, but as airline travel became the more preferred mode of transportation, Cunard decided to unleash the ship to the highest bidder. In 1967 the city of Long Beach acquired the Art Deco masterpiece for a song.

The city of Long Beach has meticulously transformed the ship from a heap of steel into one of the most celebrated ocean liners of the 20th century, inviting an entirely new generation aboard from her permanent berth in Long Beach Harbor. Her three-funnel silhouette is unmistakable and, at the age of 73, she has never looked more magnificent. Since 1971, she has transported modern-day passengers around the globe through an array of innovative tours and exhibits. Passengers can voyage into the past and spend an entire day admiring the ship's Art Deco beauty, exploring the decks from stem to stern, booking guided and self-guided tours, and reliving the glory and elegance of a bygone era.

From history to mystery, there are several tours on which to embark during the course of an afternoon. The Self-Guided Shipwalk Tour, which is included in the price of general admission, allows visitors to explore the ship from stem to stern, engine room to wheelhouse, at their own leisure. Those with a penchant for the paranormal will enjoy the Ghosts & Legends of the *Queen Mary*, a special-effects walk-through show that dramatizes actual unexplainable events that have taken place on board during the past seven decades. The 25,000-square-foot area that houses Ghosts & Legends takes guests through many of the locations where supernatural occurrences and unexplainable events have been witnessed.

Heritage House, a historic 1894 East-Lake home that was slated for demolition three decades ago, was saved from the wrecking ball and moved to the site, structurally restored, and filled with memorabilia and furnishings reminiscent of the home's era.

INTERNATIONAL SURFING MUSEUM
411 Olive St., Huntington Beach
(714) 960-3483
www.surfingmuseum.org
Southern California's surf culture is celebrated and heralded in the heart of Orange County's surf mecca, Huntington Beach. Within its confines are displays of surfing artifacts and memorabilia, the camera that captured the movie *Endless Summer* on film, an homage to surf legend Duke

Kahanamoku, classic surfboards, and more. Just down the road at the corner of Main Street and Pacific Coast Highway are the outdoor Surfers' Hall of Fame and the Surfing Walk of Fame.

MARCONI AUTOMOTIVE MUSEUM
1302 Industrial Dr., Tustin
(714) 258-3001
www.marconimuseum.org
Car enthusiasts are sure to feel in their element at this museum, founded in 1994 by Dick Marconi—hence the name. On display is a collection of historic, exotic, and classic vehicles worth more than $30 million. There are super bikes, open wheel racing cars including Formula 1 and Indy, American muscle cars, vintage racing cars, and high performance vehicles classified as exotic. A

For a nominal fee, guests can enjoy additional tours such as the Behind-the-Scenes Guided Tour, which takes visitors to areas not open to the general public, such as the first-class swimming pool. Passengers can also experience a tour of duty on a guided World War II expedition, which chronicles the ship's history during her "Grey Ghost" days when she was stripped of her finery, coated in a hue of battleship grey, and sent out to sea in order to aid the allied effort. The guided Haunted Encounters tour guides modern-day passengers to some of the ship's most haunted areas where paranormal activity has been reported. Floating alongside the *Queen Mary* is the *Scorpion*, a Cold War–era Soviet submarine that was once shrouded in secrecy. A stark contrast to the elegant Art Deco ocean liner, the seven compartment vessel invites guests to squeeze in to tour its torpedo and sonar rooms and imagine life at sea amid extremely cramped quarters.

Though no longer a mechanical marvel, the *Queen Mary* still remains a "city afloat." Between tours and exhibits, passengers can relax at one of the ship's award-winning restaurants or lounges. Champagne Sunday Brunch, a weekly event that takes place inside the first-class dining room where such notables as the Duke and Duchess of Windsor noshed, features an array of international food stations and children's buffet.

Further unlocking a door to the past is the magnificent Observation Bar, located on Promenade Deck at the bow of the ship. Its original Art Deco color scheme, coupled with a whimsical mural, arched bar, and vintage stools, is the ideal setting to enjoy light refreshments, panoramic sunsets, and spectacular views of the Long Beach skyline. Famous passengers, such as Clark Gable and Winston Churchill, often passed their time on board sipping libations inside this first-class lounge.

You can also slumber aboard the ship in a former stateroom where portholes reveal sea and cityscapes, while modern amenities add an element of convenience. Vintage touches, such as original faucets displaying a choice of either fresh or salt water, as well as built-in vanities, are testaments to a forgotten epoch of travel. From stem to stern, engine room to wheelhouse, the *Queen Mary* is truly a floating masterpiece. The *Queen Mary* is located at the south end of the 710 Freeway in Long Beach and is open daily from 10 a.m. For information call (562) 435-3511 or www.queenmary.com.

1999 Jaguar XJ-220S, one of only five produced, is here, too, along with a one-of-kind Ferrari FX.

NEWPORT HARBOR NAUTICAL MUSEUM
600 East Bay Ave. at the Balboa Fun Zone, Newport Beach
(949) 675-8915
www.nhmn.org

Considering that the world's largest international yacht race begins in Newport Harbor, it seems only fitting that a museum dedicated to nautical heritage should be here as well. The Newport Harbor Nautical Museum boasts hundreds of ship models, including one made of bone and human hair and another crafted from 22-karat gold and pure silver. The museum also features some 58,000 maritime photos that date back to the

1890s and chronicle the area's maritime history. A little Hollywood is thrown in for good measure since John Wayne, Humphrey Bogart, Errol Flynn, and Lauren Bacall all enjoyed a bon voyage from these waters.

OCEAN INSTITUTE
24200 Dana Point Harbor Dr., Dana Point
(949) 496-2274
www.ocean-institute.org

On weekdays the Ocean Institute hosts a number of school-age children who visit with their teachers to get a better appreciation for the sea, but on weekends the public is welcome to experience salty sea sprays, observe live specimens, and get a better understanding of migrating whales. This family-friendly museum also includes lab activities, sea creature viewings, octopus and jellyfish feedings, and living history programs based on Richard Henry Dana's book *Two Years Before the Mast*, which takes place aboard the historic brig *Pilgrim*. There are even art classes available for kids.

SHERMAN LIBRARY AND GARDENS
2647 East Pacific Coast Hwy., Corona del Mar
(949) 673-2261
www.slgardens.org
When it comes to settings, Sherman Library and Gardens wins hands down. Located in the enchanting village of Corona del Mar, part of Newport Beach proper, the museum is a hybrid of botanical beauty and historical preservation. The gardens feature plants and fauna that span the globe and are punctuated with fountains and sculptures and an exchange of seasonal flowers. There are cactus, a tropical conservatory blooming with orchids, a koi pond filled with carp, a rose garden, a fern grotto, a Japanese Garden, and an herb garden. The library is housed in a charming adobe home and contains various facets of Pacific Southwest heritage. There are some 25,000 books, pamphlets, and other printed items, including maps and photographs. The venue is a research library used by a cross-section of researchers, from young students to historians. And, because it is a research library and not a circulating library, all materials remain on-site. Sherman Library and Gardens also hosts a number of hands-on classes, such as wreath making and tropical floral design. There is also a charming cafe on the premises, Café Jardin, which is located near the central flower garden.

PARKS AND BEACHES

Orange County is a recreational haven that can be enjoyed year-round. Set against a backdrop of mountains and seascapes, you can explore and play at one of the many city or regional parks, wildlife preserves, or cemented skate parks where you can do your best Tony Hawk impersonation.

Of course, Orange County is known for its pristine beaches where surfers gather at sunrise to hang ten and active residents are seen jogging, bicycling, and skating before they hit the 9 to 5 grind. The beaches, both those run by the city and those managed by the state, provide all the conveniences needed to enjoy a day under the sun: clean restrooms and concession stands for purchasing food and beverages, as well as rental equipment, fee-based parking areas, and lifeguards. Many Orange County beaches also have cement fire rings for nighttime bonfires, a favorite OC pastime.

Orange County's parks are also well maintained and are weekend destinations for families to gather for afternoon picnics, leisurely bike rides, or hikes on wooded trails. Many might be surprised that Orange County, a well-developed region caught somewhere between urban and suburban, has rural areas for fishing, boating, and bird watching, as well as sanctuaries for wildlife, flora-filled trails for hiking, and old-fashioned fun such tossing horseshoes into a sandy pit. There are even equestrian trails for those who enjoy a trot.

Even in the most populated of areas, Orange County included, nature is present if you just bother to look. Mere feet from a busy highway are migrating birds oblivious to their city surroundings. Plant life, abundant with blooms, thrives in the shadows of high-rise buildings and residential complexes, proving that nature is sometimes found in the most unnatural of settings.

MAJOR REGIONAL AND CITY PARKS

Regional parks charge a nominal fee for vehicles—$3 on weekdays and $5 on weekends with a fee increase on major holidays. Wilderness parks are $3 to enter every day of the week. City parks are free.

CARBON CANYON REGIONAL PARK
4442 Carbon Canyon Rd., Brea
(714) 973-3160
www.ocparks.com
This remote park was once part of the long-forgotten community of Olinda, an area settled by farmers and ranchers in the 19th century. The park, which sits in a canyon surrounded by homes, remains somewhat rural and unscathed by Orange County's many building booms. The park has eight lighted tennis courts, a trio of sand volleyball courts, and a field used for active group sports. A pair of backstops is available for softball games on a first come, first-served basis. Little park goers can get an active workout at one of five fully equipped tot lots with equipment to climb and explore. There are nine covered picnic areas, a four-acre lake, a pair of fishing ponds that require anglers 16 and older to have a fishing license, an amphitheater, and barbecues. Naturalist-guided tours and group lectures are offered year-round. Open from 7 a.m. to 6 p.m. November to March and 7 a.m. to 9 p.m. April through October.

CRAIG PARK
3300 State College Blvd., Fullerton
(714) 973-3180
www.ocparks.com

Named for a longstanding public servant, Ted Craig, Phase One of Craig Regional Park was finished in 1974 and the final phase was completed in 1980. The park is lush and green with shaded turf grass, picnic areas, and trails for hiking and biking. A three-acre lake lures migratory waterfowl as well as anglers armed with a California Fish and Game License. Model radio-controlled sailboats are also permitted. Bird watchers flock to Craig Park as well as to enjoy its wildlife sanctuary where a nature center provides some insight into the park's natural habitat. There is also a botanical preserve with neatly lined rows of pruned roses that bloom April through September. The park's sports complex includes baseball fields, basketball and volleyball courts, and racquetball and handball courts as well as old-fashioned pits for tossing horseshoes. There is a trio of tot lots as well as equestrian trails plus plenty of places to picnic and barbecue. Leashed dogs are also welcome. Open from 7 a.m. to 6 p.m. November to March and 7 a.m. to 9 p.m. mid-March to November.

IRVINE REGIONAL PARK
1 Irvine Park Rd., Orange
(714) 973-6835
www.ocparks.com

Tucked among a grove of mature oak and sycamore trees with sloping foothills adding to the topography, Irvine Regional Park is a sanctuary for both humans and wildlife known to burrow among the 477 acres. This park, with its year-round pony rides and railroad adventure, which includes a 10-minute train ride, is the ultimate place for families with young children. There are several picnic areas, many sheltered, as well as trails for walking and biking, a half-dozen playgrounds, four softball fields, volleyball courts, and a lagoon. A 4-mile equestrian trail fringes the central park's perimeter with convenient parking for horse trailers. There are ponds, creeks, and footbridges, too, plus a waterfall that adds to the

Annual Park Pass

Park goers can save money by purchasing an annual day use pass and decal, which provides easy access to Orange County's regional, wilderness, and historical parks plus four OC beaches, including Aliso Beach Park, Capistrano Beach, Dana Point Harbor, and Salt Creek Beach, as well as the following regional and wilderness parks:

- Aliso and Wood Canyons
- Carbon Canyon Regional Park
- Caspers Wilderness Park
- Clark Regional Park
- Craig Regional Park
- Irvine Regional Park
- Laguna Coast Wilderness Park
- Laguna Niguel Regional Park
- Limestone-Whiting Wilderness Park
- Mason Regional Park
- Mile Square Regional Park
- O'Neill Regional Park
- Peters Canyon Regional Park
- Riley Wilderness Park
- Santiago Oaks Regional Park
- Yorba Regional Park

To purchase an annual day pass, contact the OC Parks office at (714) 973-6855 or www.ocparks.com.

park's beauty. During the holiday season Irvine Regional Park strings lights on its train and ferries children to Santa's Village for a visit with St. Nick. The park is open November through March from 6 a.m. to 6 p.m., and April through October until 9 p.m.

LAGUNA NIGUEL REGIONAL PARK
28241 La Paz Rd., Laguna Niguel
(949) 923-2240
www.ocparks.com

Located in south Orange County on an 80-acre sprawl surrounded by a lake nearly half the park's size, Laguna Niguel Regional Park was originally part of a Mexican land grant. Today it is one of the county's most lush destinations, rich with sheltered picnic areas, barbecues, pedestrian bridges leading to remote areas, and equestrian trails for those who enjoy exploring on horseback. The lake is stocked with trout during the winter as well as bass, bluegill, and catfish year-round with bait and boat rentals located at the park's boathouse. Sporty types can take to the jogging trails, sand volleyball courts, lighted tennis courts, or the horseshoe pits. The park's Kite Hill is a favorite spot for remote-controlled airplanes and gliders. There are also a handful of tot lots, and leashed dogs are welcome to accompany their human companions to the park as well. Laguna Niguel Regional Park is open November through March from 6 a.m. to 6 p.m., and April through October until 9 p.m.

YORBA REGIONAL PARK
7600 East La Palma, Anaheim
(714) 973-6615
www.ocparks.com

Situated on what was once a thriving cattle ranch belonging to settler Bernardo Yorba, Yorba Regional Park now caters to herds of people in pursuit of a leisurely afternoon. There are more than 400 picnic tables, many with permanent shading, as well as a quartet of lakes with a labyrinth of streams where visitors can fish or sail model boats. Equestrian trails traverse through this green belt and eventually connect to the Santa Ana River trail, which makes its way down toward the beach. In addition, there are many places for children to play, plus volleyball courts, horseshoe pits, baseball diamonds, and a fitness course. With some 200 barbecue stations, finding a place to grill shouldn't prove to be too much of a problem. There is also a "bark park" for pooches with one designated for larger breeds and another for smaller pups. Dogs are allowed

---

Dog Parks

Southern Californians love their dogs, and Orange County is no exception. In the past few years several dog parks have popped up, providing owners and their pooches a place to play. Most offer off-leash privileges, too, as well as water dispensers for dogs and dog waste bags.

Arbor Dog Park
Located in Seal Beach off Lampson Avenue between Valley View and Los Alamitos Boulevard

Central Bark
Located at 6405 Oak Canyon in Irvine

City of San Clemente Dog Park
Located at 301 Avenue La Pata

Costa Mesa Bark Park
Located in TeWinkle Park at the corner of Arlington Avenue and Newport Boulevard

Dog Park
Situated in Laguna Beach at Laguna Canyon Road south of El Toro Road

Fullerton Pooch Park
Located next to Hunt Library near the train tracks just off West Walnut Avenue

Garden Grove Dog Park
Located in Garden Grove Park in the 9000 block of Westminster Avenue

Huntington Central Park Dog Park
Located in Central Park in Huntington Beach at 18000 Goldenwest Street

Huntington Dog Beach
Yes . . . a beach just for dogs! Located on Pacific Coast Highway between Seapoint Street and 21st Street

Pooch Park
In Laguna Niguel at Golden Lantern near Chapparosa Park

off their leashes in this area only. The park is open November through March from 7 a.m. to 6 p.m., and until 9 p.m. April through October.

SKATE PARKS

Just like surfing, skateboarding is part of Southern California/Orange County culture and many cities have installed public skate parks to keep kids from scuffing up public benches and sidewalks. It seems to have worked, as these concrete destinations are popular with Orange County youth.

HARVARD SKATEBOARD PARK
14701 Harvard Ave., Irvine
(949) 337-6577
www.cityofirvine.org
Opened a decade ago and a collaboration between the city of Irvine and local skaters, the park is a gathering spot for kids and teens. With many admirable features, from bowls and rails to lighting for nighttime recreation, parents can watch the action from the bleachers. Free.

LAGUNA HILLS SKATE PARK
25555 Alicia Pkwy., Laguna Hills
This skate park tends to get crowded, especially in the afternoon when neighboring Laguna Hills High School lets out. Divided with an upper reservoir with 3- to 4-foot banks; a pyramid and moon crater making up its mid-section; and 2- to 8-foot banks completing the lower section, Laguna Hills Skate Park also has half-pipes, bowls, and other challenging obstacles. A youth skate session is held on Saturdays from 8 a.m. to 10 a.m. and is strictly for skaters 12 and under. Free.

LAKE FOREST ETNIES SKATE PARK
20028 Lake Forest Dr., Lake Forest
(949) 916-5870
www.city-lakeforest.com
With more than 40,000 square feet of skating space, this skate park, a collaboration with Etnies, the sports apparel and footwear company, is one of the largest in the United States and was designed by a number of pro skaters such as Mike Vallely and Ryan Sheckler.

There are multiple courses including a street course and flow course plus Combi and skull bowls. Lessons are also available, plus the park hosts band nights and other special events. Etnies Skate Park is scheduled to undergo a major expansion. Currently it's free to skate here, but non-Lake Forest residents will soon be obligated to pay a nominal fee for the privilege.

VANS SKATE PARK
The Block of Orange
20 City Blvd. West, Orange
(714) 769-3800
www.vans.com
Part of the Vans empire, makers of skate apparel and shoes, this is the ultimate park for skateboarders, and many local professionals drop by to get a workout as well. With a 20,000-square-foot indoor street course with challenging obstacles plus a 12-foot Combi pool replicated from nearby Upland Pipeline Skatepark, considered one of the best skating pools during the 1980s, and an area for beginners that offers a less intimidating environment, Vans Skate Park has something for all skill levels. There are mini ramps, too, plus an outdoor street course made of concrete with a series of ledges, stairs, manual pads, and more. When skaters need a break, they can head to the arcade located on the premises. Admission fee is charged.

BEACHES

With 42 miles of coastline, velvety sands, and hidden coves, Orange County has some of the best beaches in Southern California. The following list of beaches is arranged geographically starting near the Los Angeles County line in Seal Beach and concluding in San Clemente near the San Diego County line.

Seal Beach
SEAL BEACH
At the end of Main Street just off Pacific Coast Highway
This quiet beach doesn't get the big crowds like some of Orange County's other beaches, but it has all the conveniences needed including a

fee-based parking lot or metered parking along the street, a pier with a Ruby's Diner at the end, a fenced playground, and a location that is in close proximity to Old Town Seal Beach where additional restaurants and conveniences can be found.

Sunset Beach

SURFSIDE BEACH AND SUNSET BEACH
Off Pacific Coast Highway between Anderson and Warner Avenue
Spanning more than 3 miles is a pair of beaches that, for the most part, could be considered one long stretch of sand. Big, multi-level homes line the strand. This beach is also quiet, not really known to tourists, and close to restaurants along Pacific Coast Highway. Metered parking is available.

Huntington Beach

Huntington Beach offers a trio of beaches divided into three areas and controlled by a pair of separate agencies. While each is alluring in its own unique way, they all share a common thread—convenience. Each beach offers cold-water showers with wheelchair accessible restrooms and access ramps. You'll also find food concessions, beach volleyball courts, and oversized fire rings.

BOLSA CHICA STATE BEACH
On Pacific Coast Highway between Warner Avenue and Seapoint Avenue where Dog Beach is located
Bolsa Chica is as popular by night as it is by day, and that's because of the fleet of cement fire rings scattered along the sand and used for after-dark bonfires. Stretching some 3 miles, the beach gets its share of sunbathers and surfers all year long. There are clean restrooms, concession stands, and paid parking. The Bolsa Chica Ecological Reserve parallels the beach from across Pacific Coast Highway, and a few miles up the road is the Dog Beach. California State Parks Life-

guard Service patrols the beach year-round, with the lifeguard towers staffed during the summer months only.

HUNTINGTON CITY BEACH
Along Pacific Coast Highway past Bolsa Chica State Beach starting at Seapoint Avenue
Huntington City Beach is a 3.5-mile stretch of glistening coastline and is sandwiched between a pair of state beaches, Bolsa Chica and Huntington. Dubbed Surf City and home to many surfing competitions, this beach has an elongated municipal pier, fire pits for roasting marshmallows after dark, several restrooms and concession stands for food and beach rentals, plus a ribbon of pavement for bike riding and roller skating. Lots of parking, but the lot fills up quickly during the summer months.

HUNTINGTON STATE BEACH
Past the city beach on Pacific Coast Highway from Beach Boulevard to the Santa Ana River on the Newport Beach boundary
With Wi-Fi service now available at Huntington State Beach, you can multitask by surfing the Web from your beach chair. Huntington State Beach and the city beach blend into one long stretch of shoreline, making it hard to tell where one ends and the other begins. A nesting sanctuary for many flocks of birds, Huntington State Beach is also popular with surfers and anglers. With a fleet of fire rings, nighttime bonfires are popular here, too.

Newport Beach

Newport Beach boasts more than 8 miles of shoreline stretching from the Santa Ana River jetty all the way south to Crystal Cove State Park and is bordered by Newport Bay. All beaches are open to the public from 6 a.m. to 10 p.m. with Crystal Cove State Park closing at sunset. Fire rings and public barbecues are available near the Balboa Pier and at Corona del Mar State Beach on a first come, first-served basis.

NEWPORT BEACH
Parallels Newport Boulevard
Often touted as "Zooport" because of the constant crowds that flock here whenever the sun is out, Newport Beach stretches several miles from the Huntington Beach/Newport Beach city line all the way to the Balboa Peninsula. Swimming and surfing are good up and down the beach with fewer crowds in the blocks between 40th and 50th streets. Newport Pier, which is located near shops, services, and pubs, is located between 20th and 21st streets. Parking can be a nightmare during the summer, so allow plenty of time to locate a space.

BALBOA BEACH
Parallels Balboa Boulevard
Located near the end of the peninsula, Balboa Beach isn't the easiest to reach unless you live here or are staying nearby. The Balboa Pier, home to the original Ruby's Diner, has metered parking and there are shops and conveniences close by. Street parking is at a premium.

WEST JETTY VIEW PARK
At the end of Balboa Boulevard
Experienced surfers and bodysurfers are passionate about the Wedge, a slice of daring surf that is a result of the rock jetty located on the north side of the Newport Harbor entrance. There have been fatalities among the most experienced surfers, so keep in mind that this is no place for a beginner. The waves can break at a brisk pace and the Wedge is often hazardous for swimmers due to an unpredictable undertow. Lifeguards are on duty.

CORONA DEL MAR STATE BEACH
Jasmine Avenue and Ocean Boulevard
Skin divers, swimmers, fishermen, and even surfers commingle in the waters of this state beach. Easy to reach with a grassy area, clean restrooms, picnic spots, beach rentals, and lifeguards on duty, Corona del Mar State Beach offers a half-mile of platinum sand cradled between sheer cliffs and a jetty.

Beyond Sunbathing and Swimming

Sunbathing and swimming are the two obvious activities to do at the beach, and neither takes much effort. But Orange County beaches are the ultimate playgrounds where there are no limits on how to spend your time. Abandon your towel and beach chair, if only momentarily, and try one of these favorite beach activities.

- Do a little two-wheeling atop a beach cruiser along the ocean-front strand.
- Show 'em what you're made of in a game of beach volleyball.
- Chase silvery little fish by moonlight during a seasonal grunion hunt.
- Learn to surf from the pros by enrolling in a local surf school.
- Ditch the surfboard and learn to bodysurf instead.
- See what's biting by casting a fishing line from a jutting jetty.
- Take a stroll along the sand and do some beachcombing.
- Roast marshmallows at an after-dark bonfire.
- Glide along the strand while strapped to a pair of in-line skates.
- Play a game of Frisbee with your favorite four-legged friend at a designated dog beach.
- Try skim boarding across the moist sand.
- Scan the water's surface for schools of dolphin.

LITTLE CORONA DEL MAR STATE BEACH
South of State Beach

Little Corona is a haven for bodysurfers, snorkelers, and skin divers, but it's the tide pools teeming with sea urchins that attract throngs of naturalists. A footpath wanders down to the first tide pools where, by law, nothing can be disturbed. You can rock hop to neighboring tide pools to view the marine life. Arch Rock, a natural wonder with its window-like opening to the sea, makes for a great photo opportunity.

Laguna Beach

CRYSTAL COVE STATE PARK
South of Corona del Mar/Newport Beach along Pacific Coast Highway

With more than 3 miles of beaches and some 2,400 acres of glorious woodlands, Crystal Cove State Park is a bastion and lone survivor of undeveloped Orange County coastline. Offshore the waters are designated an underwater park and, while the beach is extremely popular with swimmers and surfers, there is so much more to discover with tide pools, hidden coves, a web of trails for biking and horseback riding, and sea kayaking. There is a pair of campsites here, too, which requires a bit of a hike to reach. Access to the beach is at Reef Point, Pelican Point, or Los Trancos—all feature parking lots and relatively easy access to the shoreline with limited restroom facilities and outdoor showers.

i Want to hang ten with the best of them? There are several surfing schools located in Orange County, including Newport Surf School (www.newportsurf school.com) and Soul Surfing School (www .soulsurfingschool.com). Both offer private and group lessons.

THE COVES: SHAW'S, FISHERMAN'S, AND DIVER'S
Shaw's Cove: Fairview Street off Coast Highway
Fisherman's and Diver's: The 600 block of Cliff Drive

A staircase trails down to the beach some 35 feet below where these hidden inlets are located. Concealed from the public, locals enjoy the privacy the Coves offer with pouches of tide pools, pounding surf, diving, and, thankfully, on-duty lifeguards. Some of the area is a marine preserve, so if you wander out onto the reef you could likely spot octopus, lobster, and maybe some crabs, but everything must remain undisturbed with fishing and trapping prohibited. There are no real conveniences nearby, so it's wise to pack a cooler of edibles and water if you plan on staying for any length of time.

Beach Flags

Along the beaches are lifeguard towers every few yards and hanging from their towers are different colored flags. While these flags add a colorful element to the lifeguards' workplace, they actually have a purpose. A red flag indicates that only expert swimmers or surfers should be in the water as the conditions are at a high hazardous level; a yellow flag signals that the waters pose a medium threat and caution should be used; a green flag is what most beach goers are looking for and it means the waters are at a low hazard and fine for everyone's general use; and the yellow flag with the black ball in the center is a universal banner—sometimes an unwelcome one—for surfers that prohibits them from using the water due to an abundance of swimmers and body boarders. Typically the black ball flag is hung during the summer when the beaches are most crowded.

MAIN BEACH
Coast Highway and Broadway
Main Beach is always bustling with groups playing a friendly game of hoops, swimmers splashing in the water, bicyclists whizzing by, and volleyball players knocking the ball back and forth across a net. Main Beach is also in the heart of Laguna Beach with plenty of places to grab a quick bite to eat and convenience stores stocked with sunscreen and beverages. Further south are the Street Beaches, which are shielded from Coast Highway and in the shadow of some opulent homes. Continuing south is Arch Cove, with more cliffside manses, swatches of sand, and pounding surf. These beaches have lifeguards on duty and are less crowded than Main Beach.

ALISO CREEK COUNTY BEACH
The 31300 block of Coast Highway in South Laguna
A contemporary fishing pier defines this simple stretch of coastline, which is known for its bodysurfing and swimming. To the south is a hidden cove for those who want a bit more privacy and less sand. There are also picnic areas, volleyball, and lifeguards on duty.

i One of Laguna's best stretches of shoreline is in front of the Montage Resort (30800 block of Coast Highway in south Laguna). Just to the right of the resort is a little hidden cove surrounded by a jagged and concealing rock. It is isolated, but easy to reach and few people seem to venture down that way. If you get hungry, you can easily walk up the slope and cross the street to the supermarket for some grab and go items.

THOUSAND STEPS
South of Aliso Creek Beach
A popular beach whose name is derived from the approximate number of steps needed to reach the sand, so just getting to and from the beach is a great workout. There really aren't 1,000 steps, but the steep staircase certainly feels like a thousand and counting. Thousand Steps is ideal for surfing, playing volleyball, sunbathing, and bodysurfing. The beach has a restroom and shower.

Dana Point
SALT CREEK BEACH PARK
Off Coast Highway below the Ritz-Carlton Hotel
Located in the shadow of the Ritz-Carlton Hotel is a bisection of half-mile beaches. The hotel, which sits atop a cliff, is the dividing point although there are no obstacles preventing you from going back and forth between the two areas. Both swatches of sand are part of Salt Creek Beach Park, but the coastline to the south is referred to as Dana Strand. Each area is great for swimming, jogging, and sunbathing. The crowds, for the most part, are manageable. On weekends there is a place to grab really good breakfast burritos, which you can eat on one of the benches leading down to the beach.

DOHENY STATE BEACH
South of Salt Creek Beach
The calm waters make this beach an ideal place for beginner surfers to learn the basics, but skilled surfers tend to scoff at the somewhat placid conditions. Five acres of lawn area are punctuated with picnic areas, beach rentals, volleyball courts, and other facilities and, with all these amenities, it's no wonder families favor Doheny State Beach. Divers can enjoy the underwater park located just offshore, and anglers can set sail from neighboring Dana Point Harbor for a day of deep-sea fishing. There are restaurants and conveniences within walking distance.

CAPISTRANO BEACH
South of Doheny State Beach along Coast Highway
Possessing its own zip code, but still part of Dana Point, Capistrano Beach abuts San Clemente and has a small beach town feel. Often referred to as Capo Beach, the sand and water are a good mix for a fun-filled afternoon with swimming, bodysurfing, surfing, and other seaside escapades.

Beach Safety Tips

Never underestimate the power of the ocean. Every year on Orange County beaches there are countless rescues, injuries, and, sadly, fatalities that might have been prevented. Having a basic knowledge and understanding of water safety will come in handy and might just save your life or someone else's.

If you're going to go in the ocean you better know how to swim and never swim alone. If at all possible, stay near a lifeguard station and never rely on flotation devices, such as rafts or arm floaties, to keep you buoyed. Young children need to be supervised and monitored at all times, regardless of whether a lifeguard is present. And just like driving, drinking and swimming don't mix so save the beer and wine for another time. Not only is it unwise to consume alcohol at the beach, it's also illegal. Some other useful tips include:

- Jump in the water feet first rather than head first. This will avoid any head, neck, or spinal injuries should the water prove to be shallow.

- If you feel you are in trouble, do not be embarrassed to wave for help. Flail your arms, shout, and make a spectacle of yourself—it's better than dying, literally, of embarrassment.

- If you want to swim long distances, make sure you do so parallel to the shoreline.

- Be careful when walking on coastal bluffs, tide pool areas, or jetties. Large waves can sweep you off your feet and often come without warning, so keep your eyes fixed on the water.

- Do yourself and others a favor by reporting dangerous conditions to lifeguards or other beach management.

Some Orange County beaches are prone to riptide conditions, which can leave swimmers extremely vulnerable. These strong currents pull swimmers away from the beach and out to sea. If you find yourself caught in a rip current, swim sideways and not against the current's pull. Once you feel free from the riptide, make your way to the shoreline. Sometimes a rip current can carry you several yards away from where you started. It's always wise to inquire about conditions before you enter the ocean.

The unpredictability of the ocean isn't the only hazard you will encounter at the beach. The sun can do some serious damage as well, so you will want to protect your skin from its powerful rays. If at all possible, limit your beach and pool time between 10 a.m. and 2 p.m. when the sun is at its strongest. Always wear sunscreen with a high SPF count and reapply liberally after swimming or every couple of hours. A good pair of sunglasses and a hat can protect both your eyes and face from any sun damage. And, just because it's overcast, don't think that the sun's rays have no damaging effect. Sometimes the worst sunburns occur on cloudy days simply because no sun protection was applied. Finally, be sure to talk to your physician about any medications you may be taking that could cause an adverse reaction due to sun exposure.

SAN CLEMENTE CITY BEACH
Stretched along the city of San Clemente's coast

Spanning almost the entire length of San Clemente proper with railroad tracks that run along the beach, this city sandpit has a jutting pier with restaurants, shops, and conveniences nearby. The beach is great for all sorts of outdoor recreation, from swimming and surfing to fishing. The further away from the pier you venture, the fewer people you're likely to encounter. A metered parking lot is located nearby. Further south at San Clemente State Beach, which ends near the San Diego County line, there is even more solitude. From a distance you can catch a glimpse of the former Western White House where President and Mrs. Nixon once lived.

WILDLIFE REFUGES AND NATURE RESERVES

BOLSA CHICA ECOLOGICAL RESERVE
Warner Avenue and Pacific Coast Highway, Huntington Beach

Huntington Beach is a land of contrasts with many unexpected pleasures, including the Bolsa Chica Ecological Reserve, which extends along the east side of Pacific Coast Highway from Warner Avenue to Seapoint Avenue. Owned by the California State Land Commission and managed by the Department of Fish and Game, this California coastal wetlands sanctuary is comprised of 330 acres and is home to nearly 200 species of birds.

A primary stop on the Pacific Flyway—the flight path for thousands of birds migrating from North to South America—Bolsa Chica is one of the finest birding locations in the entire United States. Alert visitors often spot threatened or endangered species such as peregrine falcons, snowy plovers, clapper rails, or California least terns. But Bolsa Chica, the largest remaining salt marsh in Southern California, is also home to a huge variety of marine life, including sharks, crabs, horn snails, and more. Among the best places to observe wildlife is from the footbridge and trail just off Pacific Coast Highway. Be sure to pack a pair of binoculars for optimum viewing.

In order to keep the area pristine and in its natural state, bicyclists, pets, scooters, and motorized vehicles are not permitted. Fishing is legal only in the north lot and with a fishing license; legal catch limits apply. Visitors must stay on the trails to further protect the land and wildlife.

Amigos de Bolsa Chica, a volunteer support group, offers free tours beginning at the Walkbridge near Pacific Coast Highway on the first Saturday of each month from 9 a.m. to 10:30 a.m. The Bolsa Chica Land Trust also offers free public tours of the wetlands and mesa. Tours run from 10 a.m. to noon the third Sunday of each month. Visit www.surfcityevents.com for more information.

Open daily from sunrise to sunset, the Bolsa Chica Ecological Reserve is open to foot traffic

Bolsa Chica Conservancy Interpretive Center

Located at the corner of Warner Avenue and Pacific Coast Highway is the Bolsa Chica Conservancy Interpretive Center, which offers tours, presentations, and field labs. In addition to its 200-gallon aquarium, the center boasts a variety of living exhibits that include reptiles and insects. The conservancy also hosts a monthly service day on the last Saturday of the month to help clean and restore the reserve. You may pick up a free Birder's Guide to the reserve, which can also be downloaded at www.bolsachica.org. The center is free and is open Tuesday through Friday from 10 a.m. to 4 p.m.; Saturday from 9 a.m. to noon; and Sunday from noon to 3 p.m. For more information, call (714) 846-1114 or visit online at www.bolsachica.org.

only. Trail parking is accessible from the northbound lane of Pacific Coast Highway, 1 mile south of Warner Avenue across from the Bolsa Chica State Beach entrance, or at the Interpretive Center, located approximately 1 mile away at 3842 Warner Avenue at Pacific Coast Highway.

THE ENVIRONMENTAL NATURE CENTER
1601 16th St., Newport Beach
(949) 645-8489
www.encenter.org
This wildlife preserve, located on 3.5 acres near Newport High, is teeming with 15 California native communities as well as Orange County's only Butterfly House where several native species thrive. While the Environmental Nature Center puts its energies into educating local school children through an array of on-site and offsite programs, the public is welcome to visit the center and poke around on their own, exploring the many plant communities, from desert and woodland to freshwater marsh and redwood forest. Coastal Sage Scrub is one of the many plants

found along Southern California's coastal bluffs and canyons, and is prominent at the nature center as well. There are walking trails and glimpses of wildlife. The sanctuary also hosts many programs for adults and children, including yoga for kids, how to cook using raw foods, and naturalist programs for young children.

TALBERT NATURE PRESERVE
1298 Victoria St., Costa Mesa
(949) 923-2250
www.ocparks.com
Located on the north and south sides of Victoria Street in Costa Mesa, the preserve encompasses nearly 180 acres and is divided into a half-dozen zones where clusters of plant groups thrive. Zone I is the Intensive Use Area and Zone II is the Border Planting region with vegetation grown to maintain boundaries and screen embankments. There is also a Coastal Zone, Native Grassland Zone, Alluvial Woodland Zone, and Wetland Zone each with its own purpose and habitats.

RECREATION

With 42 miles of coastline stretching from the Los Angeles County border down to the San Diego County line, coupled with what many consider the idyllic climate, 328 days of magnificent sunshine, and an average temperature that hovers around 73 degrees, is it any wonder that people spend the bulk of their time outdoors? Tennis, golf, cycling, and boating are just a few things to do in your free time. And, if the weather proves to be less than perfect, there are also places where you can still feel active such as indoor rock gyms, yoga and Pilates studios, and ice skating rinks. Of course a trip to a day spa, where you can be pampered from head to toe, is enjoyed rain or shine and is often well deserved.

ADULT LEAGUES

There is an abundance of sports leagues for kids, but what about adults who have a competitive nature? The YMCA of Orange County (www.ymcaoc.org, 714-549-9622) offers several leagues for adults including volleyball, soccer, tennis, and basketball at various facilities throughout the region. There is also the Orange County Women's Soccer League (www.ocwsl.org, 714-518-4877) for women 18 and up with four divisions determined by age, and an adults basketball league, Fast Action Basketball (www.fastactionbasketball.com, 949-443-9933). Many local parks and recreation departments also form adult leagues to include a variety of sports.

BOWLING

SADDLEBACK LANES
25402 Marguerite Pkwy., Mission View
(949) 586-5300
www.saddlebacklanes.com
Located in the Village Center in south Orange County, this full-service bowling alley includes multiple lanes, a coffee shop, lounge, and pro shop. There is also an arcade, so the entire family can come out and enjoy an afternoon or evening together. On weekends the facility is open until 1 a.m.

TUSTIN LANES
1091 Old Irvine Blvd., Tustin
(714) 731-5022
www.tustinlanesbowl.com
There are 42 new bowling lanes, several leagues, a full-service lounge with big screen television, and pool tables, plus the ever popular Rock-N-Bowl that takes place on Friday and Saturday nights. You can also book meetings here or host birthday parties.

YORBA LINDA BOWL
18171 Imperial Hwy., Yorba Linda
(714) 777-3818
www.yorbalindabowl.com
It's not enough just to bowl these days; it has to be a sensory experience as well. Even though Yorba Linda Bowl offers the ho-hum traditional bowling experience, it's better known for its Glow Bowling with thunderous sounds, loud music, and electrifying lighting. Once the game is over, the lounge offers additional entertainment with karaoke.

COOKING CLASSES

LAGUNA CULINARY ARTS
845 Laguna Canyon Rd., Laguna Beach
(949) 494-0745
www.lagunaculinaryarts.com
Located in Laguna Canyon, Laguna Culinary Arts is perfect for the home chef. With a variety of

hands-on cooking lessons, including an evening program of individual and series-style classes, there is nothing that can't be mastered in the kitchen. Class size is limited, everyone shares in the experience, an emphasis on using fresh ingredients is a major component, and there is even a focus on presentation. Date night is especially fun for couples who get to cook and enjoy a romantic meal together. There are lessons in cake decorating and the history of cheese making, in which you get a crash course in the nuances of cheese. There is an on-site cheese and wine shop, too, and Laguna Culinary Arts also offers culinary vacations. Laguna Culinary Arts recently opened a satellite location in the city of Orange, which is more convenient for those living in north and central Orange County.

ORANGE COUNTY INHOME COOKING LESSONS
(714) 743-6933
www.thebestinachef.com
Where could be a better place to learn the art of cooking than within the confines of your own kitchen? Chef Steve, a professional chef who also offers private chef services, will come to your home and teach you whatever you want to learn, from food safety to preparing low-fat and low-carb dishes. Gather your friends around the kitchen table for a group lesson/dinner party. Chef Steve also offers kids' cooking lesson at just $10 per student plus the cost of food.

PREP KITCHEN ESSENTIALS
12207 Seal Beach Blvd., Seal Beach
(562) 430-1217
www.prepkitchenessentials.com
This small store carries all the necessary tools and cookware needed to stock a kitchen, but it's the lofty in-store kitchen in the back, with its collection of prep tables and gadgets, that has earned Prep Kitchen Essentials a reputation as the go-to place for culinary classes. The breadth of classes includes learning the essentials, such as knife techniques, but there is also an abundance of fun and innovative classes that include French bistro favorites, indoor grilling, halftime party

pleasers, and more. There isn't a single freezer on the premises, so every ingredient used is fresh, organic, and hormone- and preservative-free. Best of all, every class includes grazing on the food prepared by the participants.

A STORE FOR COOKS
30100 Town Center Dr., Laguna Niguel
(949) 495-0445
www.astoreforcooks.com
Taking a soup to nuts approach, this specialty store carries a wide array of kitchen gadgets and tools, and it offers demonstration cooking classes that include wine and food pairings. Classes are often taught by local chefs and cookbook authors.

CYCLING

Orange County has two great, vehicle-free places to go two-wheeling. The Huntington Beach Ocean Strand (www.surfcityusa.com) stretches nearly 9 miles, running the entire length of the city along the beach. The paved pathway offers uninterrupted pedaling with places to stop and eat along the way. It's not just limited to bicyclists either. Skateboarders, roller skaters, stroller-pushing moms, and walkers all share the path. The other ideal place for bicyclists is the path that runs along the Santa Ana River. Extending from the Pacific Ocean in Huntington Beach and stretching all the way to the Riverside County line, the 12-foot-wide path is divided into two lanes so cyclists can ride in tandem. While the path provides a safe avenue for cyclists, solo riding isn't recommended. As infrequent as it is, you'll occasionally hear of someone being assaulted or attacked along the trail. And, on occasion, homeless camps will emerge beneath one of the street overpasses. Because the trail is so isolated with no commercial operations on the path, it's wise to ride in a group or with at least one other person.

GOLF COURSES

Orange County has an abundance of public golf courses with many that are affordable and others that offer breathtaking ocean views with most providing a challenging 18 hole experience. While there are just too many golf courses to list in this chapter, www.playocgolf.com is a great source for course information with the most up-to-date green fees and full descriptions of each facility. Courses are listed in alphabetical order.

ANAHEIM HILLS GOLF COURSE
6501 East Nohl Ranch Rd., Anaheim Hills
(714) 765-4653 (GOLF)
www.playanaheimgolf.com
Considered one of The OC's most esteemed courses and located in a tony section of the county, the 18-hole Anaheim Hills Golf Course has a lovely setting amid groves of oak and sycamore trees with natural elements surrounding it. Walking is not permitted, but green fees do include cart rentals. While there is a clubhouse, the course has no dining facility.

BLACK GOLD GOLF CLUB
17681 Lakeview Ave., Yorba Linda
(714) 961-0060
www.blackgoldgolf.com
This relatively newcomer is located within a planned community and has the highest elevation for a teeing area in all of Orange County. The course is challenging and rewarding with views that extend to Catalina Island—at least on clear days. There are 18 holes, a driving range, lessons, a clubhouse, and dining facility. Walking the course is not permitted.

COYOTE HILLS GOLF COURSE
1440 East Bastanchury Rd., Fullerton
(714) 672-6800
www.coyotehillsgc.com
This north Orange County golf course was co-designed by Payne Stewart and is embedded in a 250-acre foothill setting with waterfalls, cobblestone bridges, and sweeping views. There are 18 holes, a driving range, clubhouse, and restaurant.

MONARCH BEACH GOLF LINKS
22 Monarch Beach Resort Dr., Dana Point
(949) 240-8247
www.monarchbeachgolf.com

This 18-hole, par 70 course enjoys a Pacific Ocean location that debuted in 1983 and underwent a multimillion-dollar renovation in 2001. Designed by the legendary Robert Trent Jones Jr., and only one of two oceanfront courses in The OC (Pelican Hill is the other), Monarch Beach Golf Links' pro shop is consistently ranked among the Top 100 Golf Shops by *Golf World Business*. The 1,200-foot clubhouse, overlooking the course and pounding surf, serves breakfast and lunch daily and is operated by the nearby St. Regis Resort.

PELICAN HILL GOLF CLUB
22800 Pelican Hill Rd. South, Newport Coast
(949) 467-6800
www.pelicanhill.com
Part of the tony Pelican Hill Resort along Newport Coast, Pelican Hill Golf Club features 36 holes spanning 400 acres of incredible coastal land. The two courses, north and south, were designed by Tom Fazio and are adjacent to countless acres of permanently preserved land that adds to their beauty. With views of the Pacific at most every hole, plus gentle slopes, challenging greens, and canyon-crossing tee shots, the green fees at Pelican Hill are among the most expensive in Orange County. The daily guest fee includes a forecaddie but not gratuities. If you book a tee time at twilight the green fees are nearly half the price sans the caddie. Both courses are amenity-filled, resulting in the quintessential golf experience.

TUSTIN RANCH GOLF CLUB
12442 Tustin Ranch Rd., Tustin
(714) 730-1611
www.tustinranchgolf.com
This 18-hole championship course, designed by Ted Robinson, is punctuated with placid lakes, trickling waterfalls, and a lush terrain. The readers of the *Orange County Register* continue to cast their votes for Tustin Ranch Golf Club as among the county's best golf courses. Golfers have the choice of walking the course or utilizing golf carts. There is also a clubhouse and dining option.

HIKING

Orange County has a labyrinth of hiking trails, some easy to reach, others require a trek on your part. Most every regional park has trails for hiking (see Parks and Beaches chapter), but one of the most interesting and diverse places to go for a hike is the Bolsa Chica Ecological Reserve in Huntington Beach (www.surfcityevents.com). Owned by the California State Land Commission, the reserve extends along the east side of Pacific Coast Highway between Warner and Seapoint Avenues. These coastal wetlands are comprised of 330 acres and home to nearly 200 species of birds. Another option is Crystal Cove State Park (www.crystalcovestatepark .com) between Corona del Mar and Laguna Beach. Encompassing 2,000 acres and stretching several miles along Pacific Coast Highway, the area is an undeveloped woodland ideal for hiking or mountain biking. Peter's Canyon, a wooded regional park in Orange (www.ocparks .com/peterscanyon), is home to a number of hiking trails that offer sweeping canyon views, nature trails, and wooded paths that are home to a number of wildlife and eucalyptus groves.

ICE SKATING

With perpetual sunshine and an average temperature of 70 degrees, it is unlikely Orange County will get snow flurries anytime soon. While residents of colder climates can enjoy ice skating on frozen ponds made possible by Mother Nature, those living in Orange County have to rely on indoor ice rinks created by man. A few sheltered rinks include Orange County Ice Palace in Yorba Linda (www.ocicepalace.com, 714-692-1207), Aliso Viejo Ice Palace in south Orange County (www.avicepalace.com, 949-643-9648), and Anaheim Ice (www.anaheimice.com, 714-535-7465), where the Anaheim Ducks train. All three facilities offer skating lessons, too.

MINIATURE GOLF

BOOMERS
3405 Michelson Dr., Irvine
(949) 559-8341
www.boomers.com
Located in Irvine and visible from the freeway, this mini golf course has a pair of courses with all the usual suspects: windmills, water traps, clown's mouth, etc. It can get rather busy on the weekend as golfers queue up at the various holes, so weekdays or weekday evenings are recommended. There are also an arcade, batting cages, bumper boats, laser tag, and soft play areas, plus a rock wall, gravity games, and a McDonald's on the premises. Visit the Web site, which usually has printable coupons, for additional savings. The indoor arcade has a lot of games for all ages and most dispense tickets, depending on how you score, which are redeemable for prizes.

CAMELOT GOLFLAND
3200 Carpenter Ave., Anaheim
(714) 630-3340
www.golfland.com
Visible from the 91 Freeway at the Kraemer exit, Camelot is the largest miniature golf course in the country and offers putters five courses with varying themes and obstacles, from pagodas and castles to Spanish forts. Even with the abundance of putt-putt courses, this place can still get crowded on the weekends. Thankfully, if the courses are too congested, try your hand at laser tag or an arcade game (they have 200) or get wet and wild on the five-story waterslide.

ROCK CLIMBING

In the last decade rock climbing gyms have made their way into the mainstream and are ideal for both the novice and the pro. These safe, environmentally controlled venues are ideal when you can't get to an outdoor location. Among the offerings in Orange County are ClimbX (www.climbxhb.com, 714-843-9919) in Huntington Beach, Rock City Climbing Center in Anaheim Hills (www.rockcityclimbing.com, 714-

777-4884), and Rockreation Climbing Gym (www .rockreation.com, 714-556-7625) in Costa Mesa.

SURFING

When it comes to surfing, all beaches are not created equal. Sure, you can surf most any beach in Orange County (see the Parks and Beaches chapter for descriptions of all OC beaches), but some are better than others simply because of their geographical position. The crème de la crème of ocean swells are found at Huntington City Beach (www.surfcityusa.com), located at the foot of Main Street near the pier and home to the annual U.S. Open of Surfing. The surf is so good here that the USA Surf Team undergoes rigorous training to prepare for its many international competitions. Huntington City Beach is really for skilled surfers, although beginners can test the waters here as well. A better beach for the novice surfer is Doheny State Beach in Dana Point. It's especially alluring for long boarders. Seal Beach, Newport Beach, and Laguna Beach also have decent surfing conditions.

TENNIS

Most of the hotels in Orange County have tennis courts, but you typically have to be a guest to get any court time. Many of Orange County's public parks have tennis courts that are free to use on a first-come, first-served basis. Just show up and if there is an empty court, it's yours. For a list of regional parks visit www.ocparks.com. Both the Fountain Valley Tennis Center (714-839-5950) and the Irvine Tennis Association (949-669-0734) are also open to the public.

YOGA AND PILATES

Yoga and Pilates studios have become as popular as full-service gyms—maybe even more so in Orange County. Yoga is more than just physical exercise as it offers overall balance in regards to health and well-being. Meditation and self-realization also play instrumental roles in yoga.

Limited Surf Time

While surfing is a favorite pastime along Orange County's beaches, it's not a free for all where you can paddle out whenever the urge may strike. During the summer, life-guards hang a "black ball" flag from their towers—a yellow flag with a dominant black ball—which bars surfers from the waters due to the abundance of swimmers and body boarders. Usually surfers hit the water in the early morning or late afternoon before or after the black ball rule gets underway. During the summer a handful of Orange County beaches allow all-day surfing, including the north side of the Huntington Beach Pier all the way to Golden West Street and near the Newport Beach River Jetties just south of Brookhurst. During the winter months, the black ball rule is not in effect and surfing is permitted all day long.

Pilates, developed by Joseph Pilates in the 1920s, has its roots in core body strengthening and lengthening the spine. Dancers have long known the benefits of Pilates, but it has become a buzz-word of late for its overall sculpting effects and creating good posture. Yoga and Pilates can also work in tandem, and many studios offer both.

Pole dancing is another new way to stay in shape. Studios, such as Sheila Kelley S Factor (www.sfactor.com) in Costa Mesa or Pilates on the Pole (www.pilatesonthepole.com) in Newport Beach, have actual stripper poles available for a real workout (no worries, you're clothed the entire time), combining ballet, yoga, and the art of striptease to promote health and confidence.

ARTFORM STUDIO
24194 Alicia Pkwy., Suite A, Mission Viejo
(949) 837-9999
www.artformstudio.com
Established in 2002 in south Orange County by former dancers, ArtForm Studio offers everything from private instruction to group classes with many options in between within a state-of-the-art facility. Group classes are more flexible, allowing participants to pay as they go without making any long-term commitments. The candlelight Pilates/yoga fusion class is extremely popular with an added element of relaxation.

BODY DESIGN
210 Newport Center Dr., Suite 3, Newport Beach
(949) 719-2600
www.bodydesignonline.com
With one of the best settings to inspire exercise—distant ocean views—this Newport Beach fitness studio is as aesthetic as it is functional, with no more than 10 students per class, but you pay for the privilege as this is one of The OC's more expensive places to find your "om." Body Design also offers spa services, so it's a one-stop shop for fitness and wellness. The Hot Flash Attack class is specifically designed for women 50 years old and up.

YOGA CENTER
445 East 17th St., Costa Mesa
(949) 646-8281
www.yogacenter.org

With a fundamental approach to the art of yoga, the Yoga Center teaches authentic yoga style as it's been taught for centuries by yogis with a goal for clients to optimize their health, vitality, and inner peace. A strong emphasis is on meditation with instructors skilled in techniques to help individuals find the best approach to meditating. The center also offers retreats and monthly donation-only classes with a different topic addressed at each session.

Staying Physically—and Fiscally—Fit

If you're looking for an affordable alternative for staying fit, the parks and recreation departments throughout Orange County's many cities are a great resource. Not only will you find yoga and Pilates classes offered, but there are also fitness boot camps, Tai Chi, tennis, aquatics, and many other workout alternatives. The city of Brea in north Orange County has its own fitness center for people of all ages and abilities, with Brea residents enjoying special discounts. Irvine has a fitness center just for seniors, and Garden Grove has a number of recreation classes for every member of the family.

SPECTATOR SPORTS

When it comes to spectator sports, Orange County has everything from professional baseball and hockey to well-attended surfing competitions. The one thing it doesn't have is a professional football team. After spending 52 years in Southern California, with the last 15 seasons played at Anaheim Stadium, the Los Angeles Rams made their exodus to St. Louis in 1994 with the LA Rams departing for Oakland a year later. For nearly 15 years the region has been without a professional team and it doesn't look like one will make its home here anytime soon. If you want to watch a game from the sidelines, you'll have to settle for the bleachers at a local high school, motor up to Los Angeles to catch a UCLA Bruins or USC Trojans game, or venture south to San Diego to cheer on the Chargers.

Ah, but you can partake in the seventh-inning stretch during baseball season at Angel Stadium of Anaheim, still referred to by old-school types as the Big A. The team, today known as the Los Angeles Angels of Anaheim (say that five times fast), a name that is somewhat of an oxymoron, first played at Los Angeles's Wrigley Field in 1961, not to be confused with the more famous Chicago stadium of the same name. From 1962 to '65 the team ran bases at Chavez Ravine, home of the LA Dodgers. It wasn't until April 9, 1966, that the team had a place to call home when the California Angels, as they were then known, hosted an exhibition game against the San Francisco Giants at their brand spanking new stadium. Their first American League game took place 10 days later when they played against the Chicago White Sox. The original stadium seated 43,204 and ballooned to more than 65,000 seats in 1980 when the LA Rams moved south to Orange County. In 1998, after a year of extensive renovations, the stadium reopened as a baseball-only arena with approximately 45,000 seats and a new name, Edison International Field of Anaheim. The stadium received its present-day moniker in 2003.

Across the freeway and just a baseball-pitch from Angel Stadium is the Honda Center, where the Anaheim Ducks play during the NHL season. During the off-season, the venue, opened in 1993 and owned by the city of Anaheim, is transformed into a concert arena, circus big top, and multiple other uses. In addition to the Anaheim Ducks, the Honda Center also hosts the annual John R. Wooden Classic, when four of the nation's premier men's college basketball teams compete against one another.

BASEBALL

LOS ANGELES ANGELS OF ANAHEIM
Angel Stadium of Anaheim
2000 Gene Autry Way, Anaheim
(714) 940-2000
www.losangeles.angels.mlb.com
The Los Angeles Angels. The California Angels. The Anaheim Angels. The Los Angeles Angels of Anaheim. Which is it? With so many name changes, it's hard to keep the team's name

straight. The Anaheim Angels made the most sense since the team actually plays in Anaheim, but that name was retired when new owner Arte Moreno, who acquired the team a few years back, wanted to make Los Angeles part of the team's name. The idea caused a commotion among fans, as well as Anaheim city officials, since the team was, in their minds, the Anaheim Angels. Moreno complied with the terms of its lease with the city, which stated that Anaheim be part of the team's name, by rechristening the team Los Angeles Angels of Anaheim. Either way, locals still refer to the team simply as the Angels ignoring the longer, somewhat confusing official team name.

The Angels, which finally won its first World Series in 2002 despite starting the season with the worst record in team history, plays at Angel Stadium of Anaheim, also known as the Big A, from April to October. You would be wise to check out the team's official Web site (www .losangeles.angels.mlb.com) before purchasing tickets to see if there are any last-minute discounts. Throughout the season there are several promotional nights, such as free kids' backpacks, and select games also feature Family Night when you can get four tickets, four hot dogs, and four sodas for under $40.

HOCKEY

THE ANAHEIM DUCKS
Honda Center
2695 East Katella Ave., Anaheim
(714) 704-2500
www.hondacenter.com
Thanks to the success of the Emilio Estevez movie *The Mighty Ducks* and its subsequent sequels, the Walt Disney Company founded the Mighty Ducks of Anaheim in 1993 and was the first bona fide tenant of the Anaheim Arena, eventually renamed Arrowhead Pond and now known as the Honda Center. After the Walt Disney Company sold the team in 2005, its name was shortened by the new owners to simply the Anaheim Ducks. Part of the National Hockey League, the Ducks play October through April. Tickets can be purchased online at www.ducks.nhl.com.

HORSE RACING

LOS ALAMITOS RACE COURSE
4961 Katella Ave., Los Alamitos
(714) 820-2800
www.losalamitos.com
Long before the arrival of Angels or Ducks, Dodgers or Lakers, Kings, Clippers, or The Galaxy, Orange County was on the fast track with quar-

Go Behind the Scenes at Angel Stadium

Ever dream of sitting in the press box announcing the play-by-play to a crowd of thousands? Well, you might not get to show off your talents as the next Vin Scully or Harry Caray, but you can sneak inside some of Angel Stadium's restricted areas, including the press box, on a behind-the-scenes tour. This 75-minute trek, which is limited to 40 participants, includes a sneak peak at the press conference room, clubhouse, and dugout. During the off-season, tours are conducted every Tuesday excluding holidays at 9:30 a.m., 11 a.m., and 1 p.m. and on the same day and time during baseball season when the team is traveling. There are no Tuesday tours offered during the season if the team is playing at home. Advance reservations are required and can be made via phone up to one month in advance. You can also take your chances by purchasing your tickets on tour day, although walk-up spots are limited. Meet your tour guide outside the Home Plate Gate located between the enormous red hats. Tickets are $3 for adults, $2 for children. To make a reservation, contact the Community Relations Department at (714) 940-2070.

ter horse racing at Los Alamitos Race Course. Opened in 1950, the track offers year-round racing with overall purses reaching more than $20 million in 2008. Racing takes place in the evenings, Thursday through Sunday, with $3 general admission. Los Alamitos is also open for daytime simulcast wagering featuring racing from Southern and Northern California Thoroughbred circuits, New York circuit, Florida circuit, Kentucky circuit, and more.

SURFING

US OPEN OF SURFING
Huntington City Beach
1 Main St., Huntington Beach
(424) 653-1900
www.usopenofsurfing.com
Huntington Beach, the original Surf City, USA, is the quintessential beach town and the ideal place to witness the Hurley US Open of Surfing. The week-long event, which gets underway during mid-July, is held on the city beach along Pacific Coast Highway at the foot of Main Street. In addition to watching both men and women compete for points and prize money in the title event, you can also enjoy late-afternoon concerts, a fashion competition, the best in skateboarding, and plenty of activities, demonstrations, and product booths. This is, without a doubt, the world's largest surfing contest and has been a much anticipated summer event for more than 50 years. Best of all, it's free.

The Real Surf City, USA

A few years back Huntington Beach went to battle against Santa Cruz, another surf ghetto in Northern California, for the legal right to call itself Surf City, USA. Each coastal community claimed that it was *their* city to which Jan and Dean were referring when they penned the classic 1960s tune "Surf City." Both claimed victory and defeat. According to *Surfer* magazine, Santa Cruz is the real Surf City, USA when you take into account the surf, food, and vibe of the nation's Top 10 surf towns. However, Huntington Beach was awarded the exclusive right to use the name "Surf City, USA." Who wiped out—Santa Cruz or Huntington Beach? It depends on who you talk to. Some would say that it was no day at the beach for either.

KIDSTUFF

The OC is the ultimate playground. And, when it comes to pint-size visitors, Orange County couldn't be more kid-friendly or accommodating. There is a never-ending list of things to do, from sporting events and seaside playgrounds to interactive museums and outdoor activities. There are even cooking classes for aspiring chefs. From young children to those on the brink of adulthood, Orange County is a place of perpetual pleasures and unleashed excitement. There are, of course, the two major theme parks, Disneyland Resort and Knott's Berry Farm, which we've covered in the Attractions chapter, but consider the other possibilities—the theme restaurants, water parks, playgrounds, arcades, and performing arts.

And, when you consider Orange County averages 329 days of sunshine, an average temperature of 70 degrees, and 42 miles of pristine coastline, the best and most affordable place to go is, of course, the beach. Take the kids down to the tide pools, build a giant sandcastle, fly a kite, do a little bodysurfing, or just collect seashells on a sunny afternoon. If the weather is overcast, head to a local library or bookstore for story time or a local park for a picnic and playground opportunities. City park and recreation departments also offer an abundance of mommy and me classes, sporting opportunities for adolescents, municipal pools for swimming, and art classes.

There are also a few outdoor shopping areas with activities for children. Fashion Island in Newport Beach has a mini-train and carousel (although rumor has it that these attractions will be retired when the center emerges from a major renovation), Downtown Disney has shops and restaurants that kids of all ages will enjoy, and The Block at Orange is home to the Vans Skatepark. South Coast Plaza, Orange County's premiere indoor mall, features a pair of carousels and gigantic balloons shaped like Mickey Mouse ears available for purchase near Carousel Court. Of course, most every restaurant, fine dining excluded, is kid-friendly, offering children their own menus as well as crayons to help keep them occupied until the food arrives.

Two great resources for finding out where to take the kids are *OC Parent* and *OC Family*, which also serve as resources for finding babysitters, camps, and other essentials that parents may find helpful. Both publications can be accessed online at www.ocfamily.com and www.parentingoc.com. *Kids Guide*, www.kidsguidemagazine.com, is another excellent source.

ADVENTURE, ANIMALS, AND SOME EDUCATION

ADVENTURE CITY
10120 South Beach Blvd., Stanton
(714) 236-9300
www.adventurecity.com

Finally, a place designed especially for young children. Adventure City, just north of Knott's Berry Farm and billed as "The Little Theme Park," features fun and friendly rides that can accommodate small children and their parents. There are 10 rides in all plus activity centers, such as Thomas and Friends where children can build creative train track layouts and then put them to the test. There is also a petting farm, rock climbing wall, and arcade. Adventure City also has a birthday pavilion where parents can host a party and kids can celebrate with friends enjoying unlimited rides. During the summer the park is open all week, but in the off-season the park is open weekends only.

DISCOVER SCIENCE CENTER
2500 North Main St., Santa Ana
(714) 542-2828
www.discoverycube.org

Conceived in 1984, but not realized until its 1998 opening, the Discover Science Center teaches children an understanding of and appreciation for science, math, and technology with more than 120 hands-on exhibits and innovative programs. A favorite of teachers and parents alike, adults and children can collaborate on creating a 19-foot-long tidal wave in the Wave Tank or dare one another to recline on a bed of 3,500 nails. How often can you walk through a tornado, experience the air's lift in a wind tunnel, or calculate your exact outer-space weight should you ever venture to Mars, the Moon, or beyond our solar system? The Quake Zone demonstrates what causes earthquakes and even lets kids experience a 6.4 magnitude quake inside the Shake Shack. The museum is somewhat of an architectural icon for Orange County. A 10-story-high tilting solar cube, constructed from 2,636 steel tubes and 667 round balls, is positioned on one of its points and adds a bit of scientific interest for visitors.

KIDSEUM AT BOWERS MUSEUM
1802 North Main St., Santa Ana
(714) 480-1520
www.bowers.org

Just down the road from the Discovery Science Center is the Kidseum, Orange County's only cultural art-based venue geared towards children, located on the premises of the more adult-oriented Bowers Museum. After crossing the Rainbow Bridge that leads to the museum, toddlers and preschool-age children are introduced to artifacts and exhibits through a variety of hands-on and interactive activities including art classes, creative projects, and storytelling. There are thematic areas where little hands can touch, play, and manipulate objects. The Community Room, available for birthday parties and special events, is also the setting for art classes and cultural food tastings, while the Art Lab enriches young minds through projects, such as crafting Japanese kites. An array of musical instruments is found inside the Cultural Discovery area where puppets and games add to the experience. Kids can also don costumes, hats, and footwear from around the globe and take to the stage for some uninhibited fun. A summer art camp takes place in July and August and is designed for kids 6 to 12 years of age. Families visiting the museum can enjoy lunch at Tangata, an upscale eatery with al fresco dining, or wander off the premises to the nearby Main Place Mall for more kid-friendly noshing.

SANTA ANA ZOO AT PRENTICE PARK
1801 East Chestnut Ave., Santa Ana
(714) 835-7484
www.santaanazoo.org

Founded in 1952 with a purpose of instilling a love of nature through education, conservation, and recreation, the 20-acre Santa Ana Zoo is well known for its animal collection of mostly Central and South American creatures. Unlike zoos that are located in major metropolises, the Santa Ana Zoo is small and manageable with more than 250 animals to visit, a train to ride, and a carousel that takes you round and round. The Crean Family Farm is a true farmyard adventure where barnyard doors are flung open for kids to see small and large animals up close. It's here that children get a feel for what a zookeeper does as they witness firsthand the care that goes into feeding and nurturing the animals. Amazon's Edge is the zoo's premier exhibit and has the feel of an authentic rainforest with gushing waterfalls and a lush island setting. This exotic region is home to howler monkeys, mallards, black-necked swans, and crested screamers. A viewing deck, cradled by tall, thick bamboo, gives the feel of being in the Brazilian jungle. It was recently used as the setting in the Disney film *Old Dogs*. The Bauer Jaguar Exploration Outpost is another interesting component modeled after a real exploration outpost found in the Amazon Basin. Children learn research techniques about the animals indigenous to this region as well as weather patterns and conservation efforts. The zoo also hosts a number of events, including Boo at the Zoo in October, a "merry not scary" Halloween happening, as well as a summer concert series.

WET, WILD, AND WORTH IT

SOAK CITY
8039 Beach Blvd., Buena Park
(714) 220-5200
www.knotts.com
Owned and operated by Knott's Berry Farm with a location adjacent to the theme park, Soak City is a well-designed aptly named seasonal attraction for people of all ages. Situated on 13 acres containing nearly two dozen water-filled rides, Soak City can provide some added relief on those hot California days. A continuous old-school surf theme penetrates the park with long boards and vintage surf woody autos. Many of the rides are as heart-stopping as those found at any dry docked theme park with multi-story drops and plunges, a 750,000 gallon wave pool, and several tube and body slides with names like Riptide, Typhoon, Tornado, and Cyclone Three. Families with young children might be more comfortable meandering down the lazy river or taking refuge at Gremmie Lagoon Children's pool. Summer weekends tend to be packed, which means long lines and less space to lounge. Weekdays are less crowded. Soak City is typically open Memorial Day to Labor Day.

WILD RIVERS WATERPARK
8770 Irvine Center Dr., Irvine
(949) 788-0808
www.wildrivers.com
Just like Soak City, Wild Rivers offers the entire family seasonal fun from May through September. There are some 40 water rides, including slides, inner tube rides, a pair of wave pools, activity pools, and places to lounge. Teens can head to the faster, more thrilling attractions, such as Sweitzer Falls, which simulates a barrel ride down Niagara Falls, while small children and their parents will find rides like Water Walk to be more of a safe haven but still packed with plenty of amusement. The park features a plethora of places to grab a bite to eat and, while you can't bring food into the park, there is an area outside for picnicking. Lockers are also available.

FOOD AND FUN

MEDIEVAL TIMES
7662 Beach Blvd., Buena Park
(866) 543-9637
www.medievaltimes.com
Take a trek back to 11th-century Spain, eat grub with your hands, and cheer on your favorite knight from your arena seat. This dinner show and attraction, located in a "castle" near Knott's Berry Farm, begins when you enter the fortress and its Hall of Arms, which displays artifacts and a torture museum that illustrates life in the 11th century. You're then seated in an arena that is equipped with some surprising Hollywood-style special effects that are sure to entertain the kids. An entertaining show of jousting, swordsmanship, hand-to-hand combat, and falconry takes place between the horse-riding knights. A four-course dinner, included in the price of admission, features soup, garlic bread, a choice of roasted chicken or ribs, potatoes, dessert, and non-alcoholic beverages. Vegetarian meals are also available as is a full bar.

PIRATE'S DINNER ADVENTURE
7600 Beach Blvd., Buena Park
(714) 690-1497
www.piratesdinneradventure.com
Fans of the Johnny Depp *Pirates of the Caribbean* films will surely enjoy this dinner show attraction that puts guests right in the midst of the swashbuckling action. The high seas adventure pits the OC pirates against a new breed of swashbuckler that has invaded the region. Who will walk the gangplank? Sit back, relax, and enjoy the theatrics, aerial artistry, and duels. The show is ideal for kids as it is truly interactive, blending action and adventure with comedy and romance. There are three components to each show: the preshow and buffet, the Port of Call Feast (dinner), and, of course, the show itself. There is an adult menu, which includes two beers or unlimited soft drinks and coffee, plus a children's menu of favorite edibles. There's also a place to buy booty (pirate souvenirs).

PLAYGROUNDS

Most every park in Orange County has a playground or tot lot, so finding one won't be an issue. The playgrounds below offer more than just slides and swings, which is why we chose to include them.

BLUE GUM PARK
14 Aberdeen, Irvine
The name might refer to a certain type of tree, but kids will likely think it has to do with something to chew. Either way, this park, utilized by moms that live in the area, is cooled by mature trees that make for a great picnic canopy. The kid-friendly clubhouse is ideal for make believe, while the hanging pedestals, monkey bars, and climbing walls create an active and energetic environment. Infants and toddlers are not forgotten either as there is a pair of baby swings for little ones to rock back and forth while their older siblings run wild. A note of caution: There are no restrooms.

CENTRAL PARK WEST
Goldenwest Street between Ellis and Talbert Aves., Huntington Beach
This park is massive with busy Goldenwest Street dividing the two sprawling parcels of land that ultimately create a single park. Central Park West truly has something for everyone with an equestrian center, disc golf course, dog park, and nature center where wildlife is present as you trek through the trails. Of course, there is plenty of playground equipment with tube-style slides, swings, and other activities for kids both big and small. In addition, you'll find a pair of restaurants on either side of the street. Alice's Breakfast in the Park is open for breakfast and lunch with views of the lake, while the Park Bench Café is located near the dog park. It, too, is open most days for breakfast and lunch with menus for both humans and their canine companions. There are also plenty of trees and picnic areas, plus barbecue grills for added convenience.

COASTAL PEAK PARK
Corner of East Coastal Peak and Ridge Park Rd., Newport Beach
(949) 644-3159
Tucked away in tony Newport Coast sits this relatively new and innovative place to play adjacent to the Laguna Coast Wilderness Park. Kids should come equipped with comfortable clothes, sturdy shoes, sunscreen, and an imagination. Let the kids loose to climb the mountain rock, tinker with interactive knobs and dials, crawl across a giant swinging net, and more. Bring the trikes and bikes because there is strip of cement that encircles the play area plus lots of grass for tossing a football or Frisbee and shaded picnic areas. Best of all, this park is new enough that the equipment is well maintained and the restrooms clean.

ARCADE FUN

With gaming systems found in just about every home, arcades are a dying breed. Still, when you stumble upon one it's hard to resist playing a game of Skee Ball or shooting hoops with Pop A Shot.

THE BALBOA FUN ZONE
600 East Bay Ave., Newport Beach
(949) 673-0408
www.thebalboafunzone.com
Since 1936 the Fun Zone has been providing Orange County residents with plenty of enjoyment. In recent years, the number of rides has shrunk to just two but the arcade is still intact. Some of the vintage games have been replaced with more high-tech machines, but the old black and white photo booth still remains.

BOOMERS
3405 Michelson Dr., Irvine
(949) 559-8341
www.boomers.com
This arcade in Irvine, with a second location up the freeway in Westminster, offers an arcade plus mini-golf with two courses, batting cages, bumper boats, laser tag, and much more. They also have rides for smaller kids and soft play areas, plus a

rock wall, gravity games, and a McDonald's on the premises. If you visit their Web site, you will usually find a coupon for some added savings. Boomers tends to get crowded on weekends, especially as the day inches toward the evening. Most of the games inside the arcade spit out tickets that are redeemable for prizes. If you want to mix things up a bit, there is a bowling alley next door.

CAMELOT GOLFLAND
3200 Carpenter Ave., Anaheim
(714) 630-3340
www.golfland.com
Camelot has been going strong for more than three decades, and is the largest miniature golf course in the country with five themed courses cluttered with pagodas, castles, and Spanish forts, just to name a few. There is also laser tag, a 200-game arcade, and a five-story waterslide. Camelot also offers child care, and a visit to their Web site can save you money.

NICKEL! NICKEL! FIVE-CENT GAMES
7454 Edinger Ave., Huntington Beach
(714) 847-2191
www.nickelnickelhb.com
Unlike other arcades, Nickel! Nickel! charges a modest admission, about $2 per person, then guests can choose to play from 25 "free play" games. Most machines average one to four nickels per play and include video games and simulators. There is also a redemption counter, the largest in all of Orange County, where guests can redeem winning tickets for token prizes. There are approximately 180 games from which to select.

CURTAIN CALL FOR KIDS

ORANGE COUNTY PERFORMING ARTS CENTER
600 Town Center Dr., Costa Mesa (near South Coast Plaza)
(714) 556-2121
www.ocpac.org
Every season the Orange County Performing Arts Center offers a mix of performances that adults

find appealing, but also produces shows that the entire family can enjoy. Many of these kid-friendly performances are based on beloved works of children's literature introducing kids of all ages to the theater on their level. Puppet theater is often included as well as musicals, such as *Annie*. Choose to attend a single performance or the entire series by being a season subscriber.

THE RIB TRADER
2710 East Chapman Ave., Orange
(714) 744-9288
www.ribtrader.com
Every Friday, Saturday, and Sunday evening, this Orange County eatery presents Merlin's Magic and Comedy Dinner Theater, a two-hour show of illusion. In addition to a mouthwatering meal, children are treated to sleight of hand magic and trickery by Merlin himself.

LET'S GET COOKING

COOKAMATION
Fountain Valley
(714) 849-9164
www.cookamation.com
Working side by side with trained chefs and nutritionists, this kids-only cooking school provides a hands-on culinary education to children ages 6 to 17 with a focus on healthy eating. In addition, kids can enroll in technique classes, such as cutlery skills and pastry workshops. Each class is taught in a safe and structured environment with lessons that are age appropriate.

Classes are taught at various locations throughout Orange County. Visit Cookamation's Web site or call for details.

LAGUNA CULINARY ARTS
845 Laguna Canyon Rd., Laguna Beach
(949) 494-4006
www.lagunaculinaryarts.com
Most people are familiar with this culinary school because it offers a breadth of programs for adults, but some may be surprised to learn that it also offers culinary classes for kids. Taking a rather unique approach, classes for three- to five-year-

olds are "mommy and me" or "daddy and me" lessons that connect cooking to children's literature. Parent and child listen to a story then work together to create the dish that was featured in the story, which makes it a truly fun and enjoyable experience. There are also classes for young gourmets, which are for older children and a bit more involved. Laguna Culinary Arts also offers Snack & Learn after school courses.

YOUNG CHEFS ACADEMY
15435 Jeffrey Rd., Irvine
(949) 679-8390
www.youngchefsacademy.com
What child doesn't like to tinker in the kitchen with mom? Young Chefs offers an innovative culinary experience for inspiring chefs of all ages. Each class, taught by qualified chefs, teachers, and nutritional experts, provides interactive learning, giving kids a life-long appreciation for the culinary arts. From KinderCooks (preschoolers) to Teen Survival classes, Young Chefs Academy has a lot to offer including camps, field trips, and birthday parties for Martha Stewart wannabes.

GO WILD AT OC'S SANCTUARIES

ALISO AND WOOD CANYONS WILDERNESS PARK
28373 Alicia Pkwy., Laguna Niguel
(949) 923-2200
Not far from Laguna Beach are nearly 4,000 acres of wilderness and wide open space that were originally tribal land. Within this expanse are mature trees of mostly oak, sycamore, and elderberry; a pair of streams; 30 miles of designated trails; rare and endangered plants; and many wild animals that dwell here year round.

BOLSA CHICA WETLANDS
Pacific Coast Highway and Warner Avenue, Huntington Beach
www.bolsachica.org
Situated smack in the middle of Surf City, this wetlands preserve, its existence once threatened by developers, encompasses more than 1,200

acres of undeveloped wetlands and lowlands. It is also an ideal place to do some bird watching as it's a stop for migratory flocks and some 200 species have been spotted over the years. There are a number of docent-led tours offered, including a tour the first Saturday of each month.

CASPERS WILDERNESS PARK
33401 Ortega Hwy., San Juan Capistrano
(949) 923-2210
It's not unusual to spot a prancing deer or some other four-legged inhabitant at this 8,000-acre wilderness preserve. Punctuated with river terraces and sandstone canyons, there are groves of mature trees, bouquets of wildflowers, and the sound of running streams. There are fire rings and bike trails, designated areas for family camping, equestrian trails, playgrounds and tot lots, and interpretive programs. The park's Ortega Highway location, a lonely road that winds between Orange and Riverside Counties, really makes it seem far removed from civilization.

SANTA ANA ZOO AT PRENTICE PARK
1801 East Chestnut Ave., Santa Ana
(714) 835-7484
www.santaanazoo.org
Orange County's only zoo rests on 20 acres boasting an impressive menagerie of animals from mostly Central and South America. In addition to its 250 inhabitants, the zoo also has a train and carousel for added amusement. For more information, see "Adventures, Animals, and Some Education" in this chapter.

THOMAS F. RILEY WILDERNESS PARK
30952 Oso Pkwy., Cota de Caza
(949) 923-2265 or (949) 923-2266
Located in a remote area of south Orange County is this 523-acre wildlife sanctuary where an abundant crop of native plants thrive as well as mature sycamore and live oak groves. There are two creeks, surrounded by rolling hills and canyons, which flow seasonally. Perhaps the tamest residents that live here are the butterflies, which have their own garden filled with plants that attract these winged creatures. There are

also horse trails to enjoy and ranger-led sunset hikes. Bring a picnic lunch to savor at one of the many tables.

PLAY BALL . . . OR HOOPS . . . OR TENNIS

Orange County is home to plenty of organized sports and leagues, including Little League (www .littleleague.org), American Youth Soccer Organization (www.ayso.com), and Pop Warner Football (www.popwarner.com). All of these national leagues have Web sites that can direct you to the correct league for your city or region. The following are some alternative options for young athletes.

Basketball

CITY OF DANA POINT YOUTH BASKETBALL
(949) 248-3530
www.danapoint.org
Open to residents and non-residents of Dana Point, this youth recreation basketball league is geared to boys and girls ages six to nine years old. Low-key instruction puts the emphasis on sportsmanship rather than keeping score.

Equestrian

BRIDGES TRAINING STABLE
2682 Oso Rd., San Juan Capistrano
(949) 858-0970
www.bridgestrainingstable.com
This riding school and training facility provides a spot-on education between rider and horse. With four instructors, a trio of trainers, and a stable of two dozen horses, Bridges specializes in hunters and jumpers, training kids eight and up in English and Western-style riding. For the novice, lesson one involves learning to move the horse forward as well as stopping, turning in either direction, backing up, walking, trotting, and downward transitions. After that, lessons inch toward more complicated moves. They also teach young ones how to train a horse. In addition, there are camps, clinics, and competitions to explore.

Football

FRIDAY NIGHT LIGHTS, LOS ALAMITOS
(562) 756-5307
www.losalfnl.com
This popular youth flag football league was founded in 2006, and each year the waiting list grows for boys and girls in kindergarten through eighth grade, who are interested in playing high quality, fun flag football. Typically each team has one practice a week in an area park, then teams come together Friday night at Oak Middle School in Los Alamitos to compete against one another. Friday Night Lights has both a fall and spring league with online registration taking place May 1 for the fall and November 1 for the spring. Local food trucks, such as In-N-Out Burger, are on hand to feed hungry spectators, and there is also a coffee truck and snack shack.

Surfing

CORKY CARROLL'S SURF SCHOOL, HUNTINGTON BEACH
(714) 969-3959
www.surfschool.net
Every Southern California kid takes to the waves at one time or another atop a surfboard. Because no one should ever underestimate the power of the ocean, instructions are always wise for beginner surfers. Corky Carroll offers private and group lessons as well as summer camp for the fledgling surfer. All programs, which are offered May to October, include the use of wetsuits and surfboards plus one-on-one coaching and supervision.

Tennis

YOUTH LEAGUE TENNIS
(818) 347-1898
www.youthleaguetennis.org
Youth League Tennis is a non-profit public benefit charitable 501 (c) 3 organization that was developed by Laura Berstein Kissirer, a former Wimbledon player.

This public league is designed for children ages 7 to 14 with a goal of playing high school tennis. Players are matched with opponents equal to their skill level in an organized, social setting. Teamwork and sportsmanship are key, and kids develop a sense of self esteem on the court.

SEASONAL AND ANNUAL EVENTS

DISNEY ON ICE
disney.go.com/disneyonice
Like clockwork, Disney on Ice manages to stage a new and different show each and every year. Orange County is always a stop for the princes, princesses, and other Disney characters starring in the production. Usually, Disney on Ice takes place at the Honda Center in Anaheim not far from, of course, Disneyland. Dates vary.

FASHION ISLAND TREE LIGHTING CEREMONY
401 Newport Center Dr., Newport Beach
(949) 721-2000
www.shopfashionisland.com
A tree lighting ceremony isn't typically a huge event, but at Fashion Island, Orange County's premier shopping destination, it's quite an extravaganza. For starters, Fashion Island usually manages to find the largest tree on the globe and adorns it in designer fashion with enormous baubles, bulbs, and tinsel. As part of the annual illumination, the arrival of Santa sends shrieks through the audience of young shoppers. The ceremony usually takes place the weekend before Thanksgiving near Bloomingdale's.

FESTIVAL OF CHILDREN AT SOUTH COAST PLAZA
3333 Bristol St., Costa Mesa
(800) 782-8888
www.southcoastplaza.com

This month-long event, which takes place during September, features an array of celebrity appearances, activities, workshops, crafts, musicals, and cultural performances. There is something taking place just about every day, including skateboard demonstrations, ceramic painting, art exhibits, and much more. In addition, the festival invites dozens of children's charities to participate by showcasing their work on behalf of children within the Orange County community.

GLORY OF CHRISTMAS
13280 Chapman Ave., Garden Grove
(714) 544-5679
www.crystalcathedral.org
Celebrating the season is this month-long pageant in December and January that blends Christmas carols, flying angels, and live animals as the nativity unfolds. The London Symphony Orchestra provides the pre-recorded music with live solo performances by both adults and children. Staged within the confines of Crystal Cathedral, a stunning all-glass, iconic structure, Glory of Christmas has grown into one of the area's most anticipated events.

RINGLING BROTHERS CIRCUS
www.ringling.com
Every summer this classic circus makes its way to The OC and puts on a dazzling and different show each year. A timeless tradition for kids of all ages, Ringling Brothers still has a ringmaster orchestrating the acts as well as elephants, tigers, and other animals. There are tightrope acts, countless clowns, daredevil stunts, and more. For the past several years the circus has called the Honda Center home.

SHOPPING

Orange County may not have invented shopping, but it sure has perfected it. In fact, shopping in The OC has been elevated to an art form. Two of Southern California's most idyllic shopping destinations, South Coast Plaza and Fashion Island, are located in Orange County and both manage to lure Angelenos down the 405 Freeway and across the county line. And, while there are some shopping areas, such as Laguna Beach and Old Towne Orange, that really have a "downtown" shopping vibe, most Orange County shoppers are bona fide mall rats, which is a good thing considering all the one-stop indoor and outdoor shopping destinations available.

This chapter has been broken down into categories, ranging from malls and lifestyle centers to cities with actual shopping destinations. We've also provided a roundup of specialty shops, such as jewelry stores, gourmet markets, and places to prowl for discarded treasures. A list of weekly farmers' markets, where local growers gather to offer the freshest fruits, vegetables, and seafood, is also included.

As the world continues to homogenize its selection of retailers you will find many of the usual suspects in Orange County. There are several Nordstrom, Macy's, Sears, JCPenney, and Target stores all within OC's boundaries. South Coast Plaza is one of two Orange County centers with a Saks Fifth Avenue (the Shops at Mission Viejo is other). Fashion Island has bragging rights to the county's sole Neiman Marcus, but South Coast Plaza and Fashion Island, just miles apart, each house a Bloomingdale's (Fashion Island also has a Bloomingdale's Home Store). Sadly, few independent booksellers or hardware stores have survived the arrival of Barnes & Noble, Borders, Home Depot, or Lowe's—all have several Orange County locations—but there are a some exceptions to that rule such as Coast Hardware in Laguna Beach, which is an old-fashioned emporium carrying all sorts of wares, and Martha's Bookstore on Balboa Island. Williams-Sonoma, Sur La Table, Anthropologie, Gymboree, Pottery Barn, Pottery Barn Kids, and many other well-known specialty stores are also found in Orange County.

Typical hours for regional malls are Monday through Friday from 10 a.m. to 9 p.m. (most department stores remain open until 9:30 p.m.), Saturday 10 a.m. to 7 p.m., and Sunday 11 a.m. to 6 p.m. Target, Home Depot, Lowe's, Barnes & Noble, and Borders tend to have more extended hours. Most stores will accept major credit cards (be prepared to show picture I.D.), debit cards, and personal checks, excluding out-of-state checks.

Major supermarkets include Ralph's, Vons, Vons Pavilions, Albertsons, and Stater Bros. Whole Foods stocks its shelves with mostly organic items, while Bristol Farms and Gelson's are two upscale markets specializing in grab and go gourmet foods as well as neatly stocked shelves offering pâtés and farm fresh eggs coupled with in-store fromageries, coffee bars, wine cellars, and other Euro-style influences.

MAJOR, ONE-STOP SHOPPING DESTINATIONS

As biased as this sounds, some of the best lifestyle centers (the new buzzword replacing the term "mall") are located in the south part of the county.

South Coast Plaza (www.southcoastplaza .com), located at Bristol Avenue and the 405 Freeway in Santa Ana on the Costa Mesa border, is comprised of two wings connected by a graceful bridge rising over Bear Street. The larger of the two buildings is the original mall and has several wings with stores scattered across two floors with a third floor near Nordstrom. Major department stores include Nordstrom, Saks Fifth Avenue, Bloomingdale's, Macy's (plus a separate Macy's Men Store), and Sears, as well as several high-end specialty stores including Jo Malone, Jimmy Choo, Max Mara, and Louis Vuitton, plus mainstream shops such as Lady Footlocker, Ann Taylor, Aveda, and Victoria's Secret. This side of the mall also has many dining options, from the casual Claim Jumper to the very upscale Moderne Marche; however, there is no central food court as the restaurants and eating options are dispersed throughout and also found in freestanding buildings outside the center. At the other end of the bridge is the smaller, gallery-style center that is part of the South Coast Plaza complex. Many of the stores, but not all, are home furnishing shops that include a two-story Pottery Barn and neighboring Crate & Barrel plus Restoration Hardware, Sur La Table, Z Gallerie, and a decent size, triple-story Macy's Home Store. Adding to the tenant mix is a two-story Borders, an upscale paperie, an Apple store, and other specialty shops. The third floor has a collection of shops including Sports Chalet and H&M. Again, this smaller annex has no central food court but does offer a handful of dining options including Champagne French Bakery, Ruby's Diner, Pacific Whey Co., and Wahoo's Fish Tacos. Both buildings have carousels for little shoppers to ride with the merry-go-round at the larger venue being much grander.

Across the street from South Coast Plaza along Sunflower Street is the al fresco **South Coast Village,** also part of this shopping compound and home to just a handful of shops and casual-to-elegant restaurants, and **Metro Pointe at South Coast** (www.metropointe .com), an outdoor esplanade containing mostly discounted or affordable retailers spanning two levels. Stores include Nordstrom Rack, Loehmann's, Marshall's, Barnes & Noble, David's Bridal, the Container Store, and several other shops and kiosks, and there are also casual dining options and a movie theater.

Moving closer to the ocean towards Newport Beach is **Fashion Island** (www.shopfashion island.com), which often appeared in the now defunct TV series *The OC.* This near-perfect, open-air shopping center, which is more than 40 years old but, like most of its clientele, has held up remarkably well, is slated to begin a major multi-million-dollar makeover that will result in a more Old-World feel with Italian-inspired fountains, faux cobblestones, and vintage street lamps with a European flair. An additional 150,000 square feet of retail space coupled with enhanced patio seating and a collection of intimate cafes will also be part of the "extreme shopping center makeover." The project, slated for completion in late 2011, will include a new 140,000-square-foot Nordstrom opening this year, but additional shops, such as Michael Stars, True Religion, and Seven for All Mankind, will open along with the West Coast flagship store of Dean and DeLuca, the purveyor of gourmet foods. Longtime tenants include Bloomingdale's, Bloomingdale's Home Store, Neiman Marcus, Anthropologie, Z Gallerie, Sony, J. Jill, and many others. Fashion Island also offers several dining options, including quick service eateries on the basement level of the multi-story indoor atrium, as well as a California Pizza Kitchen, Cheesecake Factory, and PF Chang's all clustered together. You'll also find a Yard House and a Daily Grill tucked away near Bloomingdale's plus a freestanding El Torito. Fashion Island has a carousel and kiddie train, too, which for now remain in place but may be removed permanently as part of the renovation.

Inspired by the world-famous Alhambra, the 13th-century citadel overlooking Granada, Spain, is the **Irvine Spectrum** (71 Fortune Drive, www.shopirvinespectrum.com). It is an outdoor shopping center that began mostly as an entertainment and dining venue a little more than a decade ago but reinvented itself by adding more retail options and expanding the property. In addition to many restaurants—Yard House, PF Chang's, Cheesecake Factory, and others—this open-air marketplace also contains a Nordstrom, Target, Barnes & Noble, Anthropologie, and a collection of specialty stores. There is also an entertainment component that includes the Improv, a stop for touring comedians, a multiplex theater, and a giant Ferris wheel that can be seen from the freeway. Punctuating the many pathways are dancing fountains and various performers who entertain shoppers on weekends.

It goes without saying that South Coast Plaza and Fashion Island are ranked neck and neck for the title of Orange County's Best Places to Shop with the Irvine Spectrum placing third, but there are also a handful of regional malls that, while they might not be considered shopping destinations, offer convenience for those living nearby. **Bella Terra** (7777 Edinger Ave., www.bellaterra-hb.com), located in an inland area of Huntington Beach at the Beach Boulevard exit off the 405 Freeway, is a Tuscan-themed outdoor center with a main plot for shopping and entertainment plus several dining pads and an adjacent shopping annex that includes the Cheesecake Factory and Barnes & Noble. Cobbled pathways trail towards an outdoor amphitheatre surrounded by restaurants and a multi-screen theater. Major retailers include Kohl's, REI, Cost Plus World Market, and a number of other specialized shops. Live entertainment can be enjoyed most weekends and is usually staged at the amphitheatre. **Brea Mall,** located in the northernmost part of the county, has a Nordstrom, Macy's, Sears, and JCPenney plus more than 175 specialty shops that include a mix of high-end retailers, Michael Kors and Coach

among them, as well as more middle of the road shops like Williams-Sonoma, Pottery Barn, and MAC. There is also a Glen Ivy Day Spa featuring a full menu of head-to-toe services. Dotted around the mall's perimeter are several restaurants, including a BJ's Brewery, Cheesecake Factory, and Olive Garden, plus an Embassy Suites located adjacent to the north side parking lot.

In Orange County's midsection, not far from Disneyland or Anaheim Stadium, is **Westfield Mainplace** at 2800 North Main St. in Santa Ana (www.westfield.com/mainplace) featuring 200-plus sensible retailers, such as Forever 21 and Gymboree, plus a quartet of anchors that includes Nordstrom and Macy's. There is a central food court with everything from burritos to corn dogs plus a couple of sit-down restaurants, an enclosed play area for kids on the lower level, and a discount movie theater. At the southern end of the county is **The Shops at Mission Viejo** just off the 405 Freeway in Mission Viejo—not far from the San Diego County line. While there are no retail surprises—Nordstrom, Saks Fifth Avenue, Pottery Barn, Williams-Sonoma, and a host of other national treasures—one thing that really sets The Shops at Mission Viejo apart is its level of service. The mall opens daily at 7 a.m. so local citizens can walk with a purpose and enjoy a safe and brisk workout. There is also free Wi-Fi for companions who tag along but don't have a penchant for shopping but can still multi-task. Add to the mix special parking for expectant mothers and a soft play area for children. But it's the pair of Lullaby Lounges, a place for mamas and their babies and young children, that takes on the feel of a cozy living room where mothers can feed their children, use the baby-changing tables (supplies are available for purchase if need be), take a potty break (there's a pint-sized potty for those in training), lounge on sinkable chairs and couches under soft lighting to create a calming effect for little ones, and watch kid-friendly shows on the flat-screen television. Considering shopping is mostly a female-dominated sport, perhaps this trend of nurturing mothers and their offspring will catch on elsewhere.

OFF-THE-BEATEN PATH SHOPPING

If South Coast Plaza and Fashion Island are the shopping meccas of Orange County, then places such as Corona del Mar Plaza and Crystal Cove Promenade are the anti-behemoths. Both are extremely upscale, but are not considered shopping destinations. They were built more as a convenience for the neighborhoods in which they're located. **Corona del Mar Plaza** (www .shoptheirvinecompany.com), located at 800 Avocado Ave. near Fashion Island and adjacent to Corona del Mar, features a tony enclave of shops and restaurants including Bikini, Brighton Collectibles, Sur La Table, Bristol Farms, and Sprinkles Cupcakes, just to name a few, with Gulfstream Restaurant and Tommy Bahama's Island Grille for dining. **Crystal Cove Promenade,** located between Corona del Mar and Laguna Beach at 7772 Pacific Coast Hwy. near Newport Coast, has a similar feel and tenant mix if you swap out Sur La Table for Williams-Sonoma and switch Bristol Farms with Trader Joe's. Other stores include an Ann Taylor Loft, At Ease, and Gap plus dining, such as Mastro's Ocean Club and Javier's Cantina & Grill. The best part of shopping here is the ocean view.

Moving inland is **The District at Tustin Legacy,** a new shopping and entertainment center spanning one million square feet with a mix of restaurants and retailers, such as Costco, Target, Lowe's, and Home Goods plus several restaurants including Lucille's Smokehouse Bar-B-Que, Marmalade Café, and The Winery Restaurant & Wine Bar. It's also a pet-friendly place, so dogs on leashes can enjoy the outdoor ambiance. The District also has an AMC Movie Theater and hip bowling alley. **The Lab** (www.thelab.com), which bills itself as the anti-mall, is located in Costa Mesa at 2930 Bristol St. Urban Outfitters is the only chain store located here with the other handful of retailers making their mark with cutting-edge street apparel. The culinary arts are represented with a Cuban restaurant and a sushi bar plus the bohemian Gypsy Den Café and Reading Room, featuring a menu of soup and sandwiches. **The**

Camp, located down the road from The Lab at 2937 Bristol St. in Costa Mesa, is another innovative retail compound pulling at the purse strings of shoppers who enjoy an active lifestyle. Stores include Patagonia, a store for cycling enthusiasts, a vegan restaurant, Milk + Honey featuring organic coffee, and a Bikram yoga center where yogis flex in 110-degree heat. There are a handful of other shops and restaurants, too.

The Block at Orange (www.theblockat orange.com) is a hybrid of shops, themed dining, outlet stores, and entertainment. Located at 20 City Blvd. in Orange, just off the 22 Freeway at City Drive, this sprawling outdoor center keeps its finger on the pulse of OC's youth by having the area's only Vans Skatepark plus a few retailers, such as G By Guess, that appeal to a certain adolescent age group. Adults like The Block because of the outlet shopping, from the Nike Factory Store and Off 5th (Saks Fifth Avenue's outlet) to Nieman Marcus Last Call and Hollister. The Block also has many non-discount retailers plus a slew of restaurants located inside the center and in freestanding buildings that surround it. There is also a Burkes-Williams Day Spa, Lucky Strike Lanes for bowling, and a Cohiba Cigar Lounge plus an AMC movie theater.

> **i** Homes on Balboa Island are worth millions—even the small, inland homes—but original lots on this manmade 1.71-mile-long island, which was dredged and filled before World War I, sold for a mere $250. The traditional Christmas Boat Parade began in 1908, and celebrities, such as Errol Flynn, Mae West, and Shirley Temple, all moored their yachts in the adjacent harbor.

NEIGHBORHOOD SHOPPING

If you want to avoid the typical mall scene, Orange County has some enjoyable "downtown" areas that make for a wonderful afternoon. Along the coast there is **Seal Beach,** which abuts the Los Angeles County line near Long Beach. Its Main

Street, off Pacific Coast Highway, oozes charm and has managed to keep a small town flavor by supporting local retailers and restaurateurs. The tidy blocks are filled with antiques stores, souvenir shops, day spas, clothing boutiques, and other treasure-filled storefronts coupled with a handful of pubs, wine bars, coffee houses, and Walt's Wharf, one of the area's best seafood restaurants. Up the road is **Huntington Beach,** whose Main Street is populated with surf shops, pubs, and sidewalk cafes. At the corner of Main and Pacific Coast Highway is a Hurley store and Jack's Surfboard shop. Continuing along Pacific Coast Highway in Newport Beach is Balboa Island, which you can access from Pacific Coast Highway by turning right onto Jamboree Road, and traveling a few feet down the hill and across the two-lane bridge that takes you onto the island itself. Parking on Balboa Island can be a nightmare, so be patient. Marine Avenue is where the village area is located and is filled with home stores, clothing boutiques, ice cream kiosks, art galleries, and restaurants. The only real commercial venue on the island is a single Starbucks; otherwise, most of the shops and restaurants are individually owned. Heading back to Pacific Coast Highway and to the right is the village of **Corona del Mar** with shops and some very good restaurants on either side of the street. At one end is Oysters and at the other is Five Crowns with Sherman Library and Gardens located in between. Down the road is **Laguna Beach,** where you'll find Gallery Row along the 300 to 500 blocks of Pacific Coast Highway, shops scattered around Forest Avenue and neighboring streets, and delightful restaurants at every turn. A few notable stores are Fiori, specializing in fine Italian and Greek Majolica dinnerware and accessories, and **Sherwood Gallery** for its unconventional approach to art. Further south in **San Clemente** is an enchanting two-block shopping district along Del Mar with storefronts sporting antiques, clothing, home goods, and restaurants.

The inland towns of Orange and Fullerton also have charming downtown areas. The **Orange Circle** and its Plaza look just about the same as they did some 80 years ago. The circle and its four spokes, which are created by Glassell and Chapman Avenues, are packed with antiques shops, gastropubs, home stores, sidewalk cafes, tea houses, and restaurants. Watsons, a century-old drugstore, offers a side of nostalgia with its original soda fountain that still serves up a mean chocolate shake made by hand. Harbor Boulevard cuts a swath through **Downtown Fullerton** where the bulk of the action is located between Chapman and Commonwealth Avenues as well as along neighboring streets. There are a lot of vintage clothing stores, antiques shops, casual to upscale restaurants, pubs, and a lively nightlife scene.

Downtown Disney

Designed like a faux town and leading to the gates of Disneyland and California Adventure, Downtown Disney (www.downtowndisney.com) strikes a nice balance with children and adults. There are a number of shops, such as Kitson Kids, Build-A-Bear Workshop, World of Disney, and LEGO, that appeal to children, while Quiksilver and Roxy, Sephora, and many of the restaurants will please parents. There is also a movie theater and usually some sort of entertainment element at play. On summer evenings Downtown Disney is a great destination to watch Disney's fireworks show and it costs absolutely nothing to do so.

FARMERS' MARKETS

The ultimate place for organic fruits and vegetables, fresh-picked flowers, and other homegrown goods is the local farmers' market. Most every community hosts a weekly market either in a parking lot or on city streets that are cordoned off. A few tips: bring your own paper or canvas bags; most vendors accept cash only; shop the various stalls before making a purchase because prices and quality can vary; and don't be afraid to ask for a sample to test for flavor and freshness. California certified farmers' markets have their participating vendors inspected by the county agricultural commissioner to ensure that they actually grow the products they're selling. You can visit the Orange County Certified Farmers' Market Web site at http://orange.cfbf.com/cfm.htm. Farmers' markets are open rain or shine, year-round unless otherwise noted. The following markets are arranged by day of the week, then in alphabetical order by city.

Tuesday

Brea
BREA BOULEVARD AND BIRCH STREET
4 p.m. to 8 p.m.

Irvine
HISTORIC PARK AT THE IRVINE RANCH
13042 Old Myford Rd.
9 a.m. to 1 p.m.

Wednesday

Fullerton
INDEPENDENCE PARK
801 West Valencia Dr.
8 a.m. to 1:30 p.m.

Tustin
Corner of El Camino Real and 3rd Street
9 a.m. to 1 p.m.

Westminster
WESTMINSTER MALL, GOLDENWEST AND BOLSA
Adjacent to Target Store
12 p.m. to 5 p.m.

Thursday

Costa Mesa
ORANGE COUNTY FAIRGROUNDS
88 Fair Dr.
9 a.m. to 1 p.m. (rain or shine)

Downtown Anaheim
CENTER STREET PROMENADE AND LEMON AVENUE
12 p.m. to 8 p.m.

Fullerton
100 BLOCK OF EAST WILSHIRE BETWEEN POMONA AND HARBOR BOULEVARD
4 p.m. to 8:30 p.m.

Orange
THE VILLAGE AT ORANGE
1500 East Village Way between Katella and Lincoln on Tustin Street
9 a.m. to 1 p.m.

Friday

Anaheim
KAISER PERMANENTE, LAKEVIEW AND RIVERDALE
10 a.m. to 2 p.m.

Huntington Beach
PIER PLAZA
Main Street and Pacific Coast Highway (next to the pier)
1 p.m. to 5 p.m.

Laguna Hills
LAGUNA HILLS MALL PARKING LOT
The 5 Freeway and El Toro Road
9 a.m. to 1 p.m.

Saturday

Buena Park
BUENA PARK MALL
Sears Lot 8308 on the Mall
9 a.m. to 2 p.m.

Corona del Mar
MARGUARITE AND PACIFIC COAST HIGHWAY
10 a.m. to 1 p.m.

Dana Point
PACIFIC COAST HIGHWAY AND GOLDEN LANTERN
9 a.m. to 1 p.m.

🔍 Close-up

LA's Fashion District

Orange County doesn't really have a discount district. Of course, you'll find places like TJ Maxx and Marshall's, but you won't find any outlet malls to speak of. If you want to venture into Los Angeles you can shop for designer clothes at close to wholesale prices at the Fashion District (www.fashiondistrict.com). Located in downtown Los Angeles, this 90-block area is bounded by 7th Street to the north, Santa Monica Freeway to the south, Spring and Main Streets to the west, and San Pedro Street to the east. It's every man and woman for themselves amidst this bargain hunters' paradise where you'll find some 1,000 stores selling to the general public for a fraction of what you would pay at department stores. Retailers in this area are independent, so you'll find unique items that you're not likely to find at the mall and the overhead is low, which trickles down to the price tag. Shoppers can expect to save 30 to 70 percent off retail prices on apparel and accessories for the entire family, plus textiles and fresh flowers. Saturday tends to be the district's busiest day of the week for those sleuthing to make a deal and many wholesale-only stores will open their doors to the general public. Santee Alley, a pedestrian-only breezeway, has the feel of a bazaar and it is perfectly acceptable to haggle for a better price here and throughout the entire Fashion District. Specific days are marked for sample sales, which are held monthly in participating showrooms in the California Market Center, Cooper Design Space, Gerry Building, and The New Mart. These buildings are all located near the intersection of 9th and Los Angeles Streets. Serious shoppers should enlist the services of Urban Shopping Adventures (213-683-9715, www.urbanshoppingadventures .com), which offers owner-led, custom walking tours of the Fashion District. Treks last about three hours and include some additional discounts that can only be obtained by tour goers. If you are in the market for a wedding dress, then Urban Shopping Adventures will deliver you to the doorstep of discount bridal shops. If you're into quilting, Urban Shopping Adventures will escort you to the best textile manufacturers. Whatever you're looking for, a tour can be created specifically for you. Let the hunt begin! Rates start at $36 per person with upgrades that include lunch or shuttle transportation.

Irvine

IRVINE CENTER
On the corner of Bridge and Campus (across from UCI)
8 a.m. to Noon

Laguna Beach

LUMBERYARD PARKING LOT NEXT TO THE CITY HALL
8 a.m. to Noon; 8 to 11 a.m. in July and August

Sunday

Laguna Niguel

PLAZA DE LA PAZ SHOPPING CENTER
On the Corner of La Paz and Pacific Park
9 a.m. to 1 p.m.

GARDEN SHOPS

ROGER'S GARDENS
2301 San Joaquin Hills Rd., Corona del Mar (Newport Beach)
(949) 640-5800
www.rogersgardens.com

Calling Roger's Gardens a garden shop is like calling the food halls at Harrod's in London a grocery store. It's so much more that the title doesn't do it justice. Situated on nearly eight acres filled with flowers, shrubs, and plants plus rooms of art, antiques, gourmet food, and linens, a trip to Roger's Gardens will ignite your creative and horticultural side. It's especially enjoyable at Christmas when the staff really deck the halls and then some. Throughout the year the shop hosts seminars and workshops, too.

GOURMET SHOPS

Two gourmet markets, which have locations throughout Southern California including Orange County, are **Bristol Farms** at 810 Avocado Ave. in Corona del Mar/Newport Beach (949-760-6514, www.bristolfarms.com) and **Gelson's** (www.gel sons.com) with three OC locations in Dana Point, Irvine, and Newport Beach. **Trader Joe's** (www .traderjoes.com), a reasonably priced market that sells gourmet foods under its own label but produced by some of the most respected purveyors, is located throughout Orange County and has an incredible selection of foods. The following are some independently owned gourmet stores.

FROG'S BREATH CHEESE STORE
143 North Glassell St., Orange
(714) 744-1773
www.frogsbreathcheese.com
This aromatic fromagerie carries a large selection of gourmet cut-to-order specialty cheeses plus aged prosciutto, artisan salami, vinegars, olive oils, cheese condiments, and much more. There is also an impressive and extensive salt bar with grains from around the world, from Sel Gris to Black Lava. The store offers wine and cheese tastings and a Cheese of the Month Club.

LUCCI'S
8991 Adams Ave., Huntington Beach
(714) 968-4466
www.luccisdeli.com
From the outside this Italian specialty foods store looks like just another storefront tucked inside a bland strip mall, but Lucci's is the go-to place for authentic Italian ingredients and features a deli, market, and bakery. Serving Southern California since 1946, Lucci's has an abundance of heat and eat items, a deli stocked with more than three dozen varieties of meat and cheese, and a bakery filled with fresh cannoli, breads, and more.

PARIS IN A CUP
119 South Glassell St., Orange
(714) 538-9411
www.parisinacup.com
Why schlep to Paris when you can shop for French items at this enchanting boutique where shelves are neatly stocked with fig jams and lemon curd. After you've had a chance to look around, stay for a proper tea featuring finger sandwiches, salads, and pastries.

SAPPHIRE PANTRY
1200 South Coast Hwy., Laguna Beach
(949) 715-9889
www.sapphirellc.com
Looking as if it were ripped from the streets of some European village, the Sapphire Pantry, an annex of the popular Sapphire restaurant located next store, is a haven for gourmands in search of the best culinary treats. There are more than 100 varieties of artisan cheeses, flaky croissants, Arabica coffee beans roasted to perfection, Italian and Spanish meats, and savory grab and go sandwiches.

Orange County Marketplace

Located at the Orange County Fairgrounds (88 Fair Dr., Costa Mesa) and open every weekend, Saturday and Sunday from 7 a.m. to 4 p.m., except when the fair is underway during July, the Orange County Marketplace is one of the county's premier swap meets with more than 1,100 merchants, some with multiple stalls, and 4 miles of aisles. You'll find everything from decorative flags and name brand perfumes to houseplants, hair care products, and handmade furniture. There is plenty of free parking, food kiosks, and clean restrooms. Admission is a modest $2 and kids 12 and under are free.

ZINC CAFÉ & MARKET
350 Ocean Ave., Laguna Beach
(949) 494-6302
www.zinccafe.com
This Laguna Beach institution has a loyal following. You can grab a seat at one of the few umbrella-shaded tables, or load up a market bag with an array of pantry favorites to enjoy at home, from salts and homemade marshmallows to an abundance of prepared foods displayed in cold cases that require nothing more than a few minutes in the oven. While you're waiting for everything to be boxed up (they also offer local delivery) enjoy an oversized and frothy cappuccino.

JEWELERS

LEFT TURN JEWELRY
305 Forest Ave., Laguna Beach
(866) 954-5338
www.leftturnjewelry.com
We all know and love Tiffany, Harry Winston, Cartier, and Van Cleef & Arpels and, not surprisingly, all these gems of jewelers are located at South Coast Plaza. But for something with even more bling, OC residents turn to designer and visionary Judy Klimek at Left Turn Jewelry for one-of-a-kind creations, from necklaces and earrings to bracelets. And once a piece has been sold it's gone forever because each design is a work of art with no two pieces alike.

ANNUAL EVENTS

If there was ever a place to celebrate, regardless of the occasion, it's Orange County. From old-fashioned fairs and culinary gatherings to surf competitions and feting whales, there is an event, party, gathering, or soiree to pencil in on the calendar. Most of the events are not newsworthy, at least not on the national front, but they are certainly of importance and highly anticipated by those who live in The OC.

There are ethnic celebrations, annual tours of art studios, parades that take place on land and on water, and marathons that attract runners from around the globe. These listings include events that happen each and every year. Some are held on a single day, but most, like the Sawdust Festival in Laguna Beach, continue for several days or even weeks. While Orange County has enough gatherings to fill an entire calendar and then some, we've included some worthy events in neighboring counties that can easily be reached within a day.

This list is meant to serve as a resource but, as with anything, dates and times can change. And events, even if they've been ongoing for years, can even be cancelled due to lack of funds or interest. Both the *Orange County Register* (www.ocregister.com) and *Los Angeles Times* (www.latimes.com) have weekly entertainment guides that publish on Friday and are also available online. You can also check with the different convention and visitors bureaus (see the Daytrips chapter for information) to confirm that an event is taking place. *OC Weekly* (www.ocweekly.com) and *LA Weekly* (www.laweekly.com), both tabloid-size, cutting-edge publications distributed weekly for free in newstands, are also good sources for local happenings.

Events are listed by month in alphabetical order. Call to confirm dates and admission prices.

JANUARY

THE ANNUAL TOURNAMENT OF ROSES PARADE
Colorado Ave., Pasadena
(626) 419-ROSE
www.tournamentofroses.com
Held on New Year's Day, unless January 1 happens to land on a Sunday in which case the parade takes place on January 2, the Rose Parade features the pageantry and tradition of floral floats, high-stepping equestrians, and marching bands from across the United States. You can either purchase tickets for bleacher seats or watch for free curbside along Colorado Boulevard.

WHALE WATCHING EXCURSIONS
Dana Wharf, Dana Point
(800) 590-9994

Thar she blows—at least from now through April, hundreds of migrating California gray whales make their way from the chilly Arctic seas to the warm waters of Baja, Mexico. Daily excursions leave from Dana Wharf in Dana Point and passengers take to the high seas in search of these magnificent creatures.

FEBRUARY

CHINESE NEW YEAR PARADE
Chinatown, Los Angeles
(213) 617-0396
www.lagoldendragonparade.com
Hosted by the Chinese Chamber of Commerce of Los Angeles, this annual parade has been going strong for more than a century. Typically taking place the third weekend of February, spectators are treated to a tapestry of floats, march-

ing bands, dignitaries, entertainers, and cultural groups. The Chinese New Year Lunar Festival coincides with the parade.

QUEEN MARY SCOTTISH FESTIVAL
1126 Queens Hwy., Long Beach
(562) 435-3511
www.queenmary.com
Held during Presidents Day Weekend, this two-day event celebrates the Scottish culture with haggis, highland dancing, bagpipes, and a proud display of tartan plaid. A self-guided tour of the *Queen Mary*, which was built along Scotland's River Clyde, is included in the price of admission.

SURF CITY USA HALF-MARATHON
Huntington Beach
(888) 422-0RUN (0786)
www.runsurfcity.com
This is the perfect launching pad for March's LA Marathon. Held on Super Bowl Sunday, but with plenty of time to catch the game, this Huntington Beach happening includes live surf bands, a beer garden, Super Bowl parties, and a course that runs along the coast. A beachside expo and barbecue takes place on Friday and Saturday before the race.

TẾT FESTIVAL
Garden Grove Park
9301 Westminster Ave., Garden Grove
(714) 890-1418
www.tetfestival.org
Hosted by the Union of Vietnamese Student Associations, the annual Tết Festival, held mid-month, ushers in the Lunar New Year marking the start of spring and one of the most observed Vietnamese holidays. Those who flock to the Tết Festival are treated to cultural customs, ceremonies, and an array of traditional Vietnamese foods.

MARCH

FESTIVAL OF WHALES
Dana Point Harbor, Dana Point
(949) 472-7888

Cali Holidays

California observes the following holidays, which result in the closure of banks, government offices (including the post office), and public schools.

New Year's Day: January 1

Martin Luther King Jr. Day: The third Monday in January

Presidents Day: The third Monday in February

Caesar Chavez Day: March 31

Easter Sunday: March or April

Memorial Day: The last Monday in May

Independence Day: July 4

Labor Day: The first Monday in September

Veterans Day: November 11

Thanksgiving: The last Thursday of November

Christmas: December 25

As the mighty gray whale makes its way from the cold Arctic climate to the warm waters of Mexico, Dana Point celebrates the magnificent beast's migration with a street festival plus food, entertainment, arts and crafts, and more than 100 vendors. Things get underway the first weekend in March.

LA MARATHON
www.lamarathon.com
Thousands of runners take to the streets of Los Angeles for this stadium to sea, 26-mile marathon that takes two-legged competitors past city landmarks, interesting neighborhoods, and on to the finish line. A pre-race expo is held the Friday and Saturday prior to the race and there is a party at the finish line for racers.

RETURN OF THE SWALLOWS
Mission San Juan Capistrano
Ortega Highway and Camino Capistrano, San
Juan Capistrano
(949) 248-2048
www.missionsjc.com
The romance and folklore of this breathtaking mission present themselves every March with the return of the swallows. Legend has it that the birds originally sought sanctuary at the mission from an innkeeper who destroyed their nests elsewhere. They supposedly return each year at the same time so their young can nest safely within the confines of the mission walls. The annual Swallows Festival celebrates their homecoming with live music, community presentations, live performances, the ringing of the mission's historic bells, food, fun, and dance.

SIERRA MADRE WISTERIA FESTIVAL
North Baldwin Avenue and East Montecito
Avenue, Sierra Madre
(626) 355-5111
www.sierramadrewisteriafestival.com
In 1894 the Brugmans of Sierra Madre purchased a wisteria from nearby Wilson Nursery for 75 cents. The vine has been flourishing ever since with 1.5 million lavender blossoms weighing 250 tons. It spans more than one acre in size with 500-foot branches and 40 blossoms per square foot. *Guinness Book of World Records* recognized it as the largest blooming plant in the world, and it was named one of the seven horticultural wonders of the world along with the gardens at Buckingham Palace and the gardens at Taj Mahal. Every March the town heralds its iconic vine with an art and garden fair heralds includes 150 juried artisans, live music in six locations, and food booths.

APRIL

LOS ANGELES TIMES FESTIVAL OF BOOKS
UCLA, Westwood
405 Hilgard Ave.
(213) 237-5000
www.latimes.com
This two-day outdoor event takes place on the UCLA campus in the Westwood neighborhood of Los Angeles and is absolutely free. Begun in 1996 with a goal to unite authors and publishers with book lovers, the event has grown to be one of the most prestigious literary gatherings in the country. Authors from all genres, be it celebrity chefs who have penned a best selling cookbook or a well-known author hitting the publicity trail, are on hand for readings, book signing, lectures, and more. In past years the likes of Julie Andrews, Maria Shriver, and many others have made appearances. An entire section is strictly for children who enjoy reading or being read to, and roaming characters, live entertainment, and book signings abound for little ones as well.

RAMONA PAGEANT
Ramona Bowl
26400 Ramona Bowl Rd., Hemet (Riverside
County)
(800) 645-4465
www.ramonabowl.com
Since 1923 Helen Hunt Jackson's classic novel *Ramona* has been brought to life at the annual Ramona Pageant in the town of Hemet. Staged in the historic Ramona Bowl, a California State Landmark, the canyon setting and hillside provide the backdrop to a poignant love story that unfolds between Ramona and her Indian hero. The cast, which includes more than 400 adults and children, is a sellout each year.

**SANTA BARBARA COUNTY
VINTNERS' FESTIVAL**
(805) 688-0881
www.sbcountywines.com
Held in early April on the grounds of one of the celebrated wineries of Santa Barbara County, this long weekend lingers with activities that include special winery events and a Vintner's Visa, which allows you access to the plethora of tasting rooms. The festival itself will appeal to the most discriminating gourmand with a selection of fine wines, sumptuous food, live music, strolling entertainment, demonstrations, and a silent auction full of prize opportunities.

TOYOTA GRAND PRIX OF LONG BEACH
The streets of Downtown Long Beach
Ocean Avenue and Shoreline Drive
(562) 981-2600
www.gplb.com
Located just over the county line in downtown Long Beach, the Toyota Grand Prix is an exciting three-day event held mid-April and featuring revved up NASCAR action. One day is dedicated to the qualifying races, another is earmarked for celebrities to go fender-to-fender to the finish line, and the final day is the actual race itself. What makes this race so unique, at least when it first began in 1977, is that the race actually takes place on city streets and not some designated course designed for NASCAR racing. The race includes an expo and several food outlets with bleacher seating. You can purchase tickets for the entire three days or cherry pick and attend only one day of racing.

MAY

DOHENY BLUES FESTIVAL
Doheny State Beach
25300 Dana Point Harbor Dr., Dana Point
(949) 360-7800
www.omegaevents.com
This mid-month event is a kick-off to summer with headlining musicians, various attractions, an international food court, a microbrew tasting station, and wine lounge. Bonnie Raitt, John Lee Hooker, John Fogerty, Brian Setzer, and B. B. King have all graced the stage of this two-day rockin' event. Best of all, the toe-tapping takes place on the beach.

GARDEN GROVE STRAWBERRY FESTIVAL
The Village Green
Euclid Street and Main Street, Garden Grove
(714) 638-0981
www.strawberryfestival.org
Heralding the plump and juicy strawberry is this annual and much anticipated festival held Memorial Day Weekend. This four-day event, which kicks off Friday and concludes on Monday, features a parade and countless carnival rides

as part of the celebration honoring the city's strawberry-growing history. There's entertainment, C-list celebrities, and lots of food and fun.

LAGUNA BEACH CHARM HOUSE TOUR
Laguna Beach, locations vary
(949) 472-7503
www.villagelaguna.org
Once a year Village Laguna, a non-profit group dedicated to preserving the charm and enchantment of Laguna Beach, selects five or so buildings

Grunion Runs

Grunion runs are not so much an annual event, but more of a seasonal spectacle and reason to hit the beach at night. From about March until about August, these silver fish, about 5 to 7 inches in length, appear close to the new or full moon and the runs usually hit their peak one to two nights afterwards allowing the fish to take advantage of the high tides that will carry them up the beach. These creatures become stranded on purpose and the females burrow themselves partway into the sand using their tails. In the meantime, the males cluster around the females to fertilize their eggs. The fish are then carried back to the sea by another wave and their eggs hatch two weeks later during the next high tide. The grunions run at just about every beach, including Seal Beach, Sunset Beach, Huntington Beach, Newport Beach, Laguna Beach, and San Clemente. The **Ocean Institute** (949-496-2274 or www.ocean-institute.org) in Dana Point holds a child-parent grunion night event in the summer.

of significance, from cottage-style and contemporary to oceanfront abodes, whose residents or caretakers open up their doors to the public. Those who appreciate history and architecture will certainly enjoy an afternoon of sleuthing through these vintage treasures.

SOKA UNIVERSITY'S ANNUAL INTERNATIONAL FESTIVAL
Soka University
1 University Dr., Aliso Viejo
(949) 480-4081
www.soka.edu

Held in early May on the breathtaking grounds of Soka University, this event has an abundance of international food stalls, exhibitors, games, and activities. Collectors will enjoy the art exhibition and ceramic sale, while children keep entertained with a super slide, bounce house, street painting, and a dragon race.

JUNE

MARIACHI FESTIVAL
Mission San Juan Capistrano
El Camino Real and Ortega Hwy., San Juan Capistrano
(949) 234-1321
www.missionsjc.com

It's the battle of the mariachi bands as bedecked musicians battle it out for cash prizes. The event takes place on the mission grounds in the courtyard with a full day of live musical entertainment, bilingual puppet shows, workshops hosted by Ballet Folklorica, and, of course, authentic Mexican cuisine. The mariachi band that takes first place opens up the evening's Music Under the Stars concert.

SAWDUST FESTIVAL
935 Laguna Canyon Rd., Laguna Beach
(949) 494-3030
www.sawdustartfestival.org

The makeshift village of booths and stalls is filled with an array of artwork and many artists man their own booths day after day and night after night. On display and available for purchase are original works of art including ceramics, glass, sculpture, photography, print, mixed media, watercolor and oil, furniture, clothing, and jewelry. The festival also features demo booths, hands-on art workshops, an art booth for children, refreshments, live music and more.

"Rejects Festival"

Founded in 1965 as a protest to the established Festival of Arts' jurying system, the inaugural Sawdust Festival had only a few dozen exhibitors earning it the name of "Rejects Festival" by the local press. The show must go on, but didn't in 1966; however, it returned in 1967 with great success and led to the artists moving to its established location on Laguna Canyon Road. The media named it the Sawdust Festival after artists spread sawdust on the ground to combat the dust and mud. The festival is truly a grassroots and community event where all exhibiting artists must be residents of Laguna Beach. Because the show is non-juried, amateurs feel comfortable displaying their work alongside accomplished artists, which creates an eclectic and funky mix of media. The Sawdust Festival prides itself on being more of a happening rather than a "wine and cheese" art exhibit. Music fills the air, there are daily demonstrations including the art of glass blowing, and food booths add to the ambiance. The festival runs late June to Labor Day.

TEMECULA VALLEY BALLOON AND WINE FESTIVAL
Lake Skinner Recreation Area
37701 Warren Rd., Winchester (Temecula Valley)
(909) 676-6713
www.tvbwf.com
For 25 years the Temecula Valley Balloon and Wine Festival has helped draw attention to this bucolic and winegrowing region in Riverside County. Held the first weekend in June, the event appeals to the young and old alike with 50 vibrant hot-air balloons launched in the early mornings. A wine and cheese garden features premium locally produced vintages including sparkling wines, as well as food demonstrations, pairings, and fromage samplings. There are entertainment and activities for kids and adults including a tethered balloon ride, which has you soaring 100 feet above the imbibers below.

JULY

FESTIVAL OF THE ARTS—PAGEANT OF THE MASTERS
650 Laguna Canyon Rd., Laguna Beach
(949) 494-1145
www.foapom.com
Touted as the "place where art comes to life," the Pageant of the Masters is a theatrical celebration of the art of tableaux vivants or "living pictures," in which classical and contemporary works are brought to life with real people clad in garb found in the paintings and posed to look exactly like their brush-stroked counterparts. The event takes place in an outdoor amphitheater in Laguna's canyon and includes a professional orchestra, original score, live narration, incredible set and lighting design, and a staff of hundreds of dedicated volunteers. It truly is artistry in motion. This event takes place throughout July and August.

FRENCH FESTIVAL
Oak Park at Alamar and Castillo, Santa Barbara
(805) 564-PARIS
www.frenchfestival.com

Summer Concerts

Because of Southern California's incredible weather, coastal Orange County taking first place, the summer lends itself to concerts under the stars. Most every night of the week, if you really wanted to, you could find some venue where you could spread a blanket, uncork a bottle of wine, and do a little toe-tapping by moonlight. At **Fashion Island** (949-721-2000) in Newport Beach free concerts are held on Wednesday evenings; **Huntington Beach** (714-960-3483) has Surfin' Sundays with free, live music at Pier Plaza at the foot of the pier from 1 to 4 p.m.; and in **San Clemente** on Thursday evenings free concerts are held on the beach north of the San Clemente Pier (949-361-8264). Of course, the legendary **Hollywood Bowl** in Los Angeles has an excellent roster of performers, including several performances by the LA Philharmonic, and is one of the best places to enjoy music by moonlight (www.hollywoodbowl.com).

In honor of Bastille Day, a celebration of the French Revolution, it's vive la France as Francophiles gather at Oak Park for a bit of joie de vivre. This is one of the west coast's largest French fêtes and features dozens of chefs creating French food, from crepes to begneits, plus there's beer a la France, champagne (of course!), and live entertainment on a trio of stages including cabaret, jazz, and the strains of Edith Piaf. Wandering mimes, jugglers, accordion players, and booths featuring French products are all part of this free event. *Bon vivant!*

AUGUST

OLD SPANISH DAYS
Downtown Santa Barbara
(805) 962-8101
www.oldspanishdays-fiesta.org
Old Spanish Days, sometimes referred to as Fiesta Days, is held the first weekend in August and celebrates the history, customs, and traditions of the American Indian, Spanish, Mexican, and early American settlers. There are parades, outdoor concerts, operas staged in historic churches, and a "marketplace" featuring food, Mexican crafts, art, and much more. One of the best events is the Sunday afternoon concert held on the lawn of the elegant courthouse, which marks the end of a whirlwind weekend.

STREET SCENE
East Village, Downtown San Diego
(619) 233-5008
www.street-scene.com
The Street Scene in downtown San Diego is a scene in every sense of the word. For years it was held in the historic Gaslamp Quarter, but outgrew that space a few years back and moved a few blocks east near Petco Park, where the San Diego Padres play. Held the last weekend of August, from late afternoon until midnight, Street Scene features headlining acts. Past performers have included the Black Eyed Peas and Public Enemy. In addition to music and merrymaking, there is plenty of food and drink for sale by local restaurateurs as well as arts and crafts booths.

SEPTEMBER

FESTIVAL OF CHILDREN
South Coast Plaza
3333 Bristol Ave., Costa Mesa
(877) 492-KIDS (5437)
www.festivalofchildren.org
For the entire month of September children of all ages are celebrated at this annual event that not only provides children and their families with endless entertainment that includes 100 special events, celebrity appearances, live performances,

hands-on learning, and more, but it also benefits more than 50 children's charities having a direct impact on the community at large. Moms will especially enjoy the location—South Coast Plaza—and might be able to get a little shopping in before or after the event.

INTERNATIONAL STREET FAIR
Old Towne Orange
Chapman and Glassell Avenues
www.orangestreetfair.org
What begin as a small community event in the 1970s has blossomed into one of the most anticipated Labor Day Weekend events of Orange County. Held on the historic plaza in Orange, the International Street Fair is really a food fair with just about every ethnicity and cuisine represented. The event fans out in a four-square-block area and features arts and crafts booths, live entertainment, wine and beer kiosks, and community groups.

OKTOBERFEST
Old World
7561 Center Ave., Huntington Beach
(714) 647-7107
www.oldworld.ws
If you can't go to Munich, let Munich come to you at the annual Oktoberfest. Sink your teeth into authentic bratwurst smothered in mustard and sauerkraut, then chase it down with a bold German beer. There are oompah-pah bands, stein-holding contests, traditional German dancing, and, of course, the crowd-pleasing chicken dance. The event takes place for most of September and October and is limited to weekends.

TALL SHIPS FESTIVAL
Ocean Institute, Dana Point Harbor
(949) 496-2274
www.tallshipsfestival.com
Touted as the largest annual gathering of tallships on the West Coast, this Ocean Institute–hosted event, which happens for two days in mid-September, is living history at its best. There are encampments of blacksmiths, scrimshaw artists, and privateers who are more than eager to

share with you their talents. Live music, art displays, and food round out this family-fun outing. Modern-day buccaneers are welcome to explore the tallships and gather around members of the crew to listen to tales and high sea adventure lore. Shuttle service is available from Salt Creek Beach Park (Pacific Coast Highway and Selva Road) and Dana High School.

TASTE OF NEWPORT
Fashion Island
600 Newport Center Dr., Newport Beach
(949) 729-4400
www.tasteofnewport.com
For three spectacular days in late September foodies and grazers gather at Fashion Island to sample the best of the best Orange County restaurants have to offer. There are 30 casual to fine dining restaurants, 15 wineries, some excellent microbrews, fruity and flavorful drinks, and live entertainment. No one walks away feeling hungry or parched.

OCTOBER

ORANGE COUNTY'S CHILDREN'S BOOK FESTIVAL
Orange Coast College
2701 Fairview Rd., Costa Mesa
(714) 838-4528
www.kidsbookfestival.com
There's nothing like escaping through the pages of a good book, and the earlier kids can appreciate the written word in lieu of the controller belonging to a video game the better. This festival, which reaches out to children of all ages, invites authors, illustrators, and storytellers to engage children with their words, art, and talent. There are also animals, costumed characters from the literary world, crafts, food, and lots of entertainment.

WEST HOLLYWOOD HALLOWEEN PARTY
Santa Monica Boulevard from Doheny to La Cienga, West Hollywood
(310) 289-2525
www.visitwesthollywood.com

Spooky Events for Kids and Adults

Halloween has become an event enjoyed as much by adults as it is by children. **Knott's Berry Farm** (www.knotts.com) was one of the first theme parks to create an event, Knott's Scary Farm, that both older kids and their parents could enjoy. Held throughout the month of October on most evenings, the entire theme park is transformed into a ghoulish hell and is one of Southern California's most popular events. Other theme parks, such as **Universal Studios** (www.universalstudios hollywood.com) and **Disneyland** (www.disneyland.com), which does a mild, family-friendly Halloween happening, have gotten into the act as well. The *Queen Mary's* **Shipwreck** (www.queenmary.com), which takes place aboard the historic *Queen Mary* ocean liner in Long Beach, a ship that is rumored to be haunted, is also an extremely popular event that has more appeal for adults. Usually the experience ends with guests spilling into a dance party inside the ship's Exhibition Center. There are other haunted houses throughout the region, but these are put on by local organizations as part of fundraising efforts.

This adults-only Halloween bash is one of the biggest fêtes in all of Southern California. Held on Halloween night beginning at 6 p.m., it's hard to tell what's more entertaining—the live musical acts or the party goers who arrive in outlandish (sometimes naughty) outfits and take to the streets of LA's gay neighborhood to party into the

Hotel Reservation Tips for Big Events

Attending a major event usually warrants a spike in hotel reservations. If you're planning a vacation to Orange County to coincide with one of the region's major events, such as the **Tournament of Roses Parade, Pageant of the Masters,** or a **Huntington Beach surf competition,** you'll want to go ahead and book as far in advance as possible. This is especially true if you want be near the epicenter of the gathering. For example, if you want to stay in a hotel or resort in Laguna Beach during the summer, book your room by late winter or early spring. Laguna Beach properties can and will sell out during the summer months regardless of whether guests are attending one of the seasonal events or not. While the **Rose Parade** is miles away in Pasadena, thousands of people flock to Southern California to see it firsthand. This doesn't necessarily mean they'll be able to—or even want to—secure a hotel room in Pasadena. The Rose Parade for most people is just one stop among many, and travelers from afar tend to "bundle" their vacation to include as many attractions as possible. During the Christmas break, when children are out of school, **Disneyland** tops the list of places visitors want to go while in Southern California. And all those thousands of people visiting Disneyland and Orange County will want hotels with convenient locations. Don't be the one asking to be put on the cancellation list.

night. Revelers are a mix of gay and straight. This is one of those events where inhibitions are left at home and the good times go on and on and on. The event always includes the coronation of the Queen of the Carnaval—last year it was actress Ricki Lake—and one of the most outrageous costume contests this side of the Mississippi with drag queens taking center stage. It's no surprise that this party always makes the evening news.

NOVEMBER

FASHION ISLAND TREE LIGHTING CEREMONY
Fashion Island
600 Newport Center Drive, Newport Beach
(949) 721-2000
www.shopfashionisland.com
It's one of the most popular holiday traditions in Orange County and one of the most spectacular considering the enormous size of the Fashion Island Christmas tree. Dominating most of the

Atrium Lawn adjacent to Santa's House and Bloomingdale's, the event includes student performances, the arrival of Santa, and the lighting of the tree. The two-day event takes place the weekend before Thanksgiving. After the fanfare, you can get a jump on your holiday shopping or grab a quick bite at one of the many restaurants at this upscale, outdoor center.

TURKEY TROT
Dana Point Harbor, Dana Point
(949) 496-1555
www.turkeytrot.com
Here's your chance to work off that gravy and stuffing before you've even put a forkful in your mouth. The annual Dana Point Turkey Trot, California's largest Thanksgiving Day run event, takes place along the pristine coastline, across jagged cliffs and amid cool ocean breezes as trotters, along with joggers and runners, make their way to the finish line. All ages are welcome.

DECEMBER

FIESTA NAVIDAD
Old Town San Diego
2470 Heritage Park Row, San Diego
(619) 291-9383
www.oldtownsandiego.org
This two-day festival, located in the birthplace of California, celebrates family traditions with hundreds of luminaries lighting the way through Old Town plus horse and carriage rides, entertainment, and, for one evening, Las Posadas, which follows Mary and Joseph's journey to Bethlehem. Old Town hosts one of the oldest Las Posadas in the country. In addition, there is breaking of piñatas, visits from Santa, church choirs and bell ringers, evening museum tours, and more.

LOS POSADOS FAMILY FESTIVAL
Bowers Museum
2002 North Main St., Santa Ana
(714) 567-3600
This two-hour event is usually held the second Sunday of December and is a traditional Mexi-can celebration that follows Mary and Joseph's journey to Bethlehem. Luminaries are aglow, and music, dance, food, and art round out the celebration.

NEWPORT BEACH CHRISTMAS BOAT PARADE
Newport Harbor, Newport Beach
(949) 729-4400
www.christmasboatparade.com
For five consecutive nights during select evenings of December, Newport Harbor is ablaze in lights adorning boats of all shapes and sizes. The parade, which lasts about two and a half hours and has been hailed by the *New York Times* as "one of the top 10 holiday happenings in the nation," includes 250 vessels and hundreds of illuminated waterfront estates that participate in the Ring of Lights decorating competition. The parade is free for spectators, but boaters pay an entry fee. Newport Landing (www.newportlanding.com/lights .htm) offers cruises to the general public who want to be part of the action.

DAYTRIPS

Orange County is blessed with a central location where, within two hours or less, you can be strolling along the streets of an old mining town, delving beneath the sea off an enchanted island, sipping pinot noir among verdant vineyards, or basking in the sun under a leafy palm tree. Southern California doesn't just have one resort area, it has many multifaceted destinations that lend themselves to an afternoon outing or, if time allows, a mini getaway. It's not out of the realm of possibility to surf in the morning, ski in the afternoon, and retire in the evening beneath the desert sky. Of course, this would take some precise planning on your part not to mention pristine traffic conditions to make it a reality, but the point is that these destinations, which vary so drastically in climate and terrain, are all just a short distance from one another. Sometimes the roads leading to the local mountains may require chains in order to make the trek up the hill due to fresh fallen snow, but otherwise road conditions throughout Southern California, aside from everyday vehicle congestion that can add time to your drive, are rarely jeopardized due to weather conditions.

LOS ANGELES

Unlike other cities that have tidy boundaries that center around a downtown region, Los Angeles is a sprawling metropolis with pretzel-like freeways that traverse the landscape, a jagged skyline framing its downtown, and a mosaic of styles, influences, and cultures. There are the typical must-see landmarks, such as the **Walk of Fame** and **Grauman's Chinese Theatre** along Hollywood Boulevard, and lesser known but equally significant destinations, such as **Olvera Street** in downtown. The city itself isn't walkable because there is just too much ground to cover, but if you drive to a specific neighborhood, such as the **Fashion District** in downtown or the crossroads of Hollywood and Highland, the epicenter of **Hollywood,** you can park your car and explore on foot once you arrive.

Olvera Street and Union Station

Its official name is El Pueblo de Los Angeles State Historic Park, but locals simply call it Olvera Street. Recognized as the oldest section of the city, this is where Los Angeles can trace back to its beginnings to when the first pueblo was established on

these grounds under the rule of King Carlos II of Spain in 1781. In 1930 many of the modest buildings and adobe structures were in jeopardy until preservationist Christine Sterling helped to rescue the enclave from demolition by establishing the area as a Mexican-style marketplace. Among Olvera Street's architectural treasures are the **1818 Avila Adobe,** the **Pelaconi House,** the city's oldest brick house dating back to 1855, and the 1877 **Sepulveda House,** an East Lake Victorian-style structure. Interspersed with these abodes are shops, kiosks that sell Mexican wares including marionettes and pottery, and restaurants that serve authentic fare and blended margaritas. Info: 849 North Alameda St., www.olvera-street.com, (213) 628-1274. Free admission.

Across from Olvera Street on the other side of Alameda is **Union Station,** a magnificent 1939 train depot built in the Spanish Colonial Revival style coupled with Art Deco influences. An imposing clock tower and fleet of arched entryways are set against a landscape of fig trees, Mexican fan palms, and blooming birds of paradise. For many years, Union Station was like a ghost town as train travel gave way to other, more modern modes of transportation. But a new era has dawned on this landmark as commuters spill in from various parts of the county and beyond during the weekdays as well as passengers from afar. Union Station is also a desirable backdrop for motion pictures and has been featured in such films as *Blade Runner* and *LA Confidential*. Info: (800) 872-7245.

Historic Los Angeles Eats

Downtown Los Angeles has two historic restaurants that locals frequent and that visitors should also experience. The first is **The Pantry** at Figueroa and 9th Street, a few blocks from STAPLES Center and LA Live, and owned by Richard Riordan, the mayor of Los Angeles from 1993 to 2001. With just a handful of tables, counter seating, and a line that can trail at times the length of the entire building, this has been LA's go-to, 24-hour breakfast place for more than 80 years. **Philippe's The Original,** with its sawdust-covered floors and communal tables, is adjacent to Union Station at the corner of Alameda and Ord. Opened in 1908, this is where the French dip sandwich was invented.

Hollywood and the West Side

Combine your visit to downtown with a trip to Hollywood and the West Side. Drive west along Sunset Boulevard, which will take you past some of the city's unique neighborhoods, such as **Echo Park** and **Silverlake,** before reaching **Sunset Junction** and veering off onto **Hollywood Boulevard.** A few miles up the road is Hollywood and Highland, an outdoor shopping center named for its location. If the center seems a bit familiar that's because it's also home to the **Kodak The-**

atre where the stars walk the red carpet en route to the annual Academy Awards ceremony that takes place inside. Tours of the Kodak Theatre are available to the public for a nominal fee. Next door to Hollywood and Highland is the legendary **Grauman's Chinese Theatre** and its **Forecourt of the Stars,** where you can compare your hand- and footprints to celebrities past and present who have cast their hands and feet in cement. A recent addition to the neighborhood is **Madame Tussaud's Wax Museum,** which is located next door. Across the street is **El Capitan,** an historic Disney-owned theater that presents Disney-only movies coupled with preshow entertainment. Next door to El Capitan is where *Jimmy Kimmel Live!* is filmed before a live audience on weekdays starting at about 7 p.m.

Up and down Hollywood Boulevard and neighboring streets are 2,000 terrazzo stars embedded in the sidewalk. This display of celebrity adoration and recognition is known as the **Hollywood Walk of Fame,** which covers 18 blocks east to west along both sides of the street, from Gower to La Brea, and an additional three blocks north and south along Vine from Sunset to Yucca. Nearby, at 1660 North Highland Ave., is the **Hollywood Museum** housed inside the famed Max Factor Building erected in 1913 and the once celebrated site of Max Factor's salon. The collection of movie artifacts and memorabilia include such items as Sylvester Stallone's boxing gloves from the movie *Rocky*, Elvis Presley's favorite bathrobe, Pamela Anderson's swimsuit from *Baywatch*, and Cary Grant's Rolls Royce, just to name a few. Info: (323) 464-7776, www.thehollywoodmusuem.com.

If you take Highland Avenue south for a couple of miles and head west on Third Street, you'll stumble upon **Farmers Market** at the corner of Fairfax and Third. Farmers Market was conceived in 1934 on a dirt lot as a means for local farmers to display their wares. Eventually wood stalls were erected beneath the clock tower, both of which still exist, and Angelenos would flock here to buy their fruits, vegetables, and beef. Today Farmers Market is still going strong with its collection of stalls that also include eateries serving

Walk of Fame

Many visitors to the Forecourt of the Stars at Grauman's Chinese Theatre are unaware of how the tradition of stars leaving their hand and footprints began. Actress Norma Talmadge and theater owner Sid Grauman can be credited with this ingenious and accidental stunt that began in 1927. Legend has it that at the theater's opening, Ms. Talmadge accidentally stepped into a block of wet cement. The quick-thinking Sid Grauman insisted the actress also sign her name in the cement, making it all look as if it were planned. The tradition took hold when Mary Pickford and Douglas Fairbanks repeated the gimmick a few weeks later. Everyone from John Wayne to Denzel Washington has made an impression here, including Groucho Marx who left an imprint of his trademark cigar and R2D2 who left his tread marks.

tour, and entertaining shows. Actually, the studio tour concept was born on this very lot in 1915 when Carl Laemmle transformed a former chicken ranch into a movie studio and began charging visitors a quarter to tour the lot and witness movie making magic up close. Lunch was included in the price of admission. The experience at Universal Studios is much different than it was nearly a century ago. For starters, visitors now tour the back lot in an open-air tram equipped with state-of-the-art high definition monitors while experiencing the collection of movie sets that includes an eerily realistic plane wreckage used in the Steven Spielberg film *War of the Worlds*, a glimpse at the legendary façade of the Bates Motel from the thriller *Psycho*, a cruise down Wisteria Lane from the television series *Desperate Housewives* that also served as the Cleaver's street in the 1950s television series *Leave it to Beaver*, and a close encounter with the man-eating shark from *Jaws*. While on the back-lot tour it's not entirely out of the realm of possibility to see a celebrity. Universal Studios also has a collection of thrilling rides that are movie-themed, including The Simpsons based on the popular cartoon series, plus roller coaster action aboard Revenge of the Mummy and Jurassic Park featuring an 80-foot raft plunge. There are also various shows and live performances throughout the day. **Universal CityWalk,** a faux city flanked with shops, restaurants, and attractions, is located just outside the studio gates and is a free admission attraction. This outdoor destination also has a multiplex cinema and various street performers. Guests of Universal Studios can have their hands stamped upon exiting the theme park, dine at one of the many CityWalk restaurants, and return to Universal Studios afterwards.

Ethnic Neighborhoods

In addition to El Pueblo de Los Angeles, also known as Olvera Street, Greater Los Angeles has some unique and interesting ethnic neighborhoods and destinations. From authentic *mercados* and kosher delis to the spices of Africa, you can literally travel the globe in one fun-filled

everything from gumbo to crepes to Mexican food. There is also a fromagerie and wine bar, and you'll see famous faces poking around here as well. A cobblestone pathway and double-decker trolley link Farmers Market to **The Grove,** which is reminiscent of a European town square with a collection of upscale stores including Nordstrom, Anthropologie, and American Girl plus several sidewalk cafes and a multiplex movie theater. The landscape is a mix of prancing fountains, arched bridges and a manmade lake.

Those on a theme park mission will definitely want to spend a day at **Universal Studios Hollywood** (www.universalstudioshollywood.com). While it remains a working studio, it's just as well known for its thrilling rides, back-lot studio

Close-up

Be Part of a Live Studio Audience

Many people visiting Southern California, and even those who live here, have a fascination with Hollywood—or at least what it represents. One way to guarantee a celebrity sighting is to be part of a TV show audience, an experience that will cost you nothing, except maybe gas and parking, because tickets are free. There are a variety of legitimate Web sites that distribute TV show tickets, but no single site handles all the studios and their shows. Audiences Unlimited (www.tvtickets.com) has tickets to many popular television shows and lists show schedules up to 30 days in advance. The Audiences Unlimited Web site allows you to order tickets online to pilot shows, award shows, and annual or one-time-only music, comedy, or variety specials. You can be part of the audience on *Dr. Phil*, *The New Adventures of Old Christine*, or *Two and a Half Men*. If you want to see a game show, www.tvtix.com has tickets to *Price is Right* and *Wheel of Fortune*, just to name a couple. Typically studios require audience members to be at least 16 years of age, 18 in some cases, but if your kids are dying to see one of their favorite Nickelodeon shows you can call the Nick Studios on Sunset Blvd. directly at (323) 468-5050 to obtain tickets; just be sure to make your request at least two weeks prior to your visit. Production schedules can frequently change and, while an average television or game show lasts about 20 minutes on TV, a taping sometimes can take hours when you factor in the retakes due to actors flubbing their lines, set and wardrobe changes, and so on.

afternoon. The boutique neighborhoods listed below are part of both Los Angeles proper as well as Greater Los Angeles. From Orange County, plan on traveling 45 minutes to an hour to and from any one of these destinations.

CHINATOWN
Bounded by Sunset Boulevard, Bernard Street, Figueroa, and Alameda
Located within walking distance to Olvera Street, Chinatown is the go-to place for hard-to-find herbs and fresh fish. The sound of clicking mahjong tiles can be heard above the storefronts, and Central Plaza, guarded by its distinctive Gate of Filial Piety at 947 North Broadway, is flanked with narrow walkways and tiny shops. Eateries, which once had an exclusive clientele of Chinese and Americans, now cater to a new crop of Vietnamese, Cambodian, and Laotian immigrants. Stores are generally open from 10 a.m. to 6 p.m. with extended hours for restaurants, and parking is found in various lots and along metered city streets.

EAST LOS ANGELES
On the east side of the Los Angeles River near downtown L.A. with First and Fourth Streets serving as main thoroughfares along with Cesar E. Chavez Avenue and Whittier Boulevard
Boyle Heights in East Los Angeles was where Jewish, Italian, Japanese, and Mexican immigrants settled in the early part of the 20th century. Yugoslavs and Russians could be found here as well, but these Jewish residents made their exodus to the Fairfax District during the 1940s. The Breed Street Shul at 247 North Breed St. is one of the only remaining Jewish relics that still exist in this once Jewish-dominated neighborhood.

The Breed Street Shul opened in 1923 and encompasses two historic synagogues, a 1915 wood frame building, and a 1923 non-reinforced brick building. It was one of the oldest synagogues on the West Coast. Although it was abandoned by its parishioners long ago, Breed Street Shul was restored and is now an historic landmark. Today Boyle Heights and the rest of East Los Angeles is mostly known for its Latino flair with the strains of mariachi music and local street vendors peddling their wares. El Mercado—the market—is located at 3425 East First St. and feels like a true Mexican marketplace. Its eye-popping exterior is graced with murals including one of actor/activist Edward James Olmos. This three-level structure is packed with Mexican goods, foods, and restaurants. Bypass the first floor and make your way to the second level to peruse the aisles of the grocery store stocked with Mexican foods and ingredients. The top level is cluttered with cafes and food stalls as well as strolling mariachis more than willing to serenade your table. Not too far from El Mercado is La Serenata de Garabaldi (1842 East First St.) where Angelenos flock to enjoy fresh and innovative Mexican-style seafood, handmade tortillas, and handcrafted margaritas.

FAIRFAX DISTRICT
Fairfax Boulevard between Beverly Boulevard and Melrose Avenue, West Los Angeles
Home to an influx of Orthodox, Hasidic, and Reform Jews, the Fairfax District is a mix of old and new. Lining Fairfax Boulevard are time-honored stores and restaurants, such as the decades-old Canter's Deli and the equally established Farmers Market with its abundance of food and vegetable stalls. CBS Television City arrived in 1952 and is where *The Young and the Restless* and *Price is Right* are taped along with other shows. With the arrival of The Grove in 2002, the Fairfax District suddenly was filled with well-heeled shoppers, celebrity gawkers, and aspiring starlets who arrive daily to shop at Nordstrom, Sur La Table, and Anthropologie. While the number of kosher delis and shops has dwindled, the Fairfax District is still considered a hub for Jewish culture with many Jewish-owned shops, markets, and bakeries. At the corner of Fairfax and Melrose Avenue is Fairfax High School, which counts Demi Moore, Jack Kemp, and Timothy Hutton among its notable alumni.

KOREATOWN
Between the 3400 and 5600 block of Wilshire
While still retaining an authentic feel, Koreatown, with its strong kimchee aroma and many norae-

bang (karaoke) studios, is transforming into a hip enclave rich with contemporary residential lofts and savory restaurants that are attracting visitors of all ethnicities. A mélange of colorful storefronts, restored bungalows, and cultural sights, such as the Korean American Museum, make Koreatown a must-stop destination. The karaoke bars, once non-descript lounges, now offer bottle service and private rooms along with *American Idol* wannabes belting out tunes in English, Korean, Chinese, Japanese, Tagalog, and Spanish. There are various lots and metered parking along city streets.

LEIMERT PARK
Bounded by Crenshaw Boulevard, 43rd Street, and Leimert Boulevard
A beacon for African-American culture, Leimert Park, located between downtown and the West Side, is much like the Harlem of the 1920s. Artists, poets, and musicians gather at neighborhood coffee shops and jazz clubs to engage in conversation and debate current affairs. Ella Fitzgerald and Ray Charles once lived here, which explains the neighborhood's vibrant music scene. There are nearly a dozen pedestrian-friendly blocks to be found within this urban village, which boasts a wealth of Afro-centric themed shops and services. A few noteworthy places include 5th Street Dick's Coffeehouse, La Casa Blue, Eso Won Books, and Africa by the Yard.

LITTLE ETHIOPIA
South Fairfax Avenue and Whitworth Drive, West Los Angeles
Home to the largest population of Ethiopians in the United States, this ethnic neighborhood looks like any other Los Angeles business district with its rows of neatly lined parking meters and storefronts graced with awnings. But the faint smell of tumeric and paprika, along with more exotic herbs and flavors, escapes from the kitchens of the many restaurants along South Fairfax luring passersby to their doorsteps for an authentic Ethiopian meal. So it should come as no surprise that the main attractions here are the restaurants where traditional dishes of chicken stewed in

pepper sauce and an abundance of vegetarian fare are served. Coffee in the Ethiopian culture is considered a ritual, much like tea is in England. Green coffee beans are washed, roasted, ground, and boiled tableside while incense burns during the ceremonial brew. Coffee is served in petite ceramic cups and the experience can last up to two hours. Aside from food, there are the markets filled with everyday Ethiopian goods: hand-woven clothing, African music, spices, and more.

LITTLE INDIA
Pioneer Boulevard between 183rd and 187th Streets, Artesia
Named for the many flowing Artesian wells that once populated this former farming community, Artesia, developed by Dutch and Portuguese farmers, is known these days for its four-block stretch of mini malls filled with Indian eateries and shops laden with silk saris, jewelry, home accessories, and other exotic imports. Turban-clad men stroll along the sidewalks with women wrapped in colorful saris displaying a rainbow of hues, from persimmon to cobalt blue, and accented with hand-sewn embellishments. Nakul Dev Mahajan, a world-renowned dancer and choreographer best known for his work on *So You Think You Can Dance*, has a studio here, too, where people of all creeds flock to learn the art of Bollywood dancing. Stores are generally open from 10 a.m. to 6 p.m. with extended hours for restaurants. Two-hour street parking is available along Pioneer Boulevard from 7 a.m. to 6 p.m. with customer parking available at various mini malls.

LITTLE TOKYO
Bounded by Los Angeles Street, Central Avenue, 1st and 3rd Streets, Downtown
This historic neighborhood is home to a thriving cultural center, theater, a renowned museum, Buddhist temple, plaza-style shopping center, and some very innovative boutiques and restaurants. Little Tokyo is a playground for Japanese Americans whose ancestors helped to establish this tidy neighborhood during the early part of the 20th century. The district is rich with sushi bars, wagashi stores that carry Japanese candy, and

ramen shops. Along 1st Street you'll find a row of 18th-century buildings that still exist as well as Yagura Tower, a replica of a Japanese fire tower. There is also the Japanese American National Museum and public art displayed on city streets.

THAI TOWN
5200 block of Hollywood Boulevard, Hollywood
While the pulse of this Asian community beats strongly at the Wat Thai Buddhist Temple in North Hollywood (12909 Cantara, 818-780-4200), just down the 101 Freeway is where you'll find a crop of Taiwanese-owned shops, marketplaces, bookstores, and cafes. Thailand Plaza (5321 Hollywood Boulevard) has it all with incense, candles, and garlands of flowers all available for purchase. Next door is Dokya Bookstore, which carries the *Bangkok Post*, Thai-language books, and books about Thailand in general. And nowhere in Los Angeles will you find more authentic Thai food than at the many restaurants that call this neighborhood home. Stores are generally open from 10 a.m. to 6 p.m. with extended hours for restaurants. Free parking is available at Thailand Plaza and metered parking is available along Hollywood Boulevard and neighboring streets.

Travel Information

To reach Downtown Los Angeles from Orange County, take I-5 north. To reach the Hollywood area, take I-5 north to the 101 Freeway north and exit at Sunset or Hollywood Boulevards and head west.

LA INC., THE CONVENTION AND VISITORS BUREAU
(213) 236-2331
www.discoverlosangeles.com

JULIAN (SAN DIEGO COUNTY)

Julian is a great discovery for both residents of Southern California and visitors. This former mining town, tucked in the folds of San Diego County's outback, enjoys four mild seasons with an occasional dusting of snow during the win-

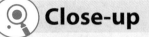 **Close-up**

Anza-Borrego State Desert Park

If time allows, you can go from eating apple pie for dessert to combing the desert floor in a matter of 45 minutes. Traveling along Highway 78 from Julian to the arid Anza-Borrego State Desert Park is a kaleidoscope of changing scenery where tall, mature trees that thrive in the higher altitude give way to cacti and sage as you near the desert terrain. The park, established in 1933 in an effort to preserve the habitat of the bighorn sheep, covers some 600,000 acres with a tapestry of trails and topography. Within the park is Borrego Springs, a resort community with lodging options and an expansive visitors center at the west end of Palm Canyon Drive. The center, with its collection of exhibits, maps, and books, is a valuable resource for visitors. The staff is equally knowledgeable, offering valuable tips to maximize your time, and a brief slide presentation will further familiarize you with the area. The labyrinth of hiking trails caters to all levels of ability, and the largest natural palm oasis in the U.S. is located within the park as well. In addition to self-guided tours, you can also scour the park on horseback or as part of a guided off-road vehicle expedition. If you plan on making Julian and Anza-Borrego State Desert Park a two-day experience, you can stay at the 15-room Julian Gold Rush Hotel, the oldest continuously operating lodge in all of Southern California (760-765-0201, www.julianhotel.com), or the adobe-style Borrego Valley Inn (760-767-0311, www.borregovalleyinn.com).

ter. The town was established around 1870 by the Bailey brothers and their cousins, the Julian brothers, and grew when gold was discovered and prospectors arrived in hopes of striking it rich. Soon there were stores, hotels, livery stables, saloons, and blacksmith shops with the first apple orchards planted as well. While the mines, long ago abandoned, may have brought Julian attention, it's the apple industry that has city folks making their pilgrimage to this alpine town.

During harvest season, which takes place in the fall, Julian gets very crowded on weekends as people stroll past the false-front stores, wooden sidewalk, and historic buildings along **Main Street.** You can belly up to the marble counter at the 120-year-old Julian Drug Store for an old-fashioned malt or head to the nearby cider mill to watch apples being pressed for cider or dunked into vats of caramel. A slice of freshly baked apple pie is enjoyed at Mom's Pies, with its big picture window along the sidewalk and workers assembling pies behind the glass, and the Julian Pie Company, which tops its slices with cinnamon ice cream and offers indoor seating or outdoor seating on its front porch or back patio.

You can also take a horse-drawn carriage ride through town and along the outskirts or embark on a guided tour of the **Eagle and High Peak Mines** that takes you into the confines of a 1,000-foot rock-hard tunnel where you can see how the mining and milling processes were used more than a century ago. You may want to make some time for wine tasting at Julian's two vineyards situated along Julian Orchards Road near town, **J. Jenkins Winery,** and **Menghini Winery.**

Travel Information

To reach Julian from Orange County, take I-5 south to Highway 78 east.

JULIAN CHAMBER OF COMMERCE
(760) 765-1857
www.julianca.com

BIG BEAR LAKE

Skiing isn't likely the first thing that comes to mind when thinking of Southern California, but the local mountains can produce quite a few inches of snow during the winter, creating a winter wonderland just 90 minutes or so from the beaches of Orange County. Located in the San Bernardino Mountains is Big Bear Lake, which is enjoyable both summer and winter.

Gold was discovered in Big Bear around 1860 and an influx of prospectors arrived. Although the fortune hunting was short lived, loggers and cattle ranchers were able to carve out a living. The first hotel opened shortly after the dam was built in 1884, but Big Bear remained rather dormant for the next several decades. When the first ski resort opened in 1949, Big Bear began to experience growth and today, while still a somewhat sleepy town, it's a great destination for local skiing. There are two major ski resorts: **Bear Mountain** and **Snow Summit.** Bear Mountain (www.bearmountain.com, 909-585-2517) has four mountain peaks with 12 chair lifts and 32 trails with an elevation of nearly 9,000 feet—the highest peak in Southern California. Its rival, Snow Summit (www.snowsummit.com, 909-866-5766), has a top elevation of 8,200 with 31 trails and a dozen chair lifts. Both resorts are generally open from Thanksgiving to Easter depending on the amount of snow. Snow Summit has nighttime skiing, too.

The summer can be one of the prettiest seasons in Big Bear. As the snow begins to melt, the mountain is littered with wildflowers as well as with hikers entering the **San Bernardino National Forest.** There is a labyrinth of trails ranging from an easy 1.5-mile loop to a strenuous 7-mile trek. The **Big Bear Discovery Center** (41397 North Shore Dr., Hwy. 38, 909-382-2790), located on the lake's north shore, is an educational and informational stop where you can purchase a $5 all-day adventure pass. This pass needs to be displayed on your vehicle in order to avoid any citations once you make your way to the hiking trails. You can also obtain camping information, maps and books, and wood-cutting permits and partake in a naturalist-led interpretive program.

The lake is teeming with boaters and fisherman. Pontoon, fishing, and sailing boats, as well as jet skis, wave runners, canoes, and paddleboats, are available lakeside to rent. **Pleasure**

Point Marina (909-866-2455) and **Big Bear Marina** (909-866-3218) are two places to rent watercraft. Alpine Trout Lake (909-866-4532) is where you can rent equipment and pay by the pound for your catch. There are also water-skiing and parasailing opportunities and **Meadow Park** offers a beach-like setting for swimmers as well as sunbathers and has a lifeguard on duty.

On the way to Big Bear Lake you can take a detour to **Lake Arrowhead,** a lower altitude location that is more high-brow than its hilltop neighbor. Considered the Newport Beach of alpine living, Lake Arrowhead has a 784-acre lake that was created during the early 1900s and is now surrounded by multimillion-dollar homes. Lake Arrowhead has no ski resorts, noted landmarks, or sightseeing opportunities, and not much in the way of nightlife either; it's just a smattering of restaurants and shops, but it's a relaxing place to find yourself. You can hike, fish, and boat with skiing located up the road in Big Bear. There is one resort and a handful of small inns plus several private cabins that can be leased for a weekend or longer. Visit www.lakearrowhead.net for a list of local property management companies.

Travel Information

To reach Big Bear and Lake Arrowhead, take the 57 Freeway north to the 10 Freeway east to the Running Springs Highway 30 exit in Redlands. Follow Highway 30 to Highway 330 to Highway 18, also known as the Rim of the World Highway. From here follow the signs to either destination. During or after a snowfall, road conditions may require you to use tire chains. These can be rented or purchased at stations before you actually begin your ascent up the mountain.

BIG BEAR VISITORS INFORMATION
(800) 424-4232
www.bigbear.com

LAKE ARROWHEAD COMMUNITIES
CHAMBER OF COMMERCE
(909) 337-3715
www.lakearrowhead.net

CATALINA ISLAND

Located just 26 miles across the sea, yet a world away from civilization, Santa Catalina Island, more commonly referred to as Catalina, offers a remarkable escape for just the day or longer. The *Catalina Flyer* sets sail from Balboa Pavilion in Newport Beach (near the end of the Balboa Peninsula) to the island several times a day. The island was first developed in the 1920s by William Wrigley, best known for his chewing gum empire. Not only did he own the island, he also was the owner of the Chicago Cubs and would bring the team to Catalina for spring training. His former estate, now a luxury bed and breakfast inn, sits on a hillside and offers commanding views.

There is only one developed town on the entire island. **Avalon,** with its quaint shops, sidewalk cafes, and collection of small inns, enjoys a waterfront location. There are a little more than 3,000 people who live on the island, but there are very few cars to be found. The reason for the vehicle shortage is that Avalon is the only city in California authorized by the state legislature to regulate the number and size of vehicles allowed on its streets. On average, there is an 8- to 10-year wait for those who want to bring a car on the island. But Avalon, which is less than 3 square miles, is so snug that two feet, a bicycle, or a golf cart can get you to just about anywhere.

At the end of Crescent Avenue, the town's main street overlooking the harbor, is the historic **Casino,** once the social epicenter of the island and now houses a museum as well as the island's only movie theater. The ballroom still has its share of gala events. Another place you'll want to visit is the **Green Pleasure Pier,** the town's only pier, built in 1909. You can dine near the foot of the pier or do some angling from its end. Catalina also offers home tours of the **Holly Hill House** as well as the casino. The **Wrigley Memorial** and **Botanical Gardens** is another oasis with a mission of preserving the island's verdant plant life. There are also a number of other activities to pursue, including golf, snorkeling, scuba diving, horseback riding, boating, kayaking, and hiking.

Catalina Bison

If you travel the island's backroads you're very likely to encounter an American bison, better known as buffalo. Herds were first brought to the island in the 1920s and used as props in Hollywood movies. The herd has grown in size and now numbers nearly 250 buffalo that roam the island freely. The Catalina Island Conservancy, stewards of the island, is responsible for managing the bison. In an effort to keep the herd from growing too large, the non-profit group gathered up some of the bison and relocated them to ranches in South Dakota. The conservancy has determined, based on studies conducted in 2004, that the island can support a healthy bison population of no more than 200. You can take a Buffalo Safari Tour, which lasts about four hours. For information, call (310) 510-4205.

The island's isthmus is where the remote **Two Harbors** is located. The *Catalina Flyer* doesn't offer service to Two Harbors; you would need to drive to San Pedro (part of Los Angeles proper and about a 40-minute drive from Orange County) if you wanted Two Harbors to be your final destination. If you want to experience both Avalon and Two Harbors, the Safari Bus links the two with stops at Little Harbor, the island airport, and the trailhead for Black Jack Junction. Service is offered daily during the summer months, while the rest of the year is less reliable in terms of scheduling. It's not cheap, either. As of this printing, one-way fares were $33 for adults and $26 for children. Unlike Avalon, which has a commercial district, Two Harbors has a bed and breakfast inn, a single restaurant, and a small market. There are also extremely rustic cabins as well as a campground for traditional tent camping or safari-style tents with cots. Another option, at least for boaters, is to moor a vessel for a few days near one of Two Harbors many coves.

There isn't much to do at Two Harbors other than kayak, scuba dive, or snorkel. History buffs can poke around the **Civil War Barracks,** built in 1864 by the U.S. Army, which deployed 83 soldiers to the isthmus to survey the land as a proposed reservation for militant Native Americans. While the plan was eventually aborted, the barracks remained and have been the backdrop for such noteworthy films as *Mutiny on the Bounty* and *Old Ironsides*. During World War II the Coast Guard used the facility as a training station for new recruits. These days, the Isthmus Yacht Club manages the facility.

Travel Information

Take the *Catalina Flyer* from the Balboa Pavilion near the Balboa Fun Zone. Reservations: (800) 830-7744. Visit www.catalinachamber.com for a complete listing of lodging options.

SANTA BARBARA

It's often touted as the American Riviera, and Santa Barbara shares an enviable climate with its European counterpart as both enjoy south-facing positions. Its architecture, a mélange of influences that include Mediterranean, Spanish Colonial, early Californian, Moorish, and Islamic, is garnished with smooth alabaster surfaces, tasteful ironwork, and red-tile roofs.

While a daytrip is completely doable, an overnight jaunt would be more fulfilling. You could spend one day touring Santa Barbara and the other motoring along the wine trail in Santa Ynez, north of the city. Downtown Santa Barbara along State Street, as well as neighboring avenues that parallel and intersect with this main drag, are filled with sidewalk cafes, individual shops, national retailers, espresso bars, and wine shops. A self-guided **Red Tile Walking Tour** will provide you with a better understanding of the city's rich architecture and history. Maps for

---

Catalina Accomodations

If you're planning on doing an overnight trip to Catalina Island, consider staying at the **Inn at Mt. Ada** (310-510-2030), a luxurious five-room bed and breakfast inn and the former home of William Wrigley of Wrigley Gum fame. Included in the nightly rate is the use of a golf cart to putt around the island, a full breakfast, a deli lunch, and snack privileges throughout the day. Children 14 and older can be accommodated. The **Villa Portofino** (310-510-0555), located in town and overlooking the harbor, or the six-room **Snug Harbor Inn** (888-394-7684, www.snugharbor-inn.com) with its stylish accommodations are both good choices. Rates are astronomical in the summer due to supply and demand, but during the winter, especially midweek, bargains can be had.

---

the walking tour are available throughout the downtown area as well as at the Visitors Center across from the beach at Cabrillo Avenue and Garden Street. The tour begins at the Santa Barbara Courthouse at 1100 Anacapa St. at Anapamu where you can also enjoy a free guided tour of this remarkable Spanish-Moorish structure Monday through Saturday. You also have carte blanche to take your own tour including a trek to the top of the crowning tower that looks out over the entire city. As you continue on your Red Tile Tour, you'll encounter many historic buildings, adobe structures, vintage shopping arcades, and the storied Presidio, just to name a few. The Santa Barbara Museum of Art and historic Lobero Theater, erected in 1873 and still used today, are also included.

Santa Barbara Accommodations

If you're planning an overnight stay—or longer—Santa Barbara has everything from full-service resorts and boutique inns to Victorian bed and breakfast retreats and cottages. The **Simpson House** (800-676-1280, www.simpsonhouseinn.com) California's only Five Diamond bed and breakfast, is located near downtown and features accommodations in the original Victorian mansion or free-standing cottages plus a full breakfast, evening hors d'oeuvres (which are more like a meal), and wine. **Harbor View Inn** (805-9630780, www.harborviewinnsb.com) sits across from Stearns Wharf and is a stylish retreat with a handful of rooms offering ocean views. As for the Wine Country, there is **Fess Parker's Wine Country Inn & Spa** (805-688-7788, www.fessparker.com) located in the heart of Los Olivos.

Just above town, which can be reached on foot for the truly ambitious or by car, is the **Mission Santa Barbara** at 2201 Laguna St. Hailed as the "Queen" of the California missions, Mission Santa Barbara was the 10th mission established in the 21-mission chain. Founded by Father Junípero Serra in 1786, the imposing structure was built stone by stone by Chumash Indians who lived at the mission and were trained by the Spaniards in agriculture and animal husbandry. In 1812 and 1925 the mission suffered significant damage when earthquakes shook the region, but was eventually repaired. It is the only mission with twin bell towers and a stone façade inspired by an ancient Latin temple. The mission is still an active place of worship for local Catholics, and the compound also houses a small museum, courtyard, cemetery, and gift shop. A nominal admission fee applies to tour the mission, but the outside grounds and gift shop are open to the public. Across the street is the **Mission Rose Park** where more than 1,000 roses bloom and artists often set up their easels to capture the beauty of the mission and garden on canvas.

If you don't have time to tour the wineries in Santa Ynez, you can lace up your walking shoes and hit the urban wine trail in downtown Santa Barbara. Within blocks of each other, along State and Anacapa Streets and two located several blocks away on Milpas and Montecito Streets, are excellent wineries. The county's oldest winery is **Santa Barbara Winery** at 202 Anacapa with its tasting room just two blocks from the beach. **Coastal Winery,** with its second-story picnic deck, is located near the end of Stearns Wharf, while **Kalrya Winery** at 212 State St. is located near the foot of the wharf. **Vino Divino** at 2012 De La Vina is a delightful wine shop that hosts regular tastings and carries a number of local vintages.

If you're traveling with kids, a Red Tile Walking Tour or trek along the urban wine trail is unlikely to jolt their interest. But Santa Barbara is an extremely family-friendly town with plenty of opportunities for young visitors. The **Santa Barbara Zoo** is home to a Baringo giraffe who gets more attention than the other giraffes due to his very visible crooked neck. **Kids' World** at Alameda Park, at the corner of Micheltorena and Garden Streets, has a wonderful play area where children can use their imagination. You can rent a four-person Surrey Cycle, a canopied bicycle with two rows of side-by-side seats in the front and behind, near the foot of Stearns Wharf at the corner of Cabrillo and State Streets, then pedal over to nearby Chase Palm Park to take a whirl on the carousel. **Ty Warner Sea Center** is another place sure to pique kids' interest and, if you are headed up to wine country, **Ostrich Land** in Solvang is always a fun stop.

Santa Barbara Wine Country is a bucolic and savory region with lots of vineyards, tasting rooms, and gourmet discoveries. Highway 154 is the main artery that will deliver you to the heart of the wine country, but it's Foxen Canyon Road and Zaca Station Road where you'll encounter the bulk of the wineries: **Firestone, Curtis Winery, Fess Parker, Zaca Mesa Winery, Foxen Winery,** and **Rancho Sisquoc,** just to name a few. Just off Highway 154 is the small hamlet of Los Olivos, which has additional tasting rooms along Grand Avenue and neighboring streets, including **Andrew Murray Vineyards, Richard Longoria Wines, Los Olivos Vintners, Daniel Gehrs Wines, Kahn Winery,** and **Arthur Earl.** Los Olivos Wine & Spirits Emporium, Los Olivos Tasting Room and Wine Shop, and Los Olivos Wine Merchant all specialize in hard-to-find wine acquisitions and tastings.

i On your way up to the wine country look for the sign indicating the Chumash Painted Cave. Inside the sandstone cave are religious drawings illustrated by the Chumash Indians coupled with additional sketches of coastal fisherman that are believed to date back to the 1600s. Be prepared for some rough driving once you turn off the main road.

Lunch at Los Olivos Café and enjoy a fabulous wine country meal, or stop in to one of the gourmet markets or delis and take it to go and enjoy your meal among the vineyards with a nice bottle of wine. If you head back towards Highway 154, crossing over the highway and continuing straight, you'll eventually come upon **Neverland Ranch** on your left, the former estate of Michael Jackson. Back out to Highway 154 and heading toward Santa Barbara you'll come upon Highway 246 to your right. This road leads to Solvang and en route you'll pass Ostrich Land before arriving to the town. Once you reach **Solvang,** you can park the car and walk to everything. The town was settled in 1911 by a group of Danes, but has evolved into a kitschy attraction flanked with Old World–style buildings and windmills. There are several small inns and restaurants with the *aebleskiver*, the Danish take on the pancake, found on just about every menu.

Another mission, the **1804 Mission Santa Ines,** is located nearby along with the **Hans Christian Andersen Museum. Nojoqui Falls,** located about 5 miles south off Alisal Road, is a great place to hike and picnic and has a 164-foot waterfall. To get back to Santa Barbara (or to head back to Orange County) you can return to Highway 246, which will take you to the town of Buellton. From here you can hop on Highway 101 south to Santa Barbara or continue on towards Los Angeles and, eventually, Orange County.

Travel Information

To reach Santa Barbara from Orange County, take I-5 north to the 101 Freeway north and continue for about 75 miles. Exit at State Street.

SANTA BARBARA CONVENTION AND VISITORS BUREAU
(805) 966-9222
www.santabarbaraca.com

SAN DIEGO

If you're staying in south Orange County—Dana Point or San Clemente—your trek to downtown San Diego will only be about 60 minutes. San Diego is a laid-back city with desirable weather, plenty of attractions, and a thriving downtown, and is packed with family-friendly fun.

Downtown San Diego, once a sleepy town, has transformed into a thriving urban center with distinctive neighborhoods, excellent restaurants, upscale hotels, and more. The **Gaslamp Quarter** is a hip enclave with an active nightlife and plenty of places to eat.

Little Italy has more of a community feel, while the waterfront, near Petco Park where the San Diego Padres play their home games from April to October, feels open and spacious. Not far from the cityscape are **Balboa Park** and the world-famous **San Diego Zoo; Coronado Island,** which isn't an island at all but rather a peninsula and home to the fabled **Hotel Del Coronado; Mission Beach,** where one of only two vintage wooden roller coasters in the state is found; and **SeaWorld** near Mission Bay. Further up the coast are the coastal resort communities of La Jolla, Del Mar, and Carlsbad, home of **LEGOLAND.**

An entire day can be spent in Balboa Park, which is larger than New York City's Central Park and older than San Francisco's Golden Gate Park. Within its boundaries are some two dozen museums, including the San Diego Museum of Art, the Ruben E. Fleet Science Museum, and the Japanese Friendship Garden, used as a teahouse during the 1915–'16 Panama-California Exposition and now a place of tranquility with a Zen garden and koi pond. The San Diego Zoo is also located in Balboa Park and is home to more than 4,000 rare and endangered animals. There are shows scheduled throughout the day, guided bus tour rides that take you through the zoo, and much more.

Old Town San Diego State Historical Park, located a few miles north of downtown, is not only the birthplace of San Diego but the pulse of California history. The first mission was established here by Father Junípero Serra in 1769 on Presidio Hill. Today the mission has been reduced to ruins, but can still be seen at Presidio Park. There are other buildings, such as La Casa de Estudillo, built in 1827 by the commander of the presidio, that are authentic and others that are replicas but still tell the story of early settlers. The only commercial entity within Old Town is **Bazaar del Mundo** (619-291-4903, www.old townsandiego.org), a Mexican-style marketplace flanked with adobe replicas and a center courtyard, and its collection of shops, restaurants, and strolling mariachis.

Across the bay from downtown San Diego is **Coronado Island,** which is actually a peninsula that can be reached via ferry or from the Coronado Bay Bridge from I-5. Its hub is Orange Avenue, where there are a number of shops, sidewalk cafes, and pubs. The Hotel Del Coronado (619-435-6611, www.hoteldel.com), a turreted landmark built along the beach in 1888, is the place to stay while in San Diego. Non-guests can also enjoy the property with a free self-guided tour that reveals the hotel's history with vintage photos of kings and queens, American presidents, foreign dignitaries, and Hollywood stars. There are guest records and hotel artifacts that chronicle how times have changed since the hotel welcomed its first guest. The hotel lobby, in all its Victorian elegance, still uses the original birdcage elevator to ferry guests to their rooms. The hotel is rumored to be haunted, particularly Room 3312, where in 1892 Kate Morgan spent her last night alive. She was discovered on the beach dead from a gunshot wound. Guests have reported strange occurrences, from flickering lights and strange scents to unexplained voices and the faint sound of footsteps.

Coronado's architecture is something to be admired. Beautiful homes, from varying periods, grace the residential streets. One that is particularly noteworthy is the gabled Meade House at 1101 Star Park Circle near town. Built in 1896, it served as the winter home for author L. Frank Baum who penned the classic tale of *The Wizard of Oz* and its series of books. Baum wrote four of his books while on the island and, coincidentally, designed the crown chandeliers that dangle inside the Hotel Del.

Mission Beach, where many San Diego State students live when school is in session, is home to the Giant Dipper Roller Coaster at Belmont Park. This is one of only two wooden seaside roller coasters remaining in California (the other is in Santa Cruz). It sat dilapidated for many years and was about to meet its fate with a wrecking ball when concerned citizens rallied around to save the coaster. It reopened to fanfare in 1990 and is still as thrilling as ever.

History buffs will enjoy time spent aboard the **San Diego Aircraft Carrier Museum** (619-544-9600, www.midway.org) where the USS *Midway* is anchored at Navy Pier. Visitors can take a "boiler to bridge" self-guided audio tour of the longest-serving aircraft carrier in U.S. Navy history and examine some 40 exhibits.

Reaching back a bit further in history in Point Loma, **Cabrillo National Monument** commemorates explorer Juan Rodriguez Cabrillo's inaugural landing at San Diego Bay on September 28, 1542. It marked the first time Europeans had set foot on what was to become the western part of the United States. There is a small museum, views of San Diego, and the Point Loma Lighthouse (619-557-5450), built in the 1880s, with ranger-led talks and tours.

San Diego really appeals to kids because of its theme and animal parks. There is **SeaWorld** (619-226-3901, www.4adventure.com) on Mission Bay with its 150-acre sprawl of marine life and shows throughout the day including one with Shamu, the killer whale. **LEGOLAND** (858-918-5346, www.legoland.com), located in San Diego's North County region, features more than 50 rides and attractions and is designed for kids up to age 10. **San Diego Wild Animal Park** (760-747-8702, www.sandiegozoo.org) in Escondido, also in North County, features a safari-like atmosphere where visitors can get up close to zebras, giraffes, and lions while traveling in an open-air bus. There are shows and other attractions here as well. During the summer the Wild Animal Park hosts Snore and Roar, when kids and their parents can sleep beneath the stars within mere feet of the roaming animals. And, of course, San Diego Zoo, previously mentioned in conjunction with Balboa Park, is another favorite destination for children.

Aside from Hotel Del Coronado, you may want to consider staying at the **Crystal Pier Hotel and Cottages** (800-748-5894, www.crystalpier.com) located on the pier in Pacific Beach. The vintage cottages, blue and white clapboard abodes, all have their own kitchens and patios teetering on the edge of the ocean. **La Costa Resort and Spa** (760-438-9111, www.lacosta.com) once an adults-only haven, has really transitioned into an upscale place for both parents and kids. The swimming pool for kids includes water slides and a sandy beach area; plus, the X-Box game lounge, with pool tables and air hockey, is a place just for teens. Mom and dad can play golf, tennis, or hit the spa. The resort is also close to LEGOLAND.

Balboa Park Freebies

"Free" seems to be a word everyone can understand. Many of the museums located within Balboa Park offer free admission on select Tuesdays, including:

First Tuesday:
Reuben H. Fleet Science Center

Second Tuesday:
Museum of Photographic Arts
San Diego Historical Society
Museum and Research Archives

Third Tuesday:
Japanese Friendship Gardens
San Diego Museum of Art
San Diego Museum of Man
Mingei International Museum
San Diego Art Institute

Fourth Tuesday:
San Diego Automotive Museum
Hall of Nations free film
San Diego Hall of Champions
Sports Museum

Travel Information

To reach San Diego from Orange County, travel south on I-5.

SAN DIEGO CONVENTION AND VISITORS BUREAU
(619) 232-3101
www.sandiego.org

PALM SPRINGS AND THE DESERT RESORT COMMUNITIES

Palm Springs makes for a better weekend getaway than a daytrip. Part of the vast Coachella Valley and the desert resort communities—which also include Cathedral City, Desert Hot Springs, Indian Wells, Indio, La Quinta, Palm Desert, and Rancho Mirage—Palm Springs exudes a sexy, retro vibe. Many of the mid-century hotels have been revamped into über cool resorts. With temperatures rising no more than 70 degrees, late fall and early spring are the ideal times to visit the region. Most people make the pilgrimage to Palm Springs to lounge poolside, play a round of golf on one of many courses, engage in a game of tennis, or sequester themselves inside the confines of a luxury spa. And, while that all sounds incredibly dreamy, Palm Springs and the surrounding area have a lot to offer visitors when it comes to the great outdoors and great indoors.

If you plan on spending a night or two, there is an abundance of lodging options in all price ranges and interests. High-end retreats include the eight-room and intimate **Willows Historic Palm Springs** Inn (760-320-0771, www.thewillows historicpalmsprings.com) the former manse of actress and William Randolph Hearst mistress Marion Davies, which is best suited for couples. You can also rent a private home, one that belonged to John Phillips of the Mamas and the Papas, or stay in Frank Sinatra's former home located in the Movie Colony area. Joe DiMaggio and Marilyn Monroe's Spanish hacienda is also available and includes five bedrooms. Time & Place Homes (866-244-1800) can assist with the arrangements. Resorts ideal for families include **Miramonte Resort & Spa** (760-341-2200, www.miramonteresort.com) in Palm Desert and **Renaissance Esmeralda Resort and Spa** (760-773-4444, www.renaissanceesmeralda .com), two large, full-service resorts with great pools and locations.

Motorists heading into Palm Springs on Highway 111 are quick to notice the mid-century sign that advertises the entrance to the **Palm Springs Aerial Tramway.** Conceived during the 1930s and completed some 20 years later in 1953, the tram ferries passengers to the top of Mt. San Jacinto. There are two 80-passenger gondolas with revolving floors that frame 360-degree views as you make the steep incline to the top passing through five climate zones. Once you arrive, it's a short hike through the forest of fir trees belonging to Mt. San Jacinto State Park before reaching the mountaintop restaurant. The peak, located at an elevation of 8,516 feet, is typically 40 degrees

cooler than the desert floor and the mountain gets a dusting of snow during the wintertime. Even in the summer it's smart to bring a light jacket or sweater with you, and in the winter think hat, gloves, and a warm coat. How long you decide to stay is up to you, but you might want to dine "atop the world" at the upscale Peaks or the more casual Pines Café. Cocktails are served at the Lookout Lounge, and you can purchase advance Ride 'n' Dinner packages.

Those with a fear of heights can stay grounded by scouring one of the largest collections of World War II propeller-driven planes at the **Palm Springs Air Museum** (760-778-6262, www.palmspringsairmusuem.org). The static display of vintage aircraft is housed in a pair of air-conditioned buildings and, because they are consistently maintained, are in flying condition more than a half-century later. In addition, there is an interesting display of vintage photographs and memorabilia that tells the history of aviation during World War II.

A self-driving tour of Palm Springs reveals an incredible breadth of architecture, from classic to mid-century, which is what Palm Springs is known for. Many blocks are packed with buildings or homes designed by Richard Neutra, William Cody, Donald Wexler, or Albert Frey, including the Frey-designed Tramway Gas Station. A full-color, foldout map, produced by the Palm Springs Modern Committee, includes the name, address, architect, and year each structure was built as well as snapshots and short profiles of the area's best-known architects. Maps are just $8. Visit www.psmodcom.com for more details.

The **Village Green Heritage Center** (760-323-8297, www.palmspringshistoricalsociety .com) is a complex containing two original 19th-century homes. The **McCallum Adobe,** built in 1885 and occupied by one of the desert's earliest settlers, is filled with personal artifacts and Indian wares, while Miss Cornelia White's House, constructed in 1894 from railroad ties, contains many of the original owner's possessions, from the family Bible to the city's first telephone.

Palm Springs has some majestic sites for those who enjoy the outdoors. **Indian Canyons**

(800-790-3398), with its four gorges, is located about 5 miles from the center of town. There are jagged cliffs, palm fronds, and waterfalls that pour into natural pools. There is also a trading post, picnic grounds, plenty of hiking trails that follow babbling streams, and horse trails. Arriving at Indian Canyons takes a bit of effort and only three of the four canyons are accessible to visitors, including Andreas Canyon, a ravine with etchings sketched by primitive Indians and indentations from native women who crushed beans and nuts against the hard surfaces. Seven Sisters, the name of the natural pools that connect with the gushing waterfalls in Andreas Canyon, features natural rock formations with 20-foot drops into the water below. Finally, Palm Canyon, which covers 15 miles of terrain, has some 3,000 palm trees with some as old as 2,000 years. This canyon also has additional natural pools and hiking trails.

The **Living Desert** (760-346-5694, www.livingdesert.org) in nearby Palm Desert rests on a 1,200-acre sprawl of arid land and is home to some 400 animals and 130 desert-dwelling species. Similar to a zoo, but with creatures that are, for the most part, indigenous to the region, you might encounter coyotes, bighorn sheep, Oryx, giraffes, zebras, cheetahs, and meerkats. There is also Village WaTuTu, a replica of an existing northeast African village, with huts whose walls are made from mud and whose thatched roofs are made from grass. The Living Desert is especially of interest to children with its play area and master storytellers who weave tales of African and Native American folklore. The creatures in Village WaTuTu are also native to Africa. There are docent-led tours of the complex's hospital where animals are treated behind a glass partition. Participants can observe medical procedures and examinations conducted on animals of all sizes.

The Coachella Valley is known as the "Date Capital of the World," a reference to the fruit that thrives in this region. **Oasis Date Gardens** (760-399-5665), a 175-acre working date ranch located in Indian Wells, is known for its date shakes, market stocked with plump dates and olives, and free ranch tours.

This region also has a breathtaking scenic drive that travels through the desert forest making a 130-mile loop. The **Palms to Pines** journey travels along Highway 74 through Lake Hemet, on to Highway 243 where the Indian Vista overlook is found, and through the San Gorgonio Pass and Banning before connecting to I-10 and back onto Highway 111, the paved thread that connects the desert communities. Along the way you may spot deer, bighorn sheep, or even some rare birds. Among the oak trees are mule deer, acorn woodpeckers, alligator lizards, and more. It's an extremely diverse and interesting landscape with places to pull off and view the scenery.

As you motor near Palm Springs along I-10 near Highway 111 you'll notice rows and rows of **steel windmills,** which number about 4,000. These futuristic structures deliver electricity throughout the Coachella Valley. Take a 90-minute eco-tour, aboard an electric windmill-powered tram to learn about the benefits of wind power. Reservations are required (760-251-1997, www.windmilltours.com).

Palm Springs Accommodations

Many people use Orange County as a home base for exploring other parts of Southern California. While Palm Springs is easily doable in a day, it's much more relaxing if you can spend a night or two. There are several hotels and resorts within the Palm Springs area including The **Willows Historic Palm Springs Inn** (760-320-0771, www.thewillowshistoricpalmsprings.com), built in 1924 and once occupied by Marion Davies. It's an incredible home turned intimate inn fashioned after an Italian villa.

Travel Information

To reach Palm Springs from Orange County, head east on the 91 Freeway to I-10 and follow the signs to Palm Springs.

PALM SPRINGS DESERT RESORTS CONVENTION AND VISITORS AUTHORITY
(760) 770-9000
www.palmspringsusa.com

VENTURA AND OJAI

About 30 minutes south of Santa Barbara is Ventura, whose formal name is San Buenaventura. The two towns couldn't be more different. Santa Barbara exudes wealth in an understated way, while Ventura is more of a working class town. In the past decade, downtown Ventura has had a remarkable transformation. Where empty storefronts once stood there are now new shops, restaurants, and even a movie theater. A few blocks away is the beach, which is a popular destination for surfers and boogie boarders.

Spend an afternoon wandering down Main Street, between Ventura and Chestnut Avenues, where there is a bulk of antiques shops, restaurants, and coffeehouses. At 211 East Main St. is the **San Buenaventura Mission,** the 21st and final mission founded by Father Junípero Serra. Erected in 1782, it calls modern-day worshipers to its gates by the wooden bells that sit in its belfry. The grounds, gift shop, and sanctuary are open to the public, and a modest donation of $1 is suggested.

Highway 33, located near downtown, takes you up to **Ojai** (pronounced *Oh-Hi*), which is a delightful bucolic region spanning just 4.4 square miles. This best-kept secret, just a 30 minute ascent from Ventura, is easily manageable by foot, but the Ojai Trolley Service does provide transportation in and around town for just a quarter.

Downtown Ojai is home to the Mission Revival–style **Arcade,** erected in 1917 by Ohio glass magnate Edmund D. Libbey and considered the town's focal point. This colonnaded building features a collection of shops, tearooms, and wine bars. Book lovers can slip away a couple blocks up the road to prowl the shelves for tattered covers belonging to the many tomes at Bart's Books. This outdoor bookstore at 302 West Matilija St. carries used and rare books, and it is possible to spend hours at Bart's thumbing through an old paperback or hardbound book.

In recent years Ojai has gained a reputation as a haven for spiritual gurus, and there are many shops and galleries advertising the benefits of crystals and other metaphysical items. Ojai is a fledgling artists' colony as well, and there is no shortage of art galleries. You'll also find a web of trails for hiking and horseback riding.

Ojai Valley Inn and Spa

One of Ojai's best assets is its only full-service resort, the Ojai Valley Inn and Spa (805-646-1111 or www.ojairesort.com). The resort has a reputation for its understated elegance and architecture as well as its amenity-filled grounds. Ojai Valley Inn is no stranger to golfers and spa aficionados. There is an artist's cottage on the grounds as well where guests can blend their own essential oils or dabble with a paint brush and easel. If you think your trip calls for an overnight stay, the rooms are capsules of luxury with tiled floors and roomy baths. A few miles away are the resort's ranch and stables, where guests can saddle up for a horseback ride. The resort has three excellent restaurants including one that overlooks the fairways and another housed at the spa. If nothing else, swing by the Ojai Valley Inn and Spa to enjoy a cocktail at Jimmy's Pub, which also has views of the golf course.

A day in Ojai is all about enjoying the outdoors. Libbey Park, located across from the Arcade, is a great place to bring the kids to play. The Ojai Valley Trail, which can be picked up in town at Fox Road, is open from dawn to dusk.

About 20 miles away is the small community of Fillmore, where you'll encounter the **Fillmore & Western Railway Company** (805-524-2546, www.fwry.com). The Pullman sleepers and vintage parlor cars are often used on movie sets, but when they're not on some studio back lot they ferry passengers around the valley. The railway company also hosts themed events, such as murder mystery dinners and barbecue outings.

Travel Information

To reach Ojai take the 5 Freeway north to the 101 Freeway north. Once you pass through Ventura, exit onto Highway 33, which will take you right into the heart of Ojai.

OJAI VISITORS INFORMATION
www.ojaiconcierge.com

TEMECULA

Located less than an hour's drive from Orange County is one of Southern California's best-kept secrets. Temecula is a mix of vintage buildings and contemporary dwellings punctuated with some unexpected pleasures. From the aroma of ripened grapes and a flotilla of hot-air balloons to the *cha-ching* of slot machines, Temecula combines the beauty of Tuscany with the bright lights of Las Vegas. The region has grown considerably in the last decade with more residential and commercial developments, yet it still manages to retain its unhurried charm.

The movie *Sideways* put the spotlight on the vintners of Santa Barbara, leaving the remaining oenophiles to enjoy the less crowded tasting rooms of Temecula (951-699-6586, www.temeculawines.org).

The region's rolling hills are littered with vineyards yielding fabulous wines that are produced by an idyllic microclimate coupled with well-drained granite soils. Nearly 20 wineries open their doors to visitors year-round for tours and tastings. Prized varietals include Chardonnay, Syrah, and Meritage, just to name a few.

One way to explore the wine trail—safely—is from the backseat of a stretch limousine. There are several companies that offer chauffeured tours with a variety of vehicle options and gourmet picnic lunches readied in advance. One such company, Destination Temecula, will pick up and drop off tasters at any location throughout Southern California.

The heart of Temecula is the city's historic **Old Town.** Established in 1859, the town has been restored to its original splendor. If the walls of these buildings could talk, they'd whisper about the many scandals that unfolded during the 1920s and '30s: murders, bank robberies, floods, and the occasional visit by Hollywood heavyweights. Prizefighters Jack Dempsey and Jack Sharkey both worked out on the second floor of the Welty Building at Front and Main Street. And, before grapes were being crushed for merlot, moonshine was brewing

Pechanga's Feng Shui

The architects of Pechanga's High Limit Gaming Area didn't want to lay bets on its design, so they enlisted the help of a noted Feng Shui master to ensure the room and its elements evoke balance and harmony. Statues of fu dogs flank each entrance to the room, and these mythical Chinese figures are said to ward off negative energies while serving as protectors of their environments. Additional plush appointments include a water wall, a key element to maintaining Feng Shui; private VIP restrooms with individual sinks and vanities equipped in each stall; a full-service bar; and a secluded cash cage for conducting private transactions.

in the surrounding hills. Fleets of historic buildings are enjoying a new lease on life as a mix of shops, restaurants, and galleries occupy former jail cells, banks, and saloons. The Temecula Mercantile, built in 1891 from local bricks and once a one-stop shopping center for ranchers, has been magnificently transformed into an antiques mall. There are also several wonderful buildings housing sidewalk cafes, coffee houses, and wine tasting rooms.

What happens in Vegas stays in Vegas. The only problem with that philosophy is that more people from Orange County and other environs are choosing to stay elsewhere—namely **Temecula's Pechanga Resort & Casino** (www .pechanga.com, 951-693-1819). With the high cost of gasoline, not to mention the bumper-to-bumper traffic to and from Sin City, visitors are discovering the close-to-home convenience of heading to this tribal-run destination. Opened in 2002, the four-diamond resort offers a fabulous and exciting retreat with more than 500 rooms and suites plus a collection of dining options, lounges, and a decent caliber of entertainment with top musical acts and comedians taking to the stage of the 1,200-seat theater nearly every week.

But the main attraction at Pechanga is the high-tech, high-energy casino, which includes a non-smoking area separate from the main casino. Stake claim to one of 2,000 slot and video poker machines housed in nearly 200,000 square feet of space. Table games are divided among a pair of separate areas of the casino floor and include all the usual suspects: blackjack, three-card poker, and Pai Gow poker. The Poker Room hosts daily tournaments with a low buy-in and entry fees and a payout guarantee with up to 100 players. The High Limit Gaming Room reeks of serious gamblers with its VIP service, $10 to $100 slot machines, and blackjack tables where Ben Franklin's face is prominently displayed.

Travel Information

Take the 91 east to I-15 south and follow the exit signs to Temecula. It is approximately 60 miles from Orange County.

TEMECULA VALLEY CONVENTION AND VISITORS BUREAU
(951) 491-6085
www.temeculacvb.com

LIVING HERE

In this section we feature specific information for residents or those planning to relocate here. Topics include real estate, education, health care, and much more.

RELOCATION

Why would anyone want to move to Orange County? Could it be the incredible climate, its convenient proximity to both Los Angeles and San Diego, or the 42 miles of glistening coastline? Maybe it's the alluring shopping destinations, diverse communities, or the laid-back lifestyle. Whether it's one of these factors or an entire checklist, it doesn't take much to convince someone, especially those from colder climates, to head west and do some California dreamin' in The OC.

Once a land populated with grapevines and orange groves, Orange County blossomed after World War II when servicemen and women stationed in the region decided to stay put and raise families. Angelenos began their exodus from the city to the suburbs as Orange County's bedroom communities quickly evolved offering affordable, tidy tract homes and a quieter way of life. The opening of Disneyland and the arrival of Mickey Mouse in 1955 helped to catapult the region nationally and, slowly, Orange County evolved as a conservative metropolitan center and business hub.

Fast forward to a new millennium when Orange County is referred to as The OC, thanks to a popular television show of the same name. In recent years Hollywood has come calling, producing other Orange County–based "reality" shows, such as *The Real Housewives of Orange County* and *Laguna Beach*. Once considered the stepchild of Los Angeles, this so-called 'burb has more to offer than prime time drama. It has its own distinct identity that includes enclaves of waterfront homes, throngs of designer boutiques, well-heeled citizens, and a sexy surf culture that is solely its own. Add to the mix that Orange County is home to two major universities—Cal State Fullerton and UC Irvine—as well as Disneyland Resort, a collection of four- and five-star hotels, and an impressive roster of Fortune 500 companies.

Orange County's urban core is the Los Angeles–Long Beach–Santa Ana Metro area, and the county itself was one of America's fastest growing during the 1990s. With more than three million residents residing in nearly 800 square miles and 34 cities, Orange County continues to grow in population despite being one of the nation's most expensive regions. Home values more than doubled from 2000 to 2006 with the average annual rate rising nearly 13 percent, ranking Orange County as among the seven highest counties in the nation outside of New York City. In 2006 the median average home price was $309,000, but in recent years, with the economic downturn, the county has experienced a drop in residential real estate with many homes, from multimillion-dollar mansions to townhouses, foreclosing. With the first-time home buyer tax credit in place, Orange County is once again seeing a spike in home sales, but sellers trying to unload abodes priced below the $900,000 mark have a better chance at closing the deal. Those on the market for more than that sum are moving slowly, with nearly 13 months of inventory available.

REAL ESTATE RESOURCES

It used to be that realtors held all the cards simply because home buyers didn't have access to the Multiple Listing Service. Those days are gone, and now potential buyers, as well as sellers who want to conduct their own comparisons, can access the Multiple Listing Service at www.home

seekers.com or www.realtor.com. The best way to find a realtor is to drive a neighborhood and take note of the "For Sale" signs with the listing agent's name. In most cases realtors "work" specific neighborhoods and will know information such as the quality of local schools. Still, it's always best to do a little investigating on your own. The following is a list of associations where you can ask about a realtor's license and ethical practices, as well as the sale and purchase price of homes in specific areas.

CALIFORNIA ASSOCIATION OF REALTORS
(213) 739-8272
www.car.org

ORANGE COUNTY ASSOCIATION OF
REALTORS
(949) 586-6800, (714) 375-9313
www.ocar.org

OC REAL ESTATE BLOG
www.ocrealestateblog.com

PRUDENTIAL CALIFORNIA REALTY
(949) 481-3739
www.guidetolocalrealestate.com

Inc. magazine tapped 15 Orange County businesses for its prestigious list of the 500 fastest-growing companies for 2009. Out of the 15 selected, eight have their headquarters in Irvine, which *BusinessWeek* named as one of the best places in the United States to start a business.

HOME BUILDERS

During much of the 1990s, as well as throughout most of this decade, Orange County was abuzz with the sound of pounding nails and bulldozers leveling land. New developments rose out of nowhere and families were finding solace inside their new homes flanked with great rooms, gourmet kitchens, home theaters, and other such amenities. But it wasn't just master planned communities that caught the attention of potential buyers. Residential lofts, often built above storefronts or within new, faux-style downtowns, also made their way into the mainstream blurring the line between urban and suburban.

There has also been a surge of townhomes that have been incorporated into some of Orange County's more affluent neighborhoods. **Lennar,** a major builder of homes throughout the United States including many areas of Orange County, is creating what it touts as "Orange County's first urban master planned community." Central Park West, located in Irvine, will include 117 loft and brownstone homes with one to three bedrooms. More traditional single-family home developments are also replacing dirt lots in cities such as Buena Park and Orange. **Olson Homes,** based in Seal Beach, is developing Lotus Walk in Garden Grove featuring flats and townhomes starting at $300,000—which usually means one of the smaller units with zero upgrades. Orange County has also welcomed a number of master planned communities over the past decade including Quail Hill in Irvine, Talega in San Clemente, and Ladera Ranch near Mission Viejo.

Huntington Beach has also seen its share of growth, but with 2009 turning out to be one of the county's slowest years for construction since Eisenhower was in office—fewer than 1,800 building permits were issued during the first 10 months of 2009—things have not moved at the brisk pace they once did. **Brightwater** is a new 356-home community with views of the Bolsa Chica Wetlands with asking prices that start at $1.3 million. And what does $1.3 million get you in Orange County? For starters, you'll be near the coast, but certainly not waterfront, in a single family home with three bedrooms and three and a half baths spanning three levels with approximately 2,800 square feet. But many of these homes, and others built in the last 24 to 36 months, have simply sat on the market—empty—without a buyer to match. Where the sellers once called all the shots and buyers got into bidding wars with their competition, now the tide has turned and the power is in the hand of the buyer.

For information on potential new developments and home builders in Orange County, contact the Building Industry Association of Southern California at (909) 396-9993 or www.biasc.org.

REAL ESTATE FIRMS

As with most communities, Orange County has a number of national real estate firms whose offices are located in their specialized neighborhoods. Among some of the nation's well-known residential real estate firms are Prudential, GMAC, Century 21, and REMAX. Help U Sell is a niche realtor that offers lower commissions to sellers, but can also work with buyers. Each franchise operates differently, but some Help U Sell representatives will give buyers a portion of their commission if the buyer does most of the leg work in researching and viewing homes. The following realtors are strictly local operations.

BURR WHITE REALTY
2901 Newport Blvd., Newport Beach
(949) 675-4630
www.burrwhite.com
This local boutique-style, full-service firm specializes in waterfront and coastal properties and has been in business for more than 40 years. The bulk of their listings are found in Newport Beach. They also provide property and vacation management services, so those in the market to lease a dwelling can work with their staff as well.

MAIN BEACH REALTY
333 3rd St., Laguna Beach
(949) 715-2076
www.mainbeachrealty.com
Its name says it all, and this independent firm assists buyers interested in relocating to Laguna Beach, Dana Point, Laguna Niguel, and Huntington Beach. Both partners reside in Laguna Beach, so they are well versed when it comes to their core market and its inventory.

METRO ESTATES
120 Newport Center Dr., Suite 160, Newport Beach
(949) 720-9422
www.metroestates.com
This independent firm started out selling high-end luxury homes in and around Newport Beach. Since then, they have branched out to other areas and now serve all of Orange County including Costa Mesa, Irvine, and Balboa. Striking a perfect balance between corporate realtors and mom and pop operators, Metro Estates specializes in bank-owned properties.

ORANGE COUNTY COASTAL REALTORS
33522 Niguel Rd., Laguna Beach
(888) 622-8439
www.theoccoastalgroup.com
Experts when it comes to south Orange County real estate, especially the coastal regions, the staff has a combined 75 years of experience and takes a consultative approach with clients in the decision-making process.

PREFERRED HOME BROKERS
(714) 990-6060
www.preferredhomebrokers.com
This online real estate firm concentrates its efforts on north Orange County, specifically the communities of Brea, La Mirada, Orange, Yorba Linda, and Placentia. Many of its realtors are Orange County or Southern California natives and know their markets well.

WINKELMANN REALTY
114 North Harbor Blvd., Fullerton
(800) 397-3562
www.winkrealty.com
With its headquarters in downtown Fullerton and a second Orange County location in Fountain Valley, Winkelmann Realty is headed by real estate veteran Gloria Winkelmann. The first company in California to have one of its realtors designated a Senior Certified Relocation Professional, Winkelmann Realty has many north Orange County listings and provides clients with valuable information, such as the quality of local

schools and home inspection services. Relocation assistance is also a strong suit.

Real Estate Chains

Here is a list of national firms with Orange County offices.

Century 21
www.century21.com

GMAC
www.gmacrealestate.com

Help U Sell
www.helpusell.com

Keller Williams Realty
www.kw.com

Prudential
www.prudential.com/realestate

Realty Executives
www.realtyexecutives.com

REMAX
www.remax.com

Sotheby's
www.sothebysrealty.com

DESIRABLE NEIGHBORHOODS

Selecting an area to buy a home is a personal choice. It probably goes without saying that coastal properties are the most desirable as well as the most expensive. There are many factors at play in making the decision of where to settle down. Parents with school-age children typically want to be in an area where the school district has a great reputation, while price often drives the decision for first-time home buyers. The following are some of Orange County's more desirable areas.

The Coastal Communities

A waterfront home, or even a home near the beach, is about as good as it gets in terms of location. **Newport Beach, Laguna Beach, Dana Point,** and **San Clemente** are all lovely. In **Huntington Beach** there are no waterfront homes per se with the exception of a condominium complex overlooking the sand. Pacific Coast Highway divides a fleet of townhomes and single family homes from the beach, but residents still enjoy exceptional water views. In addition, Huntington Beach and **Seal Beach** both have neighborhoods with mid-century tract homes that, while not prime waterfront real estate, are nice affordable inland locations. Knowing that the beach communities are and always will be the most desirable, the following focuses on Orange County's inland communities.

Anaheim/Orange

Anaheim's city limits are broad and reach from Cypress in the west to the Riverside County line in the east. It's one of Orange County's larger cities with many mid-century developments flanked with nondescript homes, especially near Disneyland. Gwen Stefani, lead singer of No Doubt, was raised nearby and often infuses Anaheim landmarks into her song lyrics. Near Angel Stadium a new, pseudo urban development continues to grow with loft-style living, entertainment venues, and retail conveniences. In the eastern most part of the city the 91 Freeway divides the affluent area of Anaheim Hills, part of Anaheim proper, from Yorba Linda. Many of the homes in Anaheim Hills are large and custom, although you will also find upscale tract developments and condo-style living. Of course, Anaheim, home to the county's premier convention center, is appealing to visitors because of Disneyland, Anaheim Stadium, and the Honda Center where the Ducks play during the NHL season. A new addition to Anaheim is the Anaheim GardenWalk, an outdoor dining and entertainment center located near Disneyland.

The City of Orange, which neighbors Anaheim, has a sought-after neighborhood for preservationists. **Old Towne Orange,** a historic district with an enchanting plaza circle, is surrounded by vintage homes dating back to the

19th century. **The Plaza** has a weekly farmers' market and just down the street is **Chapman University,** a private liberal arts college. The City of Orange also has some very nice homes cradled in the hills just east of the plaza area.

Brea/Placentia/Yorba Linda

While this trio of towns does not offer much in the way of nightlife, the communities are very family friendly with good schools, many conveniences, and a major hospital. The area is also home to the Brea Mall anchored by Nordstrom, JCPenney, Sears, and Macy's with many upscale retailers dispersed among its five wings. Nearby are **Cal State Fullerton** and **Fullerton Community College** plus a private law school, an optometry school, and a private Christian school. Yorba Linda, located next to Placentia and Brea, gained prominence and national attention when the **Richard Nixon Library and Birthplace** opened its doors several years ago and was cast in the spotlight again when President Nixon's body lay in state. Many upscale homes are scattered among new hillside developments in this area as well. Placentia also has residential developments that back onto **Alta Vista Country Club,** one of the area's top golf courses. Brea is in the most northern part of the county abutting Los Angeles County near Diamond Bar, while Yorba Linda is one of the county's most eastern areas resting against the Riverside County Line. Placentia sits in the middle surrounded by Brea, Yorba Linda, Fullerton, and Anaheim.

Fullerton

Fullerton is another one of Orange County's larger towns and neighbors Brea, Placentia, Anaheim, and Buena Park. Neighborhoods near Cal State Fullerton are typical post-war era homes, while the Sunny Hills area is much more bucolic with horse trails and sizeable custom homes. Downtown Fullerton is the epicenter for dining and clubbing with one local magazine touting it as "Bourbon Street West," although it's much more subdued than anything taking place in The Big Easy. The residential streets north of Common-

wealth feature adorable vintage cottages and bungalows while the homes above the nearby courthouse are a mix of well-built and aesthetically pleasing abodes erected during the 1960s and '70s. Just north of downtown is **Hillcrest Park,** a wonderful place to come for picnics, softball games, or just to visit the playground. The homes that neighbor the park are also vintage structures and line narrow, winding streets. In addition to Cal State Fullerton, the town is also home to Fullerton Community College attended by Pat Nixon; Hope University, a private Christian college; Western State University College of Law; and Southern California College of Optometry.

Irvine

Tucked within 65 square miles is Irvine, one of the nation's largest planned communities. People either enjoy the conformity that comes with living in a planned community or feel stifled by it. Irvine's many neighborhoods, with names like Woodbridge and Turtle Rock, are built like "mini towns." Shops, restaurants, services, schools, and parks are built to complement each specific neighborhood or region. There are also strict guidelines homeowners must follow, such as approved exterior paint colors and no open garages except when entering and exiting. While some people welcome this uniformity, others refer to Irvine as "Stepford," referring to the 1970s-era film depicting a neighborhood of perfect homes and wives. Whatever your preference, Irvine is ideally located near the 5 and 405 Freeways and connects to Laguna Beach via Laguna Canyon Road. There are many parks, including the **Great Park** that is currently being developed in phases, good schools, a low crime rate, decent shopping, and a University of California campus. The **Villages of Irvine** is a brand new development featuring single-family homes ranging from 2,100 to 3,200 square feet plus additional townhomes, condominiums, and flats. Nearby shopping includes **Irvine Spectrum,** an open-air esplanade with Moroccan-style architecture containing Nordstrom, Anthropologie, Barnes & Noble, and many specialty stores, restaurants, and entertainment. A few miles west is South Coast Plaza and a few miles south are The Shops at Mission Viejo.

Villa Park

As Orange County's smallest city, Villa Park is known for its quiet neighborhoods and well-kept residential streets. Located in the center of the county and part of the Orange Unified School District, Villa Park has one of the lowest crime rates in the county. The city, which is void of sidewalks and street lights, is zoned for single-family residences only and many homes boast half-acre lots, which accounts for the collection of backyard swimming pools and tennis courts. There are two elementary schools, one middle school, and a single high school, Villa Park High, where actor Kevin Costner graduated in the 1970s.

RETIREMENT AND SENIOR SERVICES

Maybe it's the great weather, perpetual sunshine, or active lifestyle that keeps Orange County's senior citizens so fit. Didn't someone once say that 80 is the new 60? The following are a list of services for Orange County's mature residents.

THE ORANGE COUNTY OFFICE ON AGING
(714) 567-7500
www.ocgov.com
A leading advocate, planner, and facilitator, the Orange County Office on Aging works on behalf of the county's older citizens by partnering with various organizations to offer such programs as free or low-cost exercise classes, guidance on healthcare issues such as the recent H1N1 vaccine and its availability, transportation, counseling, adult day care, financial needs, housing, legal aid, meals, and much more. The Office on Aging also encourages its older citizens to consider volunteering their time and offers a community resource list of volunteer opportunities to match seniors with an organization or cause that is of interest to them or where their skill sets can best be used.

LIVING HERE

Senior Citizens Advisory Council

The Senior Citizens Advisory Council (SCAC) works with the Orange County Board of Supervisors, Community Services Agency, and the Office on Aging regarding matters affecting senior citizens living in Orange County. The council, which consists of 40 volunteers, three standing committees, and a 10-member executive board, meets monthly to assess the needs of seniors and advocate on their behalf.

HOUSING FOR RESIDENTS 55+

Orange County offers active seniors an array of choices for those who prefer to live in a community surrounded by older adults. Many offer sports, such as golf or tennis, and are conveniently located to retail stores and services.

Talega, a new master planned community in San Clemente, has two homeowner neighborhoods with retirement communities. **Wavecrest** is a collection of one- and two-story homes ranging in size from two to three bedrooms plus lofts. Behind its gates are a club room, swimming pool and spa, putting green, fitness center, and an agenda of social events and outings. **Waterleaf** offers similarly designed homes and is close to the Talega Club, which features recreational amenities. Visit www.san-clemente.org.

Laguna Woods Village, about 10 miles inland from the beach and formerly known as Leisure World, changed its name a decade ago when residents voted to incorporate as a city. This active adults-only community, where the average age is 78, offers a wide spectrum of activities, from horseback riding and golf to tennis and bowling. There are also transportation services available. Find out more at www.laguna woodscity.org.

On the other side of the county in Seal Beach is Leisure World, one of the first master planned retirement communities opened in 1962. Located a few miles from the beach and close to many good hospitals, Leisure World has approximately 9,000 residents accounting for nearly one-third of the city's population. Residents can choose from two types of property ownership, including cooperative units, where the owner is a shareholder in the housing corporation, or condominiums, where the owner has a deed to the dwelling. Residents, who must meet a minimum age requirement of 55, are able to use the golf course, swimming pool, and exercise room free of charge as well as host meetings and activities inside the clubhouses. There is also a fare-free minibus that transports residents to nearby shopping centers, and a health facility can be found on the premises. See www.lwsb.com.

MEDIA

Newspapers

Much of Orange County's news media is generated from Los Angeles, including the local news stations that broadcast from LA County. Usually correspondents from these broadcast outlets are assigned to cover Orange County news. The same goes for local radio. The *Los Angeles Times* has an Orange County bureau that continues to shrink as the paper, like many other news organizations, has changed its focus to create a broader presence on the Internet.

Dailies
DAILY PILOT
1375 Sunflower Ave., Costa Mesa
(714) 966-4600
www.dailypilot.com
Launched in 1907 as the *Newport News*, the *Daily Pilot* has gone through several name changes since—*Newport Harbor Pilot*, the *Orange County Daily Pilot*, and the *Newport Beach–Costa Mesa Pilot*. *Times Mirror*, which also owned the *LA Times*, purchased the paper in 1993 and began packaging it with the *LA Times* thus eliminating national

and world news altogether and concentrating on local news concerning the Newport/Costa Mesa area. Tribune acquired the *Daily Pilot*, as well as the *Los Angeles Times* and several other publications, in 2000 and, most recently, Sam Zell purchased Tribune. The *Daily Pilot* has a circulation of about 30,000 readers and has won many publishing and journalism awards.

THE *LOS ANGELES TIMES*, ORANGE COUNTY EDITION
1375 Sunflower Ave., Costa Mesa
(714) 966-5600
www.latimes.com
The *Los Angeles Times* remains a force to be reckoned with as it is the last daily paper still standing in Los Angeles, which at one time had daily newspapers in the double digits. Its Orange County edition has all the same news, sports, business, and entertainment coverage as the regular paper, but simply swaps out Los Angeles's local news with the most current events affecting Orange County. Other than this minor difference, it's the same paper in both counties. The *LA Times* main editorial office is in Downtown Los Angeles.

ORANGE COUNTY REGISTER
625 North Grand Ave., Santa Ana
(714) 796-7000
www.ocregister.com
The *Orange County Register*, for the most part, is the only act in town when it comes to extensive Orange County news coverage. It launched on November 25, 1905 as the *Santa Ana Register* and was published by a group of businessmen to serve the county's 20,000 residents. In 1935, Raymond Cyrus Hoiles purchased the paper making it the flagship of his publishing empire and, 15 years later, he founded Freedom Newspapers, Inc., after acquiring seven newspapers around the country. Together with his son, Clarence, he co-published the newspaper until his death in 1970. From 1970 to 1979 Clarence and his brother Harry were co-publishers until Clarence's son-in-law was named publisher and, eventually, Chairman of the Board for Freedom Communications.

The *Register*, which is a more conservative paper than its liberal counterpart, the *Los Angeles Times*, saw some of its biggest changes during the 1980s when it began publishing in full color, changed its name to its current moniker, and won its first Pulitzer Prize for its photographic coverage of the 1984 Olympics held in Los Angeles. Since then, the paper has won two additional Pulitzer Prizes for reporting and also celebrated its centennial in 2005. It also publishes three magazines: *Coast, Preferred Destinations*, and *Coast Kids*.

Among the paper's notable columnists are David Whiting (outdoors), Frank Mickadeit (local issues), Jonathan Lansner (real estate/housing), and Barry Koltnow (entertainment); Nancy Luna, a business reporter for the paper, covers restaurant news in print as well as through her blog, fastfoodmaven.com, where she dishes on the local restaurant scene.

Community Newspapers

Just about every community in Orange County has its own weekly newspaper where residents can get the scoop on news at the utmost local level. The Orange County Community Newspaper Group publishes an array of community newspapers which are distributed Thursdays as an insert inside the *Orange County Register*. Editions can also be accessed online at www.ocregister.com/articles/community-218948-find-news.html. Weekly community newspapers include:

Aliso Viejo News
Anaheim Bulletin
Anaheim Hills News
Brea Progress/La Habra
Canyon Life/Rancho Santa Margarita News
Capistrano Valley News
Dana Point News
Fountain Valley View
Fullerton News Tribune
Irvine World News
Ladera Post
Laguna Beach News Post
Laguna Niguel News
Leisure World News
Orange City News
Placentia News-Times

Saddleback Valley News
San Clemente Sun Post
Tustin News
Yorba Linda Star

OC Weekly

OC Weekly is a free alternative newspaper that began publishing in 1995 and has been known to challenge the system, be it an expose on an elected official or a profile piece on an elusive CEO. It also covers newsworthy topics that may not appeal to the mainstream media. In addition, you'll find great restaurant reviews, a list of the best clubs, film reviews, and more. Gustavo Arellano writes "Ask a Mexican," a popular and humorous "advice" column.

Magazines

COAST MAGAZINE
240 Newport Center Dr., Suite 290, Newport Beach
(949) 644-4700
www.coastmagazine.com
Coast is a monthly, glossy regional magazine that has been publishing for the past 17 years. Its goal is to provide readers with a look into life in The OC, covering topics and subjects that, perhaps, its competitors have overlooked. Readers enjoy dining reviews and travel features with opportunities to go inside homes of some of the region's movers and shakers. There is also a society column, covering openings and fêtes, plus health features and a look at the arts.

944
9 Executive Circle, Suite 215, Irvine
(949) 252-8944
www.944.com

A free, cutting-edge publication with a local focus and a knack for covering the best openings, *944*, like its competitors, takes its readers to heady destinations inside the best restaurants and provides front row seats to designer shows. If you want to get past the velvet rope, pick up a copy of *944* and live vicariously through its editor and staff writers.

OC FAMILY
1451 Quail St., Suite 201, Newport Beach
(949) 757-1404
www.ocfamily.com
This magazine aimed at moms is the go-to guide for everything family. It provides information on local preschools and private schools, camps, health care, how to outdo other parents when it comes to throwing the best single-digit birthday bash, maternity advice, and blogs from local moms. There is also health and fitness advice, details on kid-friendly restaurants, and social clubs designed specifically for moms and their offspring.

OC METRO
1451 Quail St., Suite 201, Newport Beach
(949) 757-1404
www.ocmetro.com
Covering Orange County's business, people, and life, the monthly *OC Metro* is a hybrid of business and lifestyle with a focus on some of the county's most influential businesspeople and companies, along with travel features and restaurant reviews. The publication is free and found at retailers, restaurants, and services throughout Orange County.

ORANGE COAST
3701 Birch St., Suite 100, Newport Beach
(949) 862-1133
www.orangecoastmagazine.com
Out of all of Orange County's magazines, *Orange Coast* produces one of the most attractive publications and is the premier lifestyle magazine for residents. Founded in 1974 as *Nieuport*, a name meant to draw attention on the newsstand, by Ron Guccione, cousin of *Penthouse* publisher Bob Guccione, *Orange Coast* has had a few owners since it launched its first issue and was recently purchased by Emmis Publishing. Each issue features a celebrity cover and interview plus a rundown on local dining, travel destinations, events, shopping, and more. The magazine is still very much centered around Newport Beach society.

ORANGE COUNTY BUSINESS JOURNAL
18500 Von Karman Ave., Suite 150, Irvine
(949) 833-8373
www.ocbj.com
Published weekly and delivering the most complete and comprehensive news and information pertaining to Orange County's companies, industries, and businesspeople, the *Orange County Business Journal* is an informative read. Anyone who does business in The OC will want to—and need to—read this journal cover to cover.

RIVIERA
3200 Bristol St., Costa Mesa
(714) 557-2700
www.modernluxury.com
Published by Modern Luxury Media, creators of edgy city magazines, *Riviera* has a more avant-garde feel than *Coast* or *Orange Coast* magazines. Each issue delves into an array of topics that appeal to its affluent readers, from celebrity profiles to the latest must-dine restaurant to cutting-edge fashion. Travel features and a look at local issues are usually found beneath its cover as well. *Riviera* also has a heavy focus on the coastal lifestyle, hence the name.

Radio

Orange County only has a couple of stations to call its own. Most radio stations broadcast from Los Angeles, and today's alternative rock station could easily transition to another format overnight. LA radio, just like other markets, is driven by listenership and advertisers.

Adult Contemporary/Soft Rock
KBPK 90.1 FM (Orange County)
KLIT 92.7 FM
KTWV (The Wave) 94.7 FM

KOST 103.5 FM
KBIG 104.3 FM

Children's
KDIS 1110 AM (Disney)

Christian
KFSH (The Fish) 95.9 FM
KBRT 740 AM

Classical
KUSC 99.5 FM

Country
KKGO 105.1

Hip-Hop/Rap
KPWR 105.5 FM

Jazz
KJZZ 87.5 FM
KKHZ 88.1 FM
KSBR 88.5 FM (Orange County)

Mexican/Spanish
KXOS 93.9 FM
KBUA 94.3 FM
KXOL 96.3 FM
KWIZ 96.7 FM (Orange County)
KLYY 97.5 FM
KLAX 97.9 FM
KRCV 98.3 FM
KSCA 101.9 FM
KBUE 105.5 FM
KMXE 830 AM
KHJ 930 AM
KTNQ 1020 AM

National Public Radio
KPCC 89.3 FM
KCRW 89.9 FM

News/Weather/Sports
KFWB 980 AM
KNX 1070 AM

Oldies
KRTH 101.1 FM

Rock/Alternative
KCBS (Jack FM) 93.1 FM

KLOS 95.5 FM
KROQ 106.7 FM

Sports Only
KAVL 610 AM
KSPN 710 AM
KXTA 1150 AM
KMPC 1540 AM

Talk
KFI 640 AM
KABC 790 AM

Top 40
KLSX 97.1 FM
KYSR 98.7 FM
KIIS 102.7 FM

Urban/R&B
KGGI 99.1 FM
KJLH 102.3 FM

International OC Radio

There is an abundance of Spanish radio stations in the Greater Los Angeles/Orange County area. But, because the region is a melting pot, you will also find AM stations that broadcast in Farsi, Korean, Chinese, and Vietnamese. To locate these as well as mainstream radio channels, log onto www.radiowatch.com for the most up-to-date programming and formatting information.

Television—Local TV and Network Affiliates
KCBS Channel 2 (CBS)
KNBC Channel 4 (NBC)
KTLA Channel 5 (The WB)
KABC Channel 7 (ABC)
KCAL Channel 9 (KCAL)
KTTV Channel 11 (FOX)

KCOP Channel 13 (KCOP)
KMEX Channel 34 (Univision/Spanish)
KOCE Channel 50 (Orange County Public and
    Community Television)
KDOC Channel 56 (Orange County Public
    Television)

Blogs and Ezines

GREER'S OC
www.greersoc.com
Greer Wylder, an OC native and former columnist for the *Daily Pilot*, has her pulse on Orange County's living. Tips on the newest and best retail stores, bargains on designer duds, dining spots not yet discovered, and Q&As with some of the county's innovators make her easy-to-navigate Web site a pleasure to visit. In addition, Greer delivers a free, subscriber-only daily e-letter called *A Daily Dose of OC.*

MONSTER MUNCHING
www.elmonster.blogspot.com
This blogger dishes on Orange County edibles and has a comprehensive list of restaurant reviews.

PUBLIC LIBRARIES

Orange County Public Libraries consist of 33 branches and are a network of community libraries located within the county's many cities and unincorporated areas. Those with an Orange County Public Library card have checkout privileges at any one of the branches as well as other library systems with reciprocal lending privileges. To apply for a library card, applicants must be a California resident and must present photo identification and provide proof of residence using a current utility bill or some other document. For a list of branches, visit http://egov.ocgov.com and click on "Departments and Agencies," then scroll down the list on the left side of the screen and click on OC Public Libraries.

DEPARTMENT OF PUBLIC SAFETY

Most cities in Orange County, including the campuses of Cal State Fullerton and UC Irvine, have their own independent police departments and/or fire departments; however, some communities, such as Yorba Linda, are serviced by other police departments or county law enforcement. The **Orange County Fire Authority** services 23 communities as well as the unincorporated areas. The **Orange County Sheriff–Coroner Department** consists of five organizational functions divided among 20 divisions including such core services as public protection/homeland security, jail operations, technical services including investigations and forensics, and administrative support.

In life-threatening emergencies, call 9-1-1 for immediate assistance. To learn more about Orange County's Department of Public Safety, visit http://egov.ocgov.com and click on "Law" at the information bar at the top of the screen.

INDEPENDENT FIRE DEPARTMENTS

ANAHEIM FIRE DEPARTMENT
201 South Anaheim Blvd., Suite 301, Anaheim
(714) 765-4000

BREA FIRE DEPARTMENT
1 Civic Center Circle, Brea
(714) 990-7600

COSTA MESA FIRE DEPARTMENT
2803 Royal Palm Dr., Costa Mesa
(714) 754-5106

FOUNTAIN VALLEY FIRE DEPARTMENT
10200 Slater Ave., Fountain Valley
(714) 593-4436

FULLERTON FIRE DEPARTMENT
312 East Commonwealth Ave., Fullerton
(714) 738-6500

GARDEN GROVE FIRE DEPARTMENT
11301 Acacia Parkway, Garden Grove
(714) 741-5600

HUNTINGTON BEACH FIRE DEPARTMENT
2000 Main St., Huntington Beach
(714) 536-5411

LAGUNA BEACH FIRE DEPARTMENT
505 Forest Ave., Laguna Beach
(949) 497-3311

LA HABRA–LA COUNTY FIRE DEPARTMENT
1320 North Eastern Ave., Los Angeles
(323) 881-2411

NEWPORT BEACH FIRE DEPARTMENT
3300 Newport Blvd., Newport Beach
(949) 644-3104

ORANGE COUNTY FIRE AUTHORITY
1 Fire Authority Rd., Irvine
(714) 573-6000

ORANGE FIRE DEPARTMENT
176 South Grand Ave., Orange
(714) 288-2500

SANTA ANA FIRE DEPARTMENT
1439 South Broadway, Santa Ana
(714) 647-5700

CHAMBERS OF COMMERCE

Most communities in Orange County have their own chambers of commerce, which can provide relocation and business information. The South Orange Regional County Chambers of Commerce Web site (www.socchambers.com) provides a list of chambers in the county's south region, while the following is a list of chambers of commerce that pertain to some of the county's key communities.

ANAHEIM CHAMBER OF COMMERCE
100 South Anaheim Blvd. #300, Anaheim
(714) 758-0222
www.anaheimchamber.org

BREA CHAMBER OF COMMERCE
#1 Civic Center Circle, Brea
(714) 529-4938
www.breachamber.com

BUENA PARK CHAMBER OF COMMERCE
6280 Manchester, #102, Buena Park
(714) 521-0261
www.buenapark.com

COSTA MESA CHAMBER OF COMMERCE
1700 Adams Ave., Suite 101, Costa Mesa
(714) 885-9090
www.costamesachamber.com

DANA POINT CHAMBER OF COMMERCE
P.O. Box 12, Dana Point
(949) 496-1555
www.danapoint-chamber.com

FOUNTAIN VALLEY CHAMBER
11100 Warner Ave. #204, Fountain Valley
(714) 668-0542
www.fvchamber.com

NEWPORT BEACH AREA CHAMBER
1470 Jamboree Rd., Newport Beach
(949) 729-4400
www.newportbeach.com

SAN CLEMENTE CHAMBER OF COMMERCE
1100 North El Camino Real, San Clemente
(949) 492-1131
www.scchamber.com

YORBA LINDA CHAMBER OF COMMERCE
17670 Yorba Linda Blvd., Yorba Linda
(714) 993-9537
www.yorbalindachamber.org

EDUCATION

When it comes to schools, Orange County has an abundance of choices, from the very young dabbling in finger paints to those earning post-graduate degrees. But the state's public education system is in the midst of a financial crisis with a staggering $18 billion in cuts to education that are affecting students at the primary and high school levels all the way up the ladder to higher education, which many claim is becoming less and less affordable.

Last year Governor Arnold Schwarzenegger announced revisions to his budget proposal that included multibillion-dollar cuts to the state's education system, making California the nation's last funding-per-pupil state. School districts are finding themselves strapped, delaying financial support and funds for such basic necessities as textbooks. Class sizes, which were reduced years ago, will increase with the possibility of shaving seven days off the school calendar. Many arts and music programs have been scaled back or eliminated altogether, physical education is no longer conducted daily, and summer school in many districts no longer exists.

The University of California (UC) and California State University (CSU) were once considered the best education systems in the United States, but are now facing multimillion-dollar shortfalls. The CSU system has created work furloughs for staff. Salary and hiring freezes, plus travel restrictions as a result of shrinking budgets, have also been implemented. In addition, student enrollment has been limited system-wide and college-bound students are borrowing more money than ever before and, not surprising, loan default rates are rapidly increasing as a result. Student protests on state college campuses are also becoming more common as students struggle to find the means to pay tuition or secure classes. The Cal Grant program, which provides financial aid to students at the university level, will be phased out altogether by 2011.

While this may be life as we know it, California public universities still get high marks for their full range of undergraduate and masters' programs, as well as doctoral degrees, and are noted for producing groundbreaking research. Both Cal Berkeley and UCLA rank among the Top 25 National Universities according to *U.S. News & World Report*. In addition to Orange County's two public universities, Cal State Fullerton and UC Irvine, both named to *U.S. News & World Report*'s list of Best Colleges, the county also has many community colleges as well as private and for-profit institutions.

This chapter takes you from diapers to doctorate degrees as we explore the educational systems and options Orange County has to offer.

CHILD CARE CENTERS

Selecting child care for your child or children can be a daunting task. You should settle for nothing less than a safe environment that encourages healthy social, emotional, cognitive and physical development. A quality child care center should be licensed by the state of California, have policies and procedures in place such as hours of operation and fee structures, employ qualified staff and caregivers with low child to adult ratios, and have established health and nutrition guideline as well as safety policies, such as food menus and sanitized changing tables for babies.

There are also warning signs you should look for. Can parents drop in unexpectedly and observe the center? Are caregivers nurturing or dismissive with children? Are there signs of physical or emotional abuse? Or does your child suddenly have an interest in sexual issues or knowledge of sexual issues that is well beyond their years? If you suspect any misconduct, you may want to reevaluate your situation as well as report any abuse to authorities immediately.

The Children's Home Society of California (CHS) is a resource and referral program serving Orange County parents who want to obtain information about child care programs. Listings on licensed family child care homes and child care centers are kept on file. The CHS hotline, (714) 543-2273 or www.chs-ca.org, provides information on child care assistance, conducts in-home provider background checks, offers parent workshops, and helps with subsidized programs.

PRESCHOOL

Preschool provides young children a foundation for such concepts as learning to share and following instructions while equipping them with the social skills needed to advance. It is likely that preschool will be their first introduction into a structured setting, too, with a teacher, rules to follow, and a curriculum. Many preschools prepare children for that next big step—kindergarten.

HARBOR TRINITY PRESCHOOL
1230 Baker St., Costa Mesa
(714) 556-4335
www.harbortrinity.org
Serving children ages two to six years old, this Christian preschool places a strong emphasis on character development as well as academically enriching students and preparing them for elementary school. Lesson plans also address specific ages of developments. Potty trainers are welcome.

MARINA VIEW PRESCHOOL
AND KINDERGARTEN
25301 Sweet Meadow Dr., Laguna Niguel
(949) 249-8687
www.marinaviewpreschool.com
This year-round school accepts children as young as one year up through kindergarten and offers a complete education with phonics, pre-reading,

and writing skills plus music, dance, and gymnastics. Foreign language is also a major part of the curriculum. Parents will feel secure in leaving their children in this state-of-the-art facility with security and monitoring cameras in every classroom.

STEPPING STONES PRESCHOOL
30605 Avenida de Las Flores,
Rancho Santa Margarita
(949) 709-5219
www.smumc.com
Situated on the grounds of a Methodist church, this preschool welcomes children 2½ to 5 years of age. With a low student to adult ratio, hands-on learning, a Christian environment, and family activities, Stepping Stones offers a well-rounded educational beginning.

TEMPLE BETH SHALOM
2625 North Tustin Ave., Santa Ana
(714) 628-4600
www.tbsoc.com
Children explore and celebrate the Jewish culture through an array of enriching developmental programs with an emphasis on physical activity, cognitive learning, and emotional growth. Instructors foster self-esteem, curiosity, imagination, caring for others, and the ability to play independently as well as with others.

ORANGE COUNTY DEPARTMENT OF EDUCATION

Partnering with Orange County's many school districts in order to provide some half-million students with a quality education of standard skills and safe learning environments, the Orange County Department of Education (OCDE) offers county-operated programs and services, such as alternative and correctional education, regional occupational programs, and special education, just to name a few. OCDE is a connecting agency among Orange County's 28 school districts as well as four community college districts consisting of 10 institutions. Orange County has more than 60 high school campuses and an ample number of elementary and middle schools.

The OCDE Web site, www.ocde.us, has information and links to the county's Distinguished Schools and Blue Ribbon Schools as well as Academic Performance Index (API) scores, plus resources for parents, teachers, and students. If you choose to home-school your child, www.ochomeschooling.org is a great resource for field trips, activities, and connecting with other parents who also home-school their children.

PRIVATE SCHOOLS

Like any populated community, Orange County has a number of tuition-based private schools for elementary, middle, and high school with some schools offering an education from kindergarten through 12th grade.

Religion-Based Schools

CORNELIA CONNELLY HIGH SCHOOL
2323 West Broadway, Anaheim
(714) 776-1717
www.connellyhs.org
This all girls, independent Catholic high school is a fully accredited, college-preparatory institution offering honors and advanced placement courses. Approaching its 50th year, Connelly remains one of Orange County's top schools for girls and has a student population of just 260.

MARINERS CHRISTIAN SCHOOL
300 Fischer Ave., Costa Mesa
(714) 437-1700
www.marinerschristianschool.org
A Blue Ribbon School with full accreditation, Mariners Christian School was founded in 1987 as an independent, non-denominational Christian school whose mission is to build a firm foundation through Christ-centered education. Students are armed with the necessary academic tools to help them prepare for the challenges of high school and higher education.

MATER DEI
1202 West Edinger Ave., Santa Ana
(714) 754-7711
www.materdei.org

With a student body of more than 2,100, this co-ed Catholic institution is the largest non-public school west of Chicago. While faith based, 83 percent of the students are Catholics, while the remaining 17 percent represent other denominations. In addition to an excellent academic standard, the school also promotes co-curricular or extra-curricular activities including athletics, school clubs, and performing arts. Most students reside in Orange County, but some commute from as far as Riverside and Los Angeles counties in order to attend this high-ranking school.

ORANGE LUTHERAN HIGH SCHOOL
2222 North Santiago Blvd., Orange
(714) 998-5151
www.lhsoc.org
Since opening its doors in 1973, Orange Lutheran High School has been a sizeable co-ed institution with a balanced approach to academics, athletics, and the arts. Accredited by the National Lutheran School Accreditation Organization and the Western Association of Schools and Colleges (WASC), whose accreditation team visited the campus in 2007 and awarded the school the WASC's highest possible rating in six years, Orange Lutheran High School has a stellar reputation among the county's private institutions. There are 1,150 students enrolled with a staff that includes 163 teachers and administrators. The school averages a 97 percent college acceptance rate.

SERVITE HIGH SCHOOL
1952 West La Palma Ave., Anaheim
(714) 774-1404
www.servitehs.org
A fully accredited, all-boys Catholic high school, Servite boasts that 99 percent of its graduates go on to attend college. Programs include honors and Advanced Placement courses in several core subjects. Servite also excels in athletics and participates in 13 interscholastic sports including football, baseball, and water polo, just to name a few, with nearly two-thirds of the student population participating in one or more sports.

Secular Schools

FAIRMONT PRIVATE SCHOOLS
(714) 765-6300
www.fairmontschools.com
As Orange County's oldest nonsectarian private school, Fairmont was founded in 1953 and serves 2,200 co-ed students from preschool through 12th grade. Academic studies are complemented by athletics, arts, and extracurricular activities. Added parental conveniences, such as extended day care and after-school academic assistance, are also available. There are six Fairmont campuses throughout Orange County including a preparatory school located in Anaheim.

THE PEGASUS SCHOOL
19692 Lexington Lane, Huntington Beach
(714) 964-1224
www.thepegasusschool.org
Established in 1984 as an independent, non-denominational school for bright and gifted children, Pegasus serves children in preschool through eighth grade and offers a rigorous academic program while cultivating interests with after-school enrichment classes. Founded by Dr. Laura Hathaway, Pegasus is accredited by the California Association of Independent Schools.

SAGE SCHOOL
20402 Newport Coast Dr., Newport Beach
(949) 219-0100
www.sagehillschool.org
With an average class size of just 15 students, Sage School, a co-ed college preparatory day school serving students from 9th through 12th grades, excels in academic excellence. Its students earn the highest SAT scores in Orange County, and extracurricular activities, including athletics and on-campus clubs, further add to the overall experience. As one of Orange County's most prestigious private schools, the institution employs full-time counselors to provide individualized guidance through the college selection and application process.

HIGHER EDUCATION

When it comes to America's most educated regions, Orange County ranks right up there with the best of them. More than 60 percent of the county's high school graduates pursue post-secondary education and 19 percent of those students attend either California State University or the University of California, most likely due to the affordability (at least for now) for state residents. And nearly one-third of Orange County residents age 25 or older hold at least a bachelor's degree, which is higher than the statewide average.

Orange County's colleges are attractive to local students as well as those who attend from other regions for obvious reasons. The beaches are within easy reach, the shopping is among the best in Southern California, there's an entertainment element (though more subdued than what Los Angeles has to offer), and the weather is simply unbeatable. The mountains and desert are less than two hours away, which adds to the flexibility. Within the county there are nearly 80 post-secondary institutions with almost a dozen public colleges and universities including community colleges, 15 private colleges, and more than 50 professional schools.

Community Colleges

Orange County's community college system is composed of four districts consisting of 10 schools. The Coast Community College District (www.cccd.edu) includes Coastline Community College, Golden West College, and Orange Coast College all offering programs in general education, occupational or technical education, community services, and student support and is one of the nation's leading community college districts with an enrollment of more than 60,000 full- and part-time students.

The North Orange County Community College District (www.nocccd.edu) encompasses some 155 square miles extending to the Riverside County line to the east and the Los Angeles County line to the west and north. The district is home to Cypress and Fullerton colleges, with a combined student population of 33,000. The Rancho Santiago Community College District (www.rsccd.org) includes Santa Ana College and Santiago Canyon College with a combined enrollment of 51,000 students with a workforce improvement program designed to enhance regional employment and vitality.

And, finally, the South Orange County Community College District (www.socccd.org) is a multi-campus district that includes Saddleback College, Irvine Valley College, and the Advanced Technology & Education Park. Some 40,000 students are enrolled with many working towards associate degrees as well as credits that are transferable to four-year colleges and universities. New to the district is the Advanced Technology & Education Park, which began initial classes in 2007 as part of an educational collaboration with tech-oriented businesses and other educational institutions.

Colleges and Universities

CALIFORNIA STATE UNIVERSITY, FULLERTON
800 North State College Blvd.
(657) 278-2011
www.fullerton.edu
Situated on 228 urban acres and known locally as Cal State Fullerton, this comprehensive regional university boasts seven colleges, more than 105 degree programs with 50 at the graduate level plus a doctorate in education, a faculty of 2,100, and a student body population of nearly 38,000 full- and part-time students. The campus continues to evolve as well with the recent addition of a state-of-the-art recreational center boasting an infinity-edge pool, rock wall, indoor basketball court and track, and the most sophisticated fitness equipment. Membership to this recreational facility is free to enrolled students with reasonable rates available to alumni, staff, and the community at large. *U.S. News & World Report* ranks CSUF among the nation's "Top Public Universities." In addition, the school has an active Greek system as well as a number of student organizations, a championship baseball team, and student housing.

CHAPMAN UNIVERSITY
One University Dr., Orange
(714) 997-6815
www.chapman.edu
Founded in 1861, Chapman opened its doors on the same day Abraham Lincoln took the oath of office. Its original name, Hesperian College, and original location, Woodland, California, in the northern part of the state, were changed when the university relocated to Orange County in 1954. Located just down the road from the Plaza area of Old Towne Orange, this leafy college blends liberal arts and professional programs to create seven schools and colleges with both undergraduate and graduate studies. Dodge College, the film and media school, is widely regarded in the industry and offers studies in creative producing, digital arts, film production, film studies, and more. Chapman University's total enrollment is a little more than 6,100 students with an average class size of just 23 students. Last year only 50 percent of its freshman applicants were accepted. The campus also has a close-knit and vibrant community with more than 60 recognized student clubs plus athletics and on-campus housing.

HOPE INTERNATIONAL UNIVERSITY
2500 East Nutwood Ave., Fullerton
(714) 879-3901
www.hiu.edu
Founded in 1928 as Pacific Bible Seminary, Hope International University, located across the street from Cal State Fullerton, is steeped in Christian beliefs. Undergraduate and graduate degree programs include business, education, ministry, music, psychology and counseling, human development, and other social sciences. Its campus is a former two-story retail and office complex that has been renovated to be more co-ed-friendly with dining facilities, student lounges, a bookstore, fitness center, library, and on-campus housing.

SOUTHERN CALIFORNIA COLLEGE OF OPTOMETRY
2575 Yorba Linda Blvd., Fullerton
(714) 870-7226
www.scco.edu

Offering a four-year, post-baccalaureate program resulting in a Doctor of Optometry (O.D.), Southern California College of Optometry is also located near the campus of Cal State Fullerton and introduces students to clinical topics where they also gain limited patient care experiences at the on-campus Eye Care Center.

ℹ️ In addition to its many colleges and universities, Orange County also has several for-profit schools, from local career colleges to publicly traded "chain" schools, such as the University of Phoenix, Kaplan, Concordia, and DeVry, offering both in-person and online instruction.

UNIVERSITY OF CALIFORNIA, IRVINE
Campus and University Drive
(949) 824-6119
www.uci.edu

U.S. News & World Report ranks UC Irvine among the nation's top 50 universities and 10th among all public universities. Home of the Anteaters, this distinguished university had the greatest impact on geoscience research during the mid-1990s. There are 14 schools where students can study a breadth of disciplines, from aerospace engineering and art history to cell biology and queer studies, while offering a number of masters and PhD programs with a reputation for graduating top doctors from its medical school. Its MBA program puts students at the center of Irvine's dynamic business culture where many Fortune 500 companies have their headquarters. In addition, Nobel Prizes have been awarded to three UC Irvine researchers for work in chemistry and physics. Parents can also feel good about sending their underage freshmen to UC Irvine, too, since the city of Irvine was named the Safest City in the Nation for the fifth consecutive year for communities with populations exceeding 100,000 according to FBI statistics, and among the Best Places to Live, ranking #4 on CNNMoney.com's list of America's best small cities. In addition to on-campus dormitories, UC Irvine also offers off campus housing with separate communities for undergraduates as well as communities specifically reserved for graduate students.

WESTERN STATE UNIVERSITY COLLEGE OF LAW
1111 North State College Blvd., Fullerton
(714) 738-1000
www.wsulaw.edu

With just 400 students, this private law school, which also neighbors Cal State Fullerton, offers small classes with both full-time and part-time programs of instruction. Students work towards their Juris Doctor (J.D.) and have the opportunity to earn a Certificate in Business Law or Criminal Law if they choose. Western State is fully accredited by the American Bar Association as well as the Senior Commission of the Western Association of Schools and Colleges.

TRADE SCHOOLS

FASHION INSTITUTE OF DESIGN & MERCHANDISE
17590 Gillette Ave., Irvine
(949) 851-6200
www.fidm.com

Students attending FIDM unleash their creative side while earning degrees in the visual arts and interior design with 16 additional majors to choose from. Many graduates go on to successful careers in cosmetic packaging, costume design for TV and movies, and designing clothes for apparel companies or launching their own lines.

LAGUNA COLLEGE OF ART + DESIGN
2222 Laguna Canyon Road, Laguna Beach
(949) 376-6000
www.lagunacollege.edu

The location of this school, tucked among the folds of Laguna Canyon just minutes from the beach, is unbeatable. Founded in 1961, LCAD offers five undergraduate majors that include a Bachelor of Fine Arts degree in Drawing and Painting, Illustration, Graphic Design, Animation, or Game Art plus a single graduate program resulting in a Master of Fine Arts in Painting.

HEALTH CARE

Orange County may not have as many medical facilities as its much larger counterpart to the north, Los Angeles, but it has a fine reputation for providing excellent health and patient care. And, while "enhancement" surgeries are sought-after procedures, OC doctors can do a lot more than a nip here and a tuck there. In fact, practicing OC doctors are responsible for such medical breakthroughs as differentiating embryonic stem cells to repair damaged tissue in spinal cord injuries; identifying vitamin nutrients to work in tandem with regular exercise in delaying the onset of neurodegenerative diseases; and discovering that tumor suppressor genes can be used to screen for cervical cancer.

Orange County is also home to an academic medical center, UC Irvine Medical Center, which is a leader in translational medicine with the latest research used to provide patients with the newest therapies and treatments. If you're a parent, you'll be glad to know that Orange County also has one of the nation's leading children's hospitals, Children's Hospital of Orange County (CHOC). CHOC is one of only 45 free-standing children's hospitals in the entire United States and was the first children's hospital in the state to offer minimally invasive robotic surgery for pediatric patients. The doctors and researchers at CHOC have made great strides in pediatric medicine, including conducting the nation's first balloon dilation of a cardiac lesion, which is now a routine procedure by cardiologists. CHOC is also one of the few centers in the entire world that employs a team, houses equipment, and has the expertise needed to diagnose and treat children with metabolic disorders and has one of the largest metabolic programs in all of California. While most hospitals cover late shifts with residents only, CHOC is one of only a few in the nation to have 24-hour board-certified care and neonatology specialists running the intensive care units. This alone is comforting to parents who have faced life and death situations with their most precious cargo.

While hospital acquisitions continue to occur and other providers continue their exodus from Southern California, the face of Orange County's health care system, which has fared far better than other communities in the state, keeps changing. It truly is the survivor of the fiscally fit with strong, more established health care systems riding out the downturn of the economic wave while smaller providers seem to be drowning and are either forced to merge or close their doors altogether. MedPartners Inc. and Tenet Healthcare Corporation are just two examples, with the former selling its remaining physician network, which includes Mullikin Medical Group and Friendly Hills clinics, and the latter selling four of its Orange County hospitals to a new company willing to pay $70 million.

Last year Orange County gained some unwanted medical publicity when "Octomom," a former Cal State Fullerton student, crossed the county line to set up home in The OC with her brood. While she may live in Orange County, she received her fertility treatments in Los Angeles where the attending physician has come under extreme scrutiny. With that said, many men and women turn to the fertility experts in Orange County to conceive. There are reputable clinics that offer screening, in vitro fertilization, and reproductive care. Orange County also has many holistic health clinics and dispensaries where qualified patients can obtain marijuana for medical needs.

And, not surprising, Orange County residents, as well as most of Southern California, place an importance on physical beauty—just watch the train wreck that takes place on Bravo's *The Real Housewives of Orange County*. A Google search or a glance between the pages of an antiquated phone book reveals page after page of doctors more than willing to perform breast augmentation, lap band surgery, tummy tucks, lifts for all parts of the body, and many other procedures. Many doctors offer what's called the Mommy Makeover, promising to restore women to their pre-pregnancy selves.

While it may appear that Orange County leads the way in cosmetic procedures, and that could quite possibly be true, its real strength in terms of medical contributions is patient care. It is home to one of the most advanced children's hospitals, excels in neonatal care, and has excellent facilities for treating cancer patients as well as those who have suffered a stroke. Orange County also has excellent resources for hospice care and those with mental health issues. Bottom line: Health care in Orange County is much more than just skin deep.

MEDICAL REFERRALS

Health Referral Line, (800) 564-8448, is a good source for finding safe, appropriate, and low-cost health care services.

2-1-1 Orange County is a beneficial community resource for locating health and human services as well as support. The service is similar to 9-1-1 except instead of a medical emergency, callers are getting non-emergency referrals and information on topics like where to go for prenatal care, urgent care, dental services, and vision needs. Information on early detection and preventive programs, substance abuse, and child development services are also available. The 2-1-1 system is designated by the California Public Utilities Commission, which provides the service 24 hours a day, seven days a week.

HOSPITALS

ANAHEIM MEMORIAL MEDICAL CENTER
1111 West La Palma Ave., Anaheim
(714) 774-1450
www.memorialcare.org
If you're staying at Disneyland and require medical attention, this is the closest hospital to the park. Serving North Orange County for more than half a century, the hospital is known for its outstanding general medical services as well as its surgical unit. Patients have their own rooms, a plus when staying at any medical facility. Specialized care includes a breadth of health options, from advanced blood management and wellness programs for working professionals to a family-center childbirth facility and women's health and wellness center. Anaheim Memorial is also the only Orange County hospital with an acute sexual assault response center. It also provides community outreach by offering educational classes and hosting regular health fairs.

CHILDREN'S HOSPITAL OF ORANGE COUNTY (CHOC)
455 South Main St., Orange
(714) 997-3000
www.choc.org
When it comes to providing acute care to the county's youngest patients, parents and medical providers turn to the experts at CHOC. This is Orange County's only hospital, aside from its satellite center at Mission Hospital in the southern section of the county, to exclusively care for infants, children, and adolescents. Opened in 1964, CHOC features a state-of-the-art 238-bed main hospital facility plus five community clinics throughout Orange County. CHOC also offers more than 100 additional programs and services and, at press time, was in the midst of building a new state-of-the-art patient care tower slated to open in 2013. When completed, it will feature pediatric surgical suites, private rooms, and a family-friendly lobby plus emergency, laboratory, pathology, imaging, and radiology services.

HOAG MEMORIAL HOSPITAL PRESBYTERIAN
One Hoag Dr., Newport Beach
(949) 645-8600
www.hoaghospital.org

Considered Orange County's premier acute-care medical center, Hoag Hospital has one of the better locations if the need arises for a hospital stay. Located on a bay view bluff in Newport Beach, this 498-bed facility boasts five renowned centers of excellence, including a cancer center, heart and vascular institute, neurosciences institute, orthopedic services, and women's health services. With more than 4,000 employees and many specialized health care providers, Hoag has earned a reputation for offering excellent care for patients requiring short-term and long-term care.

LOS ALAMITOS MEDICAL CENTER
3751 Katella Ave., Los Alamitos
(562) 598-1311
www.losalamitosmedctr.com

Founded in 1968 to help meet the health care needs of Orange County's growing community, this 167-bed medical facility offers a spectrum of services and facilities. There is a TotalCare Pavilion, an ambulatory surgery center, and the hospital facility. Within the TotalCare Pavilion is a trio of centers with one catering to the needs of cancer patients and the other two offering imaging and infusion services. Los Alamitos Medical Center also has Primary Stroke Center Coronary Artery Disease Center status.

MISSION HOSPITAL
27700 Medical Center Rd., Mission Viejo
(949) 364-1400
www.mission4health.com

This south county, full-service hospital is a 340-bed acute care center and is home to one of only three trauma centers in all of Orange County. In addition to its regional trauma status, Mission Hospital also provides 24-hour emergency care and houses a heart center with cardiac rehabilitation, a maternity ward with special care for high-risk pregnancy patients, and a breast center

that offers state-of-the-art care. It's part of the St. Joseph Health System family, which includes Children's Hospital of Orange County (CHOC). CHOC has a satellite facility on the top floor of the hospital's patient tower.

ORANGE COAST MEMORIAL MEDICAL CENTER
9920 Talbert Ave., Fountain Valley
(714) 378-7000
www.memorialcare.org/orange_coast

Serving the Fountain Valley, Huntington Beach, and surrounding communities, the 224-bed, full-service Orange Coast Memorial Medical Center recently opened the Orange Coast Patient Care Pavilion. This facility, with its state-of-the-art approach to patient care, is the only one of its kind in the area and offers comprehensive cancer and cardiovascular care, imaging, and outpatient services. The hospital also has a center for obesity, a childbirth unit, and an institute for Parkinson's and movement disorders. There is also a monthly roster of educational classes, from childbirth preparation to wellness seminars with such topics as chickenpox and shingles.

SADDLEBACK MEMORIAL MEDICAL CENTER
24451 Health Center Dr., Laguna Hills
(949) 837-4500
www.memorialcare.org/saddleback

Belonging to the same group as Orange Coast Memorial Medical Center, Saddleback Memorial Medical Center is in the southern region of the county and is a diligent provider in women's health, breast care, orthopedic and cancer services, cardiovascular, and overall wellness. It has one of the most advanced critical care centers in all of California and is known for its heart programs, OB/GYN services, and breadth of educational classes that are open to the community at large. A satellite campus in San Clemente, at 654 Camino de los Mares, serves the communities further south, including San Juan Capistrano and Dana Point, and offers 24-hour emergency services, outpatient rehabilitation, and online health information.

ST. JUDE MEDICAL CENTER
101 East Valencia Mesa Dr., Fullerton
(714) 871-3280
www.stjudemedicalcenter.org

St. Jude ranks high among Orange County hospitals and has been recognized for its success in an array of areas including cardiology and rehabilitation. Established more than half a century ago by the Sisters of St. Joseph of Orange, today St. Jude has grown to be one of the area's best centers for heart and breast care, rehabilitation, cancer, and orthopedics. In addition, it has an excellent childbirth center and is one of California's only accredited programs for brain injuries.

UCI MEDICAL CENTER
101 The City Drive South, Orange
(714) 456-7890
www.healthcare.uci.edu

The University of California, Irvine, Medical Center is Orange County's only hospital associated with a university. With access to more than 300 specialty physicians and 50 primary care doctors, UCI offers a full spectrum of acute and general-care services and is a Level I trauma center equipped to manage any type of traumatic injury round-the-clock for both adults and children. It also houses a Level III neonatal care unit and is the only comprehensive care center in all of Orange County. Named as one of "America's Best Hospitals" by *U.S. News & World Report*, UCI was the first to receive the Magnet Designation for nursing excellence in Orange County. UCI was also one of the first burn facilities in the nation and the only burn center verified by the American College of Surgeons and American Burn Association found within the county. Bottom line: When it comes to life and death situations, UCI is the go-to place for critical care.

URGENT CARE FACILITIES

It's after hours and the doctor's office is closed. You decide a medical situation certainly doesn't warrant a rush to the nearest emergency room, so what's a would-be patient to do? No need to self medicate or make a diagnosis; simply head to your neighborhood urgent care facility. Most urgent care offices are affiliated with a medical group and can provide on-the-spot treatment for colds and flu as well as other symptoms, bumps, and bruises. Urgent care facilities do not operate round-the-clock; instead, they provide medical care usually until 8 or 9 p.m. on weekdays and 9 a.m. to 5 p.m. on weekends with limited hours on holidays. Most urgent care centers also accept walk-in patients. If the situation calls for more extensive medical care than an urgent center facility can provide, the attending doctor will refer you to the nearest hospital. If it's a life threatening emergency, never hesitate to dial 9-1-1.

ANAHEIM URGENT CARE
2146 East Lincoln Blvd., Anaheim
(714) 533-2273

BRISTOL PARK MEDICAL GROUP
11420 Warner Ave., Fountain Valley
(714) 549-1300

FAMILY CARE CENTERS
1190 Baker St., Costa Mesa
(714) 668-2500

IRVINE URGENT CARE
2500 Alton Parkway, Suite 101, Irvine
(949) 752-2722

MEMORIAL PROMPT CARE
15464 Goldenwest St., Westminster
(714) 891-9008

PROCARE MD
18582 Beach Blvd., Suite 23,
Huntington Beach
(714) 964-4448

SEAL BEACH FAMILY URGENT CARE
1198 Pacific Coast Hwy. #1, Seal Beach
(562) 799-7071

SLEEPY HOLLOW MEDICAL GROUP
364 Ocean Ave., Laguna Beach
(949) 494-3740

VALLEY VIEW WELLNESS MEDICAL CENTER
12556 Valley View St., Garden Grove
(714) 897-9355

LAKE FOREST OUTPATIENT CLINIC
22471 Aspan St., Suite 103, Lake Forest
(949) 458-2715

HOSPICE

Hospice care provides terminally ill patients and their families with physical and emotional support during the final days of life. Usually the doctor who has been treating the patient will know when to recommend hospice services. Hospice care can be given at home or at a licensed facility. Those listed below aren't actual facilities, but rather administrative offices and a starting point to hospice care.

COMFORT HOSPICE CARE, INC.
12900 Garden Grove Blvd., Garden Grove
(714) 638-8846

HOSPICE
377 East Chapman Ave., Suite 280, Placentia
(800) 889-3227

HOSPICE CARE OF CALIFORNIA
(800) 889-3227

SILVERADO HOSPICE
San Juan Capistrano
(888) 328-5660

MENTAL HEALTH

MENTAL HEALTH ASSOCIATION OF ORANGE COUNTY
MHA takes a client-centered approach emphasizing wellness instead of illness in helping patients to effectively manage their disease for life through independence, self sufficiency, and empowerment. MHA has a handful of outpatient clinics throughout Orange County.

COSTA MESA OUTPATIENT CLINIC
420 West 19th St., Costa Mesa
(949) 646-9277

GARDEN GROVE OUTPATIENT CLINIC
12755 Brookhurst, Suite 116, Garden Grove
(714) 536-8277

Caring for the Homeless

The Mental Health Association of Orange County (714-668-1530, www.mhaoc.org) also does outreach to the homeless community. They offer men and women multi-service center options including back-to-work programs, housing solutions, substance abuse services, and intensive recovery services. They can also help with benefits assistance for those who qualify for SSI. In addition the organization also has its own mentoring program matching mentors with children and youth receiving mental health treatment from the County of Orange Health Care Agency.

FERTILITY CLINICS

COASTAL FERTILITY MEDICAL CENTER
4900 Barranca Parkway, Suite 103, Irvine
(949) 726-0600
www.coastalfertility.com
More than 3,000 healthy babies have been born since Coastal Fertility Medical Center came on the scene in 1982. The center provides a breadth of services for those who are reproductively challenged. From in vitro to genetic diagnosis to treating endometriosis, Coastal Fertility is one of the county's most established fertility clinics. The clinic also hosts fertility seminars that cover everything from procedures and insurance issues.

NEWPORT FERTILITY CENTER
20072 South Birch St., Suite 230, Newport Beach
(949) 222-1290
www.newportfertility.com

With full-service fertility treatment options that include reversing tubal ligation and diagnosing a patient's cause, male or female, for infertility, this center specializes in all reproductive surgeries, including laparoscopy and hysteroscopy. In vitro fertilization (IVF) is one of the center's most common practices.

HOLISTIC MEDICINE

ACHIEVE HEALTH CENTER
2302 Martin, Suite 400, Irvine
(949) 706-2300
www.achievehealthcenter.com
As an alternative to traditional medicine, Achieve Health Center evaluates patients' current health, then implements a natural treatment plan to address any underlying issues. From acne to high blood pressure, the doctors aim to help reduce stress with relaxation techniques and personalized wellness plans. Hypnotherapy and naturopathic medicine are just two of the clinic's specialties that can work in concert with traditional medicine or on their own depending on the diagnosis. The clinic's founder is a certified doctor of natural health studies and a board certified hypnotherapist.

WELL HEALTHCARE ONE
721 North Euclid St., Anaheim
(714) 408-1776
Joining ancient Far East medicine with contemporary medical practices, the Well Healthcare One clinic, with its team of licensed and certified practitioners, works with patients to achieve balance through health and healing. Treatments include acupuncture, acupressure, relaxation techniques, herbal medicine, nutrition therapy, and ways to achieve healthy living.

PAIN CARE AND CHIROPRACTIC SERVICES

NORTH ORANGE COUNTY CHIROPRACTIC AND WELLNESS CENTER
1001 East Imperial Hwy., Suite A1, Brea
(714) 256-0411
www.nocchiro.com

First-time patients to this North OC treatment center will receive a consultation and examination and, if necessary, undergo X rays to determine the best course of treatment, which could range from spinal adjustments and physical therapy to soft tissue therapy or a combination of treatments. Instructions on wellness programs, which can be done at home, are also part of the healing process and can include techniques on relieving stress, spinal alignment, healthy diet, and supplements. The clinic also provides massage therapy, acupuncture, hormone replacement therapy, yoga classes, and other wellness treatments.

PAINCARE MEDICAL GROUP
15701 Rockfield Blvd., Irvine
(949) 457-9900
www.paincaremd.com
With a focus on pain management and specializing in the treatment of neck and back pain, PainCare employs a team of medical doctors who specialize in pain management and, once evaluated, develops a treatment plan to begin the process of recovery. PainCare can administer epidural cortisone or epidural steroid injections to reduce the swelling, irritation, and pain caused by pinched nerves and herniated discs.

RITTER CHIROPRACTIC
1100 Quail St., Suite 114, Newport Beach
(949) 250-4059
www.melissaritterdc.com
Visitors to Ritter Chiropractic are under the care of Dr. Ritter, who will help to diagnose problems using nerve conduction velocity and/or diagnostic ultrasound, whether the injury stems from an auto accident or sports injury, and then decide on the best course to heal any injuries. Her treatments incorporate a variety of adjustment techniques that often include physical therapy modalities including such treatments as cervical traction, electric muscle stimulation, or core muscle rehab using a Swiss ball, just to name a few. She can also treat gastric reflux, migraine headaches, and carpal tunnel syndrome.

INDEX